17.89
YBP

KEY CONCEPTS IN CONTEMPORARY LITERATURE

Palgrave Key Concepts

Palgrave Key Concepts provide an accessible and comprehensive range of subject glossaries at undergraduate level. They are the ideal companion to a standard textbook making them invaluable reading to students throughout their course of study and especially useful as a revision aid.

Key Concepts in Accounting and Finance
Key Concepts in Business Practice
Key Concepts in Drama and Performance
Key Concepts in Human Resource Management
Key Concepts in Information and Communication Technology
Key Concepts in International Business
Key Concepts in Language and Linguistics (second edition)
key Concepts in Management
Key Concepts in Marketing
Key Concepts in Operations Management
Key Concepts in Politics
Key Concepts in Psychology
Key Concepts in Strategic Management

Palgrave Key Concepts: Literature
General Editors: John Peck and Martin Coyle

Key Concepts in Contemporary Literature
Key Concepts in Postcolonial Literature
Key Concepts in Victorian Literature
Literary Terms and Criticism (third edition)

Further titles are in preparation

www.palgravekeyconcepts.com

Palgrave Key Concepts
Series Standing Order
ISBN 1–4039–3210–7
(outside North America only)

You can receive future titles in this series as they are published by placing a standing order. Please contact your bookseller or, in the case of difficulty, write to us at the address below with your name and address, the title of the series and the ISBN quoted above.

Customer Services Department, Macmillan Distribution Ltd
Houndmills, Basingstoke, Hampshire RG21 6XS, England

Key Concepts in Contemporary Literature

Steve Padley

First published 2006 by
PALGRAVE MACMILLAN
Houndmills, Basingstoke, Hampshire RG21 6XS and
175 Fifth Avenue, New York, N.Y. 10010
Companies and representatives throughout the world

PALGRAVE MACMILLAN is the global academic imprint of the Palgrave Macmillan division of St. Martin's Press, LLC and of Palgrave Macmillan Ltd. Macmillan® is a registered trademark in the United States, United Kingdom and other countries. Palgrave is a registered trademark in the European Union and other countries.

ISBN-13: 978 1–4039–4691–1
ISBN-10: 1–4039–4691–4

This book is printed on paper suitable for recycling and made from fully managed and sustained forest sources.

A catalogue record for this book is available from the British Library.

A catalog record for this book is available from the Library of Congress.

10 9 8 7 6 5 4 3 2 1
15 14 13 12 11 10 09 08 07 06

Printed and bound in Great Britain by
Creative Print & Design (Wales), Ebbw Vale

Contents

General Editors' Preface

The purpose of **Palgrave Key Concepts in Literature** is to provide students with key critical and historical ideas about the texts they are studying as part of their literature courses. These ideas include information about the historical and cultural contexts of literature as well as the theoretical approaches current in the subject today. Behind the series lies a recognition of the need nowadays for students to be familiar with a range of concepts and contextual material to inform their reading and writing about literature.

But behind the series there also lies a recognition of the changes that have transformed degree courses in Literature in recent years. Central to these changes has been the impact of critical theory together with a renewed interest in the way in which texts intersect with their immediate context and historical circumstances. The result has been an opening up of new ways of reading texts and a new understanding of what the study of literature involves together with the introduction of a wide set of new critical issues that demand our attention. An important aim of **Palgrave Key Concepts in Literature** is to provide brief, accessible introductions to these new ways of reading and new issues.

Each volume in **Palgrave Key Concepts in Literature** follows the same structure. An initial overview essay is followed by three sections – *Contexts*, *Texts*, and *Criticism* – each containing a sequence of brief alphabetically arranged entries on a sequence of topics. *Contexts essays* provide an impression of the historical, social and cultural environment in which literary texts were produced. *Texts essays*, as might be expected, focus more directly on the works themselves. *Criticism essays* then outline the manner in which changes and developments in criticism have affected the ways in which we discuss the texts featured in the volume. The informing intention throughout is to help the reader create something new in the process of combining context, text and criticism.

John Peck
Martin Coyle

General Introduction

There are a number of difficulties inherent in constructing an overview of a literary historical period, some of which are attenuated when the period in question is the contemporary. Most notably, periodisation is a particularly problematic concept; many modules on literature degree courses focus on specific centuries, decades or other time-scales: 'the 19th-century novel', for example, or 'poetry of the 1930s'. There is inevitably something arbitrary or artificial about this kind of categorisation, however. Literary styles and preoccupations do not change neatly at the turn of a century or on the transition into a new decade. Writers do not stop writing in one way at the end of one literary historical period and start writing differently at the beginning of the next. Nevertheless, some degree of chronological structure is usually considered the most appropriate way of restricting the number of texts or authors studied to a selection representative of a given literary era.

The periodisation of contemporary literature introduces further complications. The term 'contemporary' denotes an open-ended period, up to and including the present day, but there is a marked lack of consensus about when the period can definitively be said to have begun. Numerous modules dealing with aspects of contemporary British and other English literatures are included in undergraduate and graduate degree courses at the time of writing. Some take 1945, the year in which the Second World War ended, as the starting-point; others see the 1960s, a period of immense social and cultural change in Britain and elsewhere, as a more relevant date at which to begin. The Cambridge University undergraduate course on contemporary literature is one of a number that covers an even shorter time-span, from 1979 to the present, possibly reflecting a belief that radical developments in literary theory and criticism in the last two decades of the 20th century have had a fundamental impact on the ways in which texts have come to be read, interpreted and understood.

Persuasive arguments can be offered for all of the above attempts at periodisation, not least because different literary genres or aspects of literary study undergo significant changes at different times. For the purposes of this book, I have opted to take the end of the Second World War as the point at which the contemporary period began. This is largely because of the extent to which the impact and implications of that conflict on British social, political and cultural life continued to resonate throughout the rest of the 20th century and beyond. At this point, I should make it clear that I have chosen to make British literature the main focus of this book, and explain the rationale behind that decision. Ideally, it would be desirable to trace the development of all literatures written in English since 1945, but the resulting volume would either be impossibly long or wholly inadequate in the depth of its coverage. Although this book will touch briefly on literary developments elsewhere – the rise of postcolonial writing, for instance, or the impact of Irish writing in the period – I have taken the view that to provide a detailed overview of the literature of one country will prove more useful to the reader than a book that tries to cover the literature of the entire English-speaking world. Readers requiring a different focus will, inevitably, refer to other literary guides, such as the volume on postcolonial literature in this series.

The period since 1945 has been one of substantial change in Britain, in areas such as social structure and class hierarchy, gender identity and the role of women (and men), sexual behaviour and personal relationships, moral values, attitudes towards the family, multicultural experience, and imperial decline. In all of these areas, the influence of the Second World War, and the widespread determination to recreate British society on more egalitarian lines that was inspired by the experience of wartime national cohesion, has been sustained and far-reaching; as will be shown later, this postwar consensus went largely unchallenged until the emergence of Thatcherism in the late 1970s. Chapter 1 of this book, 'Contexts', discusses the contextual background of the postwar era, and attempts to give some indication of the ways in which key political, social and cultural events of the period influenced and affected literary themes, ideas and styles.

Novels, poems and plays since 1945 have reflected the changes that were taking place in Britain in the post-Second World War period, though not always in straightforward or easily recognisable ways. The legacy of the Second World War, especially the Holocaust, and the American A-bombing of Hiroshima and Nagasaki that finally brought the conflict to a close, informed much of the literature of the period, both explicitly and implicitly, against the backdrop of the developing state of Cold War between the Allies and the USSR. In the first decade or so after the war, literature, reflecting a general sense of national psychic exhaustion resulting from the traumas and deprivations of the war years, seemed to withdraw from direct involvement with large-scale political and international concerns. Thereafter, however, writers became more prepared to engage imaginatively with the war and what it meant, especially as the full extent of the Holocaust became apparent. Social and cultural changes, and marked shifts in attitudes towards sexual identity and behaviour, including gender relationships, were also widely debated in post-Second World War literature. In addition, increased immigration, brought about initially by the need for a larger workforce to tackle the massive task of national reconstruction, gradually turned Britain into something approaching a genuinely multicultural society by the end of the 20th century. This transformation was not easily achieved, nor was it universally welcomed – racism has been a recurrent problem in British society over the period – but by the turn of the 21st century, second- and third-generation immigrants were more confident in their identity, and were making a huge contribution to many aspects of British life. Over the same period, Britain was undergoing a rapid and often painful process of imperial decline, the price paid for American intervention to ensure the successful prosecution of the war. These themes were strongly reflected in the literature of the second half of the 20th century.

The demographic identity of contemporary British writing was changing, too. Extension of opportunity in further and higher education led to the emergence of writers from working-class backgrounds; women writers also benefited in this respect, and from the rise of feminism; black British writers engaged with the ramifications of the migrant experience and the shift to a postcolonial world order. Scottish, Irish and Welsh writing, national literatures that had historically struggled for wider acceptance in the canonical literary tradition, also flourished, energised by an increasing emphasis on culturally and politically marginalised perspectives.

One consequence of the greater diversity of British writing for the student or general reader of contemporary literature is the difficulty of selecting, from the vast amount of published material, which texts and authors can most profitably be studied to gain a sense of the main developments in the period's fiction, poetry and drama. The middle chapter of this book, 'Texts', discusses the key themes, literary movements and styles of writing that characterise British literature in the postwar period, with some reference to developments elsewhere, where these have had a particular influence on British writing. The individual entries in this section are dictated to some extent by those authors whose work was already being widely studied on contemporary literature courses in universities at the time of writing. I have also attempted, however, to include discussion of the work of other authors who have not yet received that degree of recognition.

Another of the difficulties inherent in writing about or studying contemporary literature is the lack of historical distance against which to judge the works one reads; texts that may seem in the early 21st century particularly significant in the themes they explore and their stylistic techniques, may have faded from view 10 years on. Similarly, it is not always possible to anticipate how works and authors that did not receive serious attention at the time might be reassessed with the benefit of hindsight. For that reason, I have attempted to include discussion of the work of writers who have not yet received widespread academic and critical acknowledgement, but may well do so in the future.

The contemporary period of British literature, as defined above, is characterised by an increasing sense of democratisation, of challenges, from previously marginalised constituencies, to the values and judgements that historically had governed the formation of the literary canon. Developments in literary theory and criticism, especially from the late 1960s onwards, have enhanced and facilitated such challenges, raising fundamental questions about the ways in which texts can be read and interpreted, or even whether they can be interpreted at all in any meaningful sense. The different critical and theoretical approaches that have dominated the contemporary period are outlined in the final chapter of this book, 'Criticism', with a particular emphasis on those that came into being in the last 30 or so years of the 20th century.

The three chapters of this book should not be regarded as separate entities, however. Literature is shaped and informed by the historical moment and the social world in which it is created, disseminated and read. Contextual background is immensely useful for an understanding of the themes and preoccupations explored by a particular text, though it should always be remembered that literary texts are not historical documents. The worlds they depict are fictions, imaginative recreations of the social reality that they address. Literary criticism and theory offers us possible ways of reading and interpreting texts by focusing on different aspects of the fictional worlds they create: what they have to say about gender relations, class structures, questions of race or ethnicity, sexual identity and orientation, or many other aspects of human experience. They may also, as in various structuralist, poststructuralist and postmodernist approaches, question the validity of any given interpretative position, and the idea that meaning can be fixed and determinate, positions that earlier critical and theoretical approaches tended to take for granted.

Chapter 1, 'Contexts', offers a number of perspectives that might be used as a point of reference to inform a particular reading of a given text. The entry for 'migrant experience and multiculturalism', for example, charts the historical process, starting with the first waves of postwar immigration, by which ethnic and cultural diversity became a fundamental characteristic of life in Britain in the early 21st century. The contextual information here could usefully underpin a reading of a novel such as Hanif Kureishi's *The Buddha of Suburbia* (1990), a significant text in British literature in the post-imperial period. Like his protagonist, Karim Amir, Kureishi was born to an Indian father and an English mother, and his novel engages with second-generation immigrant experience from a particularly complex perspective. *The Buddha of Suburbia* is set partly in the suburban areas around London and partly in the city itself, and focuses on Karim's quest to establish a sense of identity in the light of his mixed-race background, and the experience of living in Britain, at a time when the idealism of the 1960s had given way to disillusionment and a growing sense of social unrest, often manifested in racial tension. The novel's emphasis on immigrant life and the conflicts between traditional Asian religious and cultural expectations, on the one hand, and the attitudes and values that defined contemporary British society, on the other, opens it up to readings that draw on postcolonial critical and theoretical approaches that are among those explored in Chapter 3, 'Criticism'. Such approaches demonstrate how Western perceptions of non-Western races, societies and cultures are predicated on a sense of the non-Western as a subordinate, inferior 'other'. It was by creating constructions of the colonised as inherently inferior that Western powers maintained their control in the imperial period, according to the postcolonial critic Edward Said. Kureishi's novel shows numerous ways in which Western assumptions about the non-Western 'other' survived the long process of imperial decline. Karim's first acting role, for example, is that of Mowgli in a theatrical adaptation of Kipling's *The Jungle Book*. Not dark enough for the part, he is forced by the white English director, Shadwell, to 'black up' and wear a loincloth, ironically reinforcing the Kiplingesque stereotype.

However, *The Buddha of Suburbia* also usefully demonstrates that literary texts can be open to a variety of readings, something that should be borne in mind when looking at a text through any given critical perspective. The novel also has much to say about issues of gender, and the ways in which these relate to questions of race and ethnicity: Jamila, Karim's political activist cousin, is forced into an arranged marriage; Karim's English mother is abandoned by her husband, precipitating a psychological breakdown: the role of women in the novel could, therefore, be productively explored through feminist critical procedures. Changes in sexual behaviour and perceptions of sexual identity in the post-Second World War era are also addressed in *The Buddha of Suburbia*, most notably in the mirroring of Karim's ethnic hybridity by his bisexual orientation. As a consequence, the novel could also be read in the light of approaches rooted in gender theory, or gay and lesbian criticism. *The Buddha of Suburbia* is in many ways a characteristic example of contemporary British fiction; it reflects the diversity of late-20th-century life and refers to some of the key social and cultural changes of the period, leaving it open to a multiplicity of potential critical readings, none of which can be regarded as final. The various forms of literary criticism outlined in the final section of this book should be thought of as offering possible ways of reading and interpreting a text, all of which may have some validity, depending on which aspects of the text are the centre of critical focus.

1 Contexts: History, Politics, Culture

Introduction

At the conclusion of the Second World War in 1945 the public mood in Britain reflected a desire for social change, not least to provide restitution for the sacrifices made by those on the home front as well as those in the armed forces. The British people had felt the effects of war to a severe degree: sustained aerial bombardment had inflicted widespread damage on major cities; men were dispersed to the various theatres of war; women moved out of the domestic sphere to support the war effort on the land, in factories or in the services; and family units were broken up as children were evacuated to safer locations. The privations endured during wartime led to demands that social iniquities and inequalities would be corrected in the future. Planning for a fairer society had begun as early as 1942, with the publication of the Beveridge Report, which advocated the creation of a Welfare State to improve healthcare and education and to alleviate poverty. The report's recommendations for a National Health Service, national insurance and family allowances were taken up after the Labour Party's surprising landslide victory in the 1945 general election, ousting Britain's wartime political leader, Winston Churchill. Initially, there seemed to be grounds for optimism that the necessary social and economic changes would be achieved, but Labour's promised radicalism failed to materialise: its parliamentary majority was slashed to a mere five seats in 1950, and in the following year the Conservatives returned to power, remaining there until 1964. The change of government did not affect the political commitment to the postwar settlement, however, and up to the late 1970s the major parties shared a belief in the Welfare State as the cornerstone of social policy.

While the consensus about the direction of British society remained relatively unchanged for over three decades after the Second World War, Britain's international status was more problematic. The economic consequences of war, together with America's rise as a world power, were major factors in the decline of Britain's imperial status. The United States had made a vital contribution to the winning of the war, and its

1

prosperity, at a time when ravaged European nations were counting the cost of military conflict, enabled it to offer assistance in postwar reconstruction, through which it could guide the future economic direction of Western Europe to the benefit of American interests. Britain, on the other hand, was conceding its former imperial territories, with Indian independence in 1947 the most notable example. Nevertheless, the extent of Britain's reduced world role was not fully recognised until 1956, when the government's attempt to counter Egypt's nationalisation of the Suez Canal was halted by America's threat of economic sanctions against the pound. The government's humiliating climb-down confirmed a shift in the international balance of power that had first become apparent with the beginning of the Cold War between America and the Soviet Union in the late 1940s. As Russia extended its influence in the 1950s and 1960s, seeking to challenge America's nuclear dominance, European nations found themselves caught between two antagonistic superpowers, a situation that continued until the collapse of the Soviet Union in the late 1980s. During the Cold War, nuclear proliferation on both sides fostered anxiety throughout Europe, leading to the establishment of protest movements such as CND (the Campaign for Nuclear Disarmament) in Britain.

On the domestic front, despite the undoubted achievements of the Welfare State, the promise of 'fairness for all' was far from being fulfilled by the end of the 1950s. Public confidence in the political establishment, shaken by Suez, was further weakened by defections from the intelligence services, revelations that British officials Guy Burgess, Donald Maclean and Kim Philby had been spying for the Soviet Union, and sexual scandals involving senior government figures and prostitutes, in the Profumo affair of 1963. In the following year the Conservative government was defeated, and Labour returned to power. For a time, under Harold Wilson's modernising leadership, Britain recovered its self-confidence, both politically and culturally, but even though it was returned with a larger majority in 1966, the Wilson government's radical ambitions were hindered by economic crises that culminated in devaluation of the pound in 1967. Although relative stability was restored, the Conservatives, under Edward Heath, won an unexpected election victory in 1970.

The economic downturn that began in the late 1960s intensified throughout the following decade, presenting serious fiscal problems, first to the Heath administration. Industrial action by miners and other key workers resulted in energy shortages, leading to the introduction of a three-day working week in 1973–4 that was the main factor in the downfall of the government. Labour fared little better from 1974 to 1979, under Prime Minister Wilson and his successor James Callaghan, eventually being forced to seek assistance from the International Monetary Fund, conditional on spending cuts that proved highly unpopular. Growing industrial unrest in 1979 led to a succession of strikes by public sector workers in the so-called 'winter of discontent'. Throughout the 1970s governments also faced other internal problems: social and racial tensions in the inner cities; rising poverty and unemployment; an intensification of the 'troubles' in Northern Ireland; and pressures for moves towards devolution in Scotland and Wales. The 1979 general election was, however, a political watershed, with the Conservative victory under Margaret Thatcher heralding a rejection of the political consensus that had remained in place since 1945.

Thatcherism, the doctrine that dominated British politics for the next decade, advocated a shift to a free-market economy, with as little state intervention as possible, and reorganisation of the Welfare State on free-market principles. State control of industries and utilities gave way to privatisation, and the manufacturing sector was no longer to be relied upon as the main provider of jobs and national productivity. Legislation to limit the power of the unions was introduced as a response to the recurrent industrial unrest of the 1970s. The most serious consequence of the change of political direction was a rapid increase in unemployment, which rose to around 3 million by the early 1980s, an unprecedented figure in the postwar era. Public services suffered from under-investment; riots in Bristol, Toxteth, Brixton and Moss Side testified to severe social problems; and manufacturing industries went into decline. For some people, however, the 1980s was a decade of affluence, with large amounts of money to be made from privatisation of national utilities and in the City. The Conservatives maintained a stranglehold on political power, increasing their majority in the 1983 election, on a wave of jingoistic feeling engendered by the emphatic defeat of Argentinean forces one year earlier, and retaining control comfortably in 1987. By the end of the 1980s the political landscape had changed irrevocably, forcing the political Left to rethink its core values. The Labour Party, after much bloodletting, began to present a more cohesive alternative, and Thatcher's abrasive style began to lose its appeal even within her own party, while new measures such as the community charge (or 'poll tax') provoked organised public protest and opposition. However, it was her refusal to countenance closer political and economic union with Europe that eventually brought about her downfall in 1990, when she resigned after narrowly surviving the first round of a leadership challenge.

John Major replaced Thatcher, and though he fought off Labour's challenge in the 1992 election, divisions over Europe and economic difficulties continued to pose serious problems for the Conservatives. A series of political and sexual scandals brought into question the probity of ministers and MPs. At the same time, the process of change within the Labour Party was accelerating under the leadership of Tony Blair, who built on the modernising work of his predecessors, Neil Kinnock and John Smith. The party under Blair moved closer to the centre-ground of British politics, establishing closer ties with business, and distancing itself from its historical alliance with the trade unions. The Labour landslide victory in the 1997 election was widely expected, though the scale of the Conservatives' defeat – their worst in electoral history – surprised many, even 'New Labour', as it now called itself.

British politics had undergone a huge transformation by the end of the twentieth century. Like Margaret Thatcher, Blair imposed his personal stamp on government, with a style of leadership close to the American 'presidential' model. What was also different about this Labour administration, compared to its postwar predecessors, was the retention of free-market principles. Those who hoped for a return to the ideals of the postwar consensus were to be disappointed, though there was an increased commitment to improving health and educational provision. Blair's government also benefited from greater economic stability than previous Labour administrations had enjoyed, and although change for the better had not been as noticeable as many had hoped, Labour was in a strong position to repeat the landslide of 1997. This was duly achieved in 2001, only months before the attack on the twin towers of the World Trade Center in New York on 11 September changed international and domestic politics as profoundly as had the Second World War. In the reprisals that followed, and particularly in the war with Iraq that began in 2003, Britain was America's staunchest ally; in the aftermath of '9/11' Britain's international status was more dependent than ever on its relationship with the United States. The Iraq war proved to be an issue of lasting significance, with mass demonstrations against the government's support for American action and British military involvement in the conflict. Arguments about the legality of the war dominated British politics in the early years of the 21st century, and the extent of public opposition to the war was reflected in the substantial reduction of Labour's majority in the 2005 general election, which brought the party its third consecutive victory.

Shortly after Labour began its historic third term – the first time the party had won three elections in a row – Britain became a target for international terrorism. On 7 July 2005, 52 people were killed in a series of suicide bomb attacks on the London transport system. The bombers, who were linked to the Muslim fundamentalist group al-Qaeda, and widely believed to be acting in response to Britain's involvement in the Iraq war, targeted three underground trains and a London bus. The perpetrators of a failed second attack two weeks later were arrested, but public anxiety about the events of July 2005 was heightened by the knowledge that some of the bombers involved in both attempts were British Asians, indicating the reach of fundamentalist groups such as al-Qaeda.

The major events and developments since 1945 outlined above – the fall of the British Empire; the rise of American influence; and the impact of the Cold War – give a sense of the changing postwar world, but within Britain other significant changes – social and cultural – took place, affecting racial, class and gender identities in particular. The period that witnessed the decline of Britain's imperial status was also characterised by an internal shift towards multiculturalism. Postwar national reconstruction required a large labour force, and to provide this Britain looked towards its empire, leading to an influx of immigrants from the Caribbean, India and Pakistan in the 1950s and 1960s. Many of these arrived with the expectation of a positive reception from the 'mother country', but were often met with hostility and racial prejudice that sometimes spilled over into violence. There were periodic calls for tighter immigration controls, and far-right political groups exploited and fostered racism, gaining worrying levels of support in some socially and economically deprived areas of Britain around the turn of the 21st century. On a more positive note, however, and notwithstanding the growing problem of militant religious fundamentalism and its impact on ethnically diverse communities, there are encouraging signs that Britain is making the transition towards a genuinely multicultural society, more diverse and tolerant than was the case some 50 years earlier, with younger, British-born blacks and Asians acquiring a more confident and assertive sense of identity, and making a huge contribution to British cultural life.

The process of social change since 1945 has also seen alterations in class structure, a consequence of the egalitarian spirit that replaced the more rigid prewar culture of deference in British society. As Britain moved from austerity towards affluence in the 1950s and 1960s, and the extension of the educational franchise brought a wider cross-section of society into higher education and the professions, entrenched notions of class status began to erode. The sense of egalitarianism was perhaps at its height from the late 1950s to the early 1970s. A retrenchment, however, took place in the 1980s, with rising unemployment, particularly in traditional working-class communities, having a negative effect on the aspirations of those affected. Although politicians at various times since the end of the Second World War have deemed class as no longer relevant, the continuing gap between rich and poor, and the diminishment of opportunity for many, after the widening of access in the earlier postwar period, should temper an over-optimistic belief in the loosening of social hierarchies, notwithstanding the general trend towards democratisation in Britain.

A third area in which substantial change has taken place, though again one that needs to be treated with caution, relates to the role and status of women. Many women had played vital roles in the production of wartime essentials, and although they were initially encouraged to return to the domestic sphere, to enable men to take up their traditional roles in the workplace, women were soon being actively recruited back into the labour force. The postwar 'baby boom', the need to meet the demands of the massive reconstruction programme required to rebuild British society, and the birth of the modern consumer age were the main reasons for the increase in employment opportunities for women. At the same time, expansion in higher education meant that more female students were able to go to university, widening their career horizons and boosting their economic power and independence.

However, the extent to which positive changes were happening for women was tempered by their continued marginalisation in the public sphere, by the obstacles they still faced in achieving parity with male work colleagues, and by the competing demands of career and family. The alternative ideologies of counter-cultural movements that were beginning to emerge in the 1960s also seemed to have little to say about female experience, forcing women to look elsewhere for a means of defining themselves in postwar society. The rebirth of feminism in the late 1960s answered this need. Much of modern feminism's initial impetus came from France and the United States, but by the early 1970s the women's movement in Britain was firmly established, and the social and cultural impact of feminism became quickly apparent as it challenged conventional perceptions of gender roles, and helped women to fulfil their personal and professional potential.

Other factors contributed to the change in women's position in society, not least the introduction of the contraceptive pill in 1961, though initially only available to married women. Not only was the 'pill' seen as empowering for women; it also played a role in facilitating what has been described as a sexual revolution in the 1960s, a period which was also characterised by liberalising reforms, such as the decriminalisation of homosexuality and the legalising of abortion, both in 1967. Typical of the trend towards greater social and cultural freedom in the 1960s were challenges to and changes in the state's role as an instrument of censorship. The 'Lady Chatterley' trial of 1960, in which Penguin Books successfully defended a charge of obscenity for publishing a paperback edition of D. H. Lawrence's *Lady Chatterley's Lover*, was seen as a defining moment in the change of attitudes to sex and sexuality. A further blow to state censorship was struck by the termination of the Lord Chamberlain's role as censor of stage productions in Britain in 1968, which allowed greater freedom to playwrights and directors to address previously taboo themes and issues.

The 1960s also saw the birth of a counter-cultural ethos in Western Europe and the United States that gave free rein to physical, sensual and intellectual expression and drew on new ideas in psychology, philosophy, sociology, music, literature and art, in opposition to 'official' politics, social attitudes and moral values. This mood was perhaps most clearly demonstrated in Paris in 1968, when student protests demanding educational reforms escalated into an alliance with French workers that paralysed the capital. The revolutionary spirit of May '68 became an enduring influence on anti-establishment thought and action, with student protests closing the London School of Economics briefly in 1969. American intervention in Vietnam, precipitating a war that lasted from 1964 to 1973, was also a major force for dissent, and led to the formation of protest groups in Britain, as elsewhere in Europe and America. In all such cases, the young were at the forefront of oppositional and counter-cultural movements, an indication of another significant postwar trend: the assumption among young people of a discrete sense of identity, with their own fashions, music and cultural references. Increased affluence gave the young substantial spending power, and in Britain factors such as the abolition of National Service, educational expansion and the growth of the Welfare State also contributed to the rise in significance of youth culture. From 1950s 'teddy boys', through the mods and rockers of the early 1960s, the hippy movement of the later 1960s, skinheads and punks in the 1970s, and rave culture in the 1990s, a sense of tribalism characterised British youth culture throughout the period, though the growth of global consumerism and commercialisation seems to have brought about a homogenisation of youth identity, as in other sections of society, towards the end of the century.

Although in many respects British society has not entirely rid itself of the inequalities that the Welfare State was set up to eradicate in the immediate aftermath of the Second World War, and notwithstanding the caveats expressed above, there is evidence in the advances made in women's roles, the beneficial effects of multiculturalism, the existence of greater social mobility and the improvements in living standards for many, to characterise the period as a whole as one of democratisation, nowhere more clearly reflected in changes in literary culture, which will be demonstrated in subsequent chapters of this book.

Further reading

Ford, Boris (ed.), *The Cambridge Cultural History of Britain*, vol. 9: *Modern Britain* (Cambridge: Cambridge University Press, 1992).
Marwick, Arthur, *British Society since 1945*, 3rd edn (Harmondsworth: Penguin, 1996).
Morgan, Kenneth O., *Britain since 1945: The People's Peace*, 3rd edn (Oxford: Oxford University Press, 2001).

British Empire, decline and loss

One of the unexpected consequences of the Allied Forces' victory in the Second World War was the subsequent diminution of Britain's status as a leading world power, reflected in a gradually accelerating process of imperial decline. The seeds of that decline were evident much earlier in the 20th century with the emergence of nationalist movements in many British colonies and imperial territories, such as India, Egypt and the Caribbean, but the strains and pressures of the war served to emphasise the fading of British imperialism. Indeed, the empire proved to be as much a burden as a benefit to the British war effort: in spite of providing an additional source of military manpower, it presented a severe problem in that it required considerable resources to safeguard its security, resources that might have been better directed elsewhere. As a result, Britain became increasingly reliant on American assistance to maintain its military presence on all fronts. In the immediate aftermath of the war, priorities closer to home took precedence over imperial ambitions, as Britain, like many of its Western European counterparts, concentrated on national reconstruction, again largely relying on American support. That support came at a price, as the United States was able to promote its own political and economic interests, which did not always sit easily with British imperial considerations.

In any event, the trend in British imperial activity after the Second World War was towards contraction rather than expansion, symbolised above all by the granting of independence to India in 1947. The event had been long anticipated, and had been official Labour Party policy since before the Second World War, becoming one of the few non-domestic priorities of the first postwar government. The loss of Britain's main imperial possession had little impact on national morale or self-image at the time. The process had been planned and discussed for so long that its conclusion seemed inevitable, and as India, like many other former imperial territories, opted to remain in the Commonwealth, the perception among the British public, which generally did not pay much attention to the machinations of empire, was that nothing much had changed.

Elsewhere, relations between coloniser and colonised were more volatile. Nationalist campaigns in Palestine and Egypt, for instance, were more confrontational and challenged Britain's imperial self-confidence. The severest blow to Britain's international prestige was delivered by the Suez crisis of 1956, which was the culmination of a period of mutual distrust between Britain and Egypt. The British government suspected Egypt's President Nasser of being in league with Soviet Russia, and with orchestrating Jordan's dismissal of Sir John Glubb, the British commander of the Arab legion. British Prime Minister Anthony Eden urged the withdrawal of joint British–American financial support for the building of the proposed Aswan Dam, in response to which Nasser announced the nationalisation of the Suez Canal, a move which would endanger international trade in the region. Britain began to prepare for military action, in collaboration with France, to gain control of the waterway and overthrow Nasser's government. A clandestine alliance was made with Israel to attack Egypt, at which point France and Britain would urge a cessation of hostilities and withdrawal from the Canal area, in the certain knowledge that Egypt could not agree to this. The way would then be left open for Britain and France to attack and occupy the Canal. The plan was duly put into operation, but far from achieving the government's intended aims, the outcome was severely detrimental to Britain's self-image as a leading world power. Condemned by the United Nations, Britain found itself isolated, but most damaging of all was the reaction of the United States, which reinforced its vehement opposition to British policy with measures designed to put serious pressure on sterling. The consequences for the British economy would have been potentially disastrous, and the government was faced with no option but to bring its military intervention to an immediate and humiliating cessation.

Where Indian independence had made little negative impression on public opinion, the Suez crisis provoked passionate debate both inside and outside parliament, with marches and demonstrations against the government's actions. The imperialist attitudes that underpinned Britain's aggressive tactics seemed to have been widely discredited by the episode, though it should also be noted that the Conservative government recovered public confidence sufficiently to remain in power for another eight years. Nevertheless, as the British Empire continued to shrink over subsequent decades, with the establishment of a growing number of newly independent states and nations, the question of

Britain's political, economic and cultural role in the world became increasingly problematic. At home, too, there were similar challenges to be met, in relation to increasing pressures for autonomy from the constituent members of the United Kingdom. By the end of the 20th century devolution had been achieved for Scotland, and Wales had its own national assembly, while the Irish situation continued to pose intractable difficulties for the British government.

Literary responses to the crisis of national self-confidence precipitated by Suez were much in evidence at the time. The tarnished image of British imperialism was one of the targets of Jimmy Porter's tirades of invective in John Osborne's *Look Back in Anger* (1956), for example, and anti-colonial sentiments pervaded other key dramatic works of the period, such as John Arden's *Sergeant Musgrave's Dance* (1959). Similarly, the passing of the British Raj also captured the literary imagination, in the work of novelists like Paul Scott, whose *Raj Quartet* (1966–75) dealt with the period of partition and independence. His final, Booker Prize-winning, novel *Staying On* (1978) focused on the aftermath of independence through the eyes of British characters that had remained in India. In less obvious ways, other British writers of the period have engaged with the mood of post-imperial loss that many critics have seen as pervading the later decades of the 20th century. Seamus Heaney, for example, has noted the concern with national identity in English poets as various as Ted Hughes, Geoffrey Hill and Philip Larkin, who in Heaney's perceptive phrase, seem 'forced to explore not just the matter of England, but what is the matter with England'.[1]

At around the same time, Indian-born Salman Rushdie was one of a number of writers striving to explore the consequences and implications of the dissolution of the British Empire, from the perspective of those once colonised by it. Rushdie's earliest works focus more exclusively on postcolonial experience in his native India, but in novels such as *The Satanic Verses* (1988) he also turns his attention, like the British poets cited by Heaney, to the 'matter with England', depicting London, rechristened 'Ellowen Deeowen', and further defamiliarised by the author's magic realist techniques, as a city in terminal decay, with a disintegrating sense of identity. The hybridity of the dual perspective that informs Rushdie's fiction is also to be found in the work of other writers from similarly mixed origins: Kazuo Ishiguro, Japanese-born but resident in Britain from the age of 6, considers the implications of Britain's post-imperial decline in *The Remains of the Day* (1989), set, very tellingly, in 1956, the year of the Suez crisis. Ishiguro's protagonist, Stevens the butler, reflects throughout the novel on his years of service to Lord Dartington, refusing to acknowledge his former employer's sympathetic attitude towards Nazi Germany in the lead-up to the Second World War. The difficulties Stevens encounters in adapting to his postwar role, as butler to the new American owner of Dartington Hall, is emblematic of the national crisis of confidence that Britain faced in trying to assimilate into the new world order after 1945.

See also   *Contexts*: Migrant experience and multiculturalism, War; *Texts*: Empire, end of, Englishness, Movement, the, Postcolonial literature; *Criticism*: Postcolonial criticism.

Further reading

Brown, Judith M., William Roger Louis and Analine M. Low (eds), *The Oxford History of the British Empire*, vol. 4: *The Twentieth Century* (Oxford: Oxford University Press, 1999).

Censorship

The question of artistic freedom of expression is one which is central to most if not all modern societies, and all societies exercise some degree of censorship, whether by state-authorised institutions and legal processes, or according to social convention and consensus. Pressure groups may also attempt to bring influence to bear in defence of their perceived interests, where they see these as compromised by other beliefs and values systems. In Britain, the period since the end of the Second World War has seen the relaxation of many forms of censorship, reflecting the general trend towards social democratisation, the decline of deference, and growing challenges to state and political authority. More liberal sexual attitudes emerged alongside greater toleration of sexual explicitness in language, art, literature, drama and film, from the 1960s onwards. This was illustrated by two landmark events in British legal history that took place almost a decade apart: the Obscene Publications Act of 1959, and the abolition of the role of the Lord Chamberlain's Office as censor of British theatrical productions in 1968. The Obscene Publications Act, for the first time, allowed literary merit to be offered as a valid defence against prosecution for obscenity. The most famous test case for the new law came in 1960, when a charge of obscenity was brought against Penguin Books for publishing an unexpurgated cheap paperback edition of D. H. Lawrence's *Lady Chatterley's Lover* (1928), a novel previously available only in a limited edition. The novel's sexual explicitness, and the demotic language in which it was expressed, provided the basis for the Crown's charge of obscenity, though the prosecution's approach was also clearly informed by outdated class assumptions, demonstrated in the question that prosecuting counsel Mervyn Griffiths-Jones put to the jury: 'Is it a book that you would even wish your wife or your servants to read?'[2] In its defence, Penguin called a number of expert witnesses, including literary critics, psychologists and leading religious figures, who attested to the novel's artistic validity. The jury found in Penguin's favour, a decision that had a profound and long-lasting impact on the literature of the period, providing writers with a wider imaginative landscape and a more extensive linguistic range in which to explore themes such as class, sexual identity and personal relationships.

While novelists in particular were liberated by the implications of the Chatterley case, until the late 1960s dramatists and theatre directors continued to be constrained by having to submit their works for approval to the Lord Chamberlain's Office. The abolition of the Lord Chamberlain's powers, under the Theatres Act of 1968, finally removed this obligation. Where dramatists such as John Osborne in the 1950s and Edward Bond in the 1960s faced protracted struggles to circumvent the censor's prohibitions without compromising their artistic vision, the generation of playwrights that emerged in the late 1960s and early 1970s – including David Hare, David Edgar and Howard Brenton – took advantage of the greater freedom available to lay the foundations for an era of vibrant and politically charged British theatre that often used dramatically effective and deliberate shock tactics to break many of the taboos that the Lord Chamberlain's Office had kept off the British stage. That is not to say that some of these playwrights did not meet with opposition of different kinds: the depiction of homosexual rape, as a metaphor for imperialist rule, in Brenton's play *The Romans in Britain* (1980) brought an unsuccessful private prosecution for gross indecency; in 1995, Sarah Kane's *Blasted* attracted considerable media controversy for representations of rape, torture and violence that shocked even veteran theatre critics.

More liberal attitudes towards censorship were to a considerable extent instrumental in the growth of the so-called 'permissive society' in the 1960s. In more recent times, however, the values associated with that decade have come under attack, firstly from a Thatcherite, and later from a Blairite, perspective, as the root cause of later social and moral ills. While censorship as such has continued to be applied with a light touch, governments have, for example, found ways in times of conflict – the Falklands War, the Northern Irish situation, the 'war against terror', and the Iraq war – to censor information or quell oppositional voices by bringing pressure to bear on the press and broadcast media. Similarly, while writers in Britain have generally enjoyed greater freedom of expression than those living in less liberal societies, there have been serious if isolated incidents in which individual writers' personal safety has been threatened. The best-known such case was that of Salman Rushdie, whose novel *The Satanic Verses* (1988) was condemned as blasphemous by Islamic fundamentalists, leading to the imposition of a *fatwa* – effectively a death sentence – by Ayatollah Khomeini of Iran, which forced Rushdie into hiding for a number of years, before it was lifted in 1998. Another writer to receive similar treatment was Gurpreet Kaur Bhatti, after the reaction of the Sikh community in Birmingham forced the closure of a local production of her play *Behzti*, in 2004. The play's depiction of rape and murder in a Sikh temple attracted fierce condemnation, and Bhatti, like Rushdie before her, was the target of death threats. Incidents of this magnitude are rare in British culture and society, whereas writers working in more repressive regimes can be faced with such dangers on a more regular basis, and often have to use more oblique strategies and literary devices to express their personal and political visions. However, the experiences of Rushdie and Bhatti illustrate that the global nature of contemporary society raises implications for the concept of censorship in the 21st century. Societies need not only to consider their own attitudes towards censorship and the ways in which it should be implemented, but also to be aware that the art and literature they produce can attract scrutiny from other powerful cultural, religious and social constituencies.

See also   *Contexts*: Religion, Sex and sexuality.

Further reading

Hyland, Paul and Neil Sammells (eds), *Writing and Censorship in Britain* (London: Routledge, 1992).
Shellard, Dominic, Steve Nicholson and Miriam Handley, *The Lord Chamberlain Regrets: A History of British Theatre Censorship* (London: British Library, 2004).

Class structure

Throughout the Second World War significant emphasis was placed on the concept of national unity, not least because of the unprecedented degree to which the home front was brought into direct involvement. Civilians experienced the effects of destruction and privation at first hand, as cities were subject to aerial bombardment; families were split up for the safety of their children; and shortages of food and essential goods were frequent and widespread. The sense that all sections of society were potentially vulnerable, that all were suffering to some degree and that all were contributing to the war effort was vital in shaping the postwar spirit of egalitarianism that gave the impetus to the creation of the Welfare State. At the point when the first postwar Labour government began to implement the proposals of the Beveridge Report, many envisaged the possibility of fundamental changes in British class structure as a result of improvements in social provision. For around 30 years the postwar consensus that informed the Welfare State held firm, though there was also considerable disaffection at its failure to achieve some of its key aims in correcting inequalities. By the late 1970s alternative social and economic models were gaining currency; the advent of Thatcherism had an impact on class structure and experience as profound as that brought about by the shift in political ideology at the end of the Second World War, if tending in a very different direction. Increased social mobility has been an incontrovertible fact of the post-Second World War era, but the extent to which traditional class hierarchies have been eradicated is debatable.

The rigid class stratifications that characterised British society before the war did not sit easily with the desire to make restitution to those who had suffered the greatest privations in the war years. As improvements in social conditions for the masses came to dominate the political agenda, and the extension of the educational franchise opened up opportunities for children and young people from working-class backgrounds, there emerged a growing belief that the class structure itself might be liable to substantial change. Although the Labour government of 1945 may have failed to sustain its early momentum after setting up the foundations of the Welfare State, leading to its loss of office in 1951, there was no doubt that material conditions had improved hugely for much of the British working class by the end of the 1950s. Employment levels were high, social services were vastly improved, and working-class people in general had greater economic power. Allied to this were increased opportunities for young people from traditional working-class backgrounds, who were gaining access to professions hitherto denied them, or entering the universities, bringing about significant changes in the social and demographic structure of those institutions. Free tuition and student grants particularly enhanced opportunities for students from working- and lower-middle-class backgrounds.

In the 1960s, hierarchical boundaries continued to be susceptible to erosion, due to the increased self-confidence and higher expectations of the traditional working class, particularly the younger generations. Other factors were also crucial: the growth of alternative social, moral and familial structures and freer attitudes towards sex and sexuality; and the challenge of the feminist movement to conventional gender identities and patriarchal structures. Class became only one of a number of markers by which British citizens defined themselves. However, the period of relative economic strength that had sustained Britain through the decade was drawing to an end by the late 1960s, and the financial crises of the 1970s, that beset both Labour and Conservative governments, was to have a damaging effect on class relationships, culminating in the dismantling of the postwar consensus that had lasted for more than thirty years.

Economic downturn and industrial unrest were recurrent features of the 1970s, posing a threat to the new-found strength and security of the working class. As public services also went into decline through lack of financial support, many of the main advances in the material life of the working class came under severe pressure, and class conflict began to re-emerge. Public service industries were in almost permanent dispute with governments of both persuasions. The miners' and power workers' disputes of the early 1970s, which precipitated the declaration of states of emergency and a three-day working week, effectively brought down Edward Heath's Conservative government in 1974. Successive Labour administrations under Harold Wilson and James Callaghan fared little better, and by the end of the 1970s relations between the government and the unions had deteriorated to a new low. The period that came to be known as the 'winter of discontent' of 1978–9 witnessed a series of damaging strikes by car workers, lorry and oil-tanker drivers, health-service workers, refuse collectors and other public service employees, in opposition to the government's wage restraint policy. The cumulative effect of this period of unrest contributed hugely to the defeat of Callaghan's government in 1979. Unemployment had been increasing at an alarming rate through the late 1970s, with damaging consequences for the working class in general and those working in manufacturing industries in particular. By the time the Conservatives returned to power, under Margaret Thatcher, the era of steady working-class advance in material and economic terms was already coming to an end.

Worse was to follow in the 1980s, as the gap between rich and poor widened and unemployment rose to over 3 million, while the decline of public services continued. One of the stated aims of the Conservative government was the curtailment of trade union power, which precipitated an intensification of class conflict and ultimately brought about the disintegration of many working-class communities. The miners' strike of 1984–5 was a watershed in the antagonistic relationship between government and unions, with the miners, led by Arthur Scargill, castigated by Thatcher as 'the enemy within' for their opposition to a proposed programme of pit closures. The dispute was long and acrimonious, ending in defeat for the union and the near-decimation of the coal industry. Other areas of the manufacturing sector experienced similar levels of unemployment, with devastating effects on the communities in which they were located. Prospects of finding any kind of employment for the working-age population of industrial towns and cities dwindled drastically, and for many commentators it seemed appropriate to think of those in such areas as constituting no longer a working class, as such, but rather an underclass, lacking in hope and with prospects and horizons greatly diminished from those of generations before them.

The attitudes of those in political authority since the 1980s towards class as a concept are instructive of how attitudes have changed. Margaret Thatcher famously declared that 'there is no such thing as Society. There are individual men and women, and there are families',[3] so denying the existence of a class structure in any meaningful sense, and her successor John Major articulated a vision of Britain as a 'classless society', suggesting that traditional ways of describing the structure of British society were no longer relevant by the 1990s. While Conservative politicians have tended to underplay the significance of class in British social and political life, there has historically been greater emphasis in the Labour movement on connecting social justice and progress to the creation of a more equitable class system. Tony Blair, however, in attempting to reposition Labour as the natural party of the middle class, has done much to erode its close identification with the interests of the working class. It is certainly the case that British society has undergone considerable structural change since the end of the Second World War, with greater movement between what were once strictly demarcated class hierarchies. The Welfare State ethos that went largely unchallenged for some 30 years delivered on many of its aims and intentions, enhancing the quality of life for many but failing to address fully the challenges facing the public services. Thatcherism's support for monetarism and the free market had devastating consequences for those affected by rising unemployment and industrial decline. Inequality remains a prevalent fact in Britain in the 21st century, which at least suggests that class continues to be a significant factor in the way society in Britain is organised.

Class is a theme that has been strongly reflected in contemporary literature, which has tended to reflect closely the political and social shifts of the period. In the 1950s, the expansion of the traditional working class into new areas and professions was manifested in the emergence of writers, dramatists and film-makers intent on representing the kinds of experience with which literature, drama and film had not been generally concerned. This led to a proliferation of novels, such as John Braine's *Room at the Top* (1957) and David Storey's *This Sporting Life* (1960), which were adapted for the screen at a time of intense creativity for the British film industry. These novels foregrounded working-class life and delineated the changing class structure of Britain in the postwar era. Playwrights such as Arnold Wesker, taking advantage of the tendency in British drama towards 'kitchen sink' realism, inspired by John Osborne's landmark play *Look Back in Anger* (1956), also drew attention to issues affecting working-class experience. As more liberal attitudes developed through the 1960s, class maintained a significant presence in fiction, poetry and drama. In the theatre in particular, aided by the lifting of censorship restrictions and the rapid growth of alternative and provincial theatre, a new wave of left-leaning playwrights, such as David Hare, Howard Barker and Trevor Griffiths, dominated British drama in the 1970s.

By the 1980s, however, disillusioned by the consequences of Thatcherism, much of the literature of the period seemed to retreat into introspective despair, though playwrights such as David Hare, for one, continued to anatomise the state of the nation, and poets like Tony Harrison and Peter Reading addressed the decline of contemporary working-class communities in the kind of vivid and uncompromising detail that also characterises some of the most imaginative Scottish fiction of the later decades of the 20th century. Working-class experience is the central theme of much of the work of James Kelman, from his first novel, *The Busconductor Hines* (1984) to the somewhat unexpected Booker Prize winner *How Late It Was, How Late* (1994), and in collections of short stories from *Not Not While the Giro* (1983) to *The Good Times* (1998). Irvine Welsh has explored the effects of social deprivation on the young underclass of Edinburgh in *Trainspotting* (1993), and has revisited some of that novel's main protagonists in later works such as *Glue* (2001) and *Porno* (2002). Class may not be a defining principle for most writers at the start of the 21st century, as it was for the new wave of novelists and dramatists who emerged in the 1950s, but it remains a significant touchstone for writers who seek to make sense of contemporary society, even if it is no longer addressed as directly as earlier in the postwar period.

See also   *Contexts*: Political protest, War, Youth Culture; *Texts*: 'Angry Young Men', Campus novel, Class, 'Kitchen sink' drama, Political commitment, Realism, Regional identity, Urban experience; *Criticism*: Cultural materialism, New Historicism, Marxist criticism.

Further reading

Roberts, Kenneth, *Class in Modern Britain* (Basingstoke: Palgrave Macmillan, 2001).

Cold War

In the aftermath of the Second World War the leaders of the victorious Allied powers, American president Harry S. Truman, British Prime Minister Winston Churchill and the Soviet leader Josef Stalin divided up the defeated German nation, with Britain, France and America occupying parts of West Germany and Russia taking control of East German territories. The rebuilding of those nations that had suffered most during the war became a key priority, one in which America, with its unparalleled economic strength and political confidence, was closely involved. Inevitable tensions arose as the two new superpowers of the postwar world, capitalist America and the communist Soviet Union, both recognised the strategic importance of extending their influence over Europe. Those tensions were exacerbated by the determination of both powers to increase their capability in nuclear weaponry. America was the first nation to create an atomic bomb, but by 1943 Russia was also beginning similar developments. In the wake of the American atomic bombing of Hiroshima and Nagasaki, that finally ended Japanese resistance and terminated the war, America and Russia became embroiled in negotiations about the future of nuclear weapons. America proposed the surrendering of all relevant materials, existing manufacturing plant and bombs to an international agency, while Russia insisted on a complete ban on bombs and fissionable material. The situation ended in stalemate, and relations between America and the Soviet Union deteriorated further.

From the perspective of Western capitalist societies the threat of a communist takeover of Europe was a crucial issue in the late 1940s, particularly as communist parties seemed to be gaining in support and influence. At the same time, Soviet communism was sweeping through Eastern Europe, taking control of Poland, Hungary, Bulgaria and Romania, and making a significant incursion into central Europe with the Russian invasion of Czechoslovakia. America's main European allies, preoccupied with domestic problems of reconstruction, lacked the financial wherewithal to defend Europe against the perceived communist threat. America's response came in the form of the Marshall Aid programme of 1947, in which financial support was pledged for European states, under conditions that would serve American political and economic interests. Unsurprisingly, the Soviet Union refused to subscribe to the terms of the plan, and further isolation followed when America pledged to defend the signatories of the North Atlantic Treaty, an agreement that led to the formation of NATO. At this point a state of 'cold war' clearly existed between America and Russia, and in the 1950s both sides stepped up their nuclear technology, developing and testing hydrogen bombs. The resultant nuclear stand-off continued through the decade, with European nations vulnerably placed between the two superpowers. A growing concern about the possibility of nuclear annihilation led to the formation and growth of peace movements, the most notable of which was the British Campaign for Nuclear Disarmament (CND), formed in 1958, partly in response to Britain's participation in the nuclear arms race, and specifically its involvement in hydrogen bomb testing.

Worldwide anxiety about nuclear proliferation reached a climax in 1962 with the Cuban missile crisis, when for a two-week period the threat of nuclear destruction loomed even larger. The American government received evidence that Soviet missile bases were being built in Cuba and responded with a declaration that there would be reprisals against Russia for any attack that originated from those bases. American president John F. Kennedy also demanded the building programme be halted and ordered a naval blockade of Cuba in an effort to stop construction. After a number of days of increasing tension the Russian leader Leonid Brezhnev agreed to American demands, and the threat of nuclear war receded. There then followed a period of relative calm as America's preoccupations shifted towards the Vietnam War.

In the late 1960s meaningful talks finally got under way between America and Russia, with a view to reducing the stockpiles of nuclear weapons. The Strategic Arms Limitation Talks (SALT) that began in 1969 culminated in a treaty imposing restrictions on the numbers of submarine-based and intercontinental nuclear missiles. After this, the uneasy 'thaw' in Cold War relations continued, and was not seriously threatened until 1983, when the US President Ronald Reagan announced his 'Star Wars' initiative, a system designed to offer protection from space against nuclear attack, which Russia claimed breached earlier treaty agreements. Two years previously Britain, as America's closest ally, became centrally implicated in the nuclear debate after agreeing to allow US Cruise guided missiles to be based in Britain at the Greenham Common military air base, in return for Trident missiles that would be used to enhance Britain's own nuclear capability. The British peace movement responded, with the setting up of a women's peace camp at Greenham Common that tried to disrupt the building of the storage facilities. The camp stayed in place long after the first arrival of Cruise missiles in 1983, and was still there when the missiles were removed, under the terms of the Intermediate Range Nuclear Forces Treaty, signed by Reagan and the reformist Russian president Mikhail Gorbachev in 1987.

It was becoming increasingly apparent by the late 1980s that the Cold War was coming to an end, aided by Gorbachev's determination to bring about substantial political change within the Soviet Union and radical upheavals elsewhere in Eastern Europe. In 1989, Gorbachev terminated the longstanding Soviet commitment to protect its interests in Eastern Europe, precipitating demonstrations that culminated in the bringing down of the Berlin Wall, which had been constructed to separate East Germany from the West in 1961. German unification followed in 1990 and a year later the Soviet Union collapsed, after the overthrow of Gorbachev by hard-line communists brought public condemnation, and the defeat of the attempted coup, effectively ending the Cold War.

Literature of the Cold War period generally demonstrated relatively little direct engagement with the events and issues that arose over that time, though novels of espionage such as John le Carré's *The Spy who Came in from the Cold* (1963), and the immensely popular James Bond novels of Ian Fleming drew productively on the machinations between East and West. Ian McEwan's *The Innocent* (1990) is a rare overt treatment of the themes thrown up by the Cold War, taking the conventions of the spy novel into the sphere of literary fiction, much as Tom Stoppard did from a dramatic perspective in his play *Hapgood* (1988). More often, however, the influence of the Cold War on contemporary writing exists on a more subliminal level. The fact of Britain's powerlessness and dependency on America during the Cold War contributed to the mood of postimperial despair that existed in the period, and was a significant theme in post-Second World War writing. For the most part, the threat of nuclear destruction that pervaded much of the Cold War era cast a dark shadow over the imagination of many British writers, and can be detected in the dystopian visions that permeate novels such as Anthony Burgess's *A Clockwork Orange* (1962) and Russell Hoban's *Riddley Walker* (1980).

See also *Contexts*: Counter-culture, Political protest, Science and technological innovation, War; *Texts*: Genre fiction, Political commitment.

Further reading

Greenwood, Sean, *Britain and the Cold War, 1945–1991* (London: Palgrave Macmillan, 2000).

Counter-culture

The term 'counter-culture' is particularly associated in the post-Second World War period with a range of cultural practices, activities and ideologies that challenged traditional values and attitudes. The term first came into widespread currency in the 1960s, with the emergence of a distinct youth culture that had its own social and sexual mores, political outlooks, fashion, art and music, much of which was influenced by events and developments elsewhere, particularly in America. As American political and economic dominance of the new world order grew, so its cultural values began to exert an influence on other Western nations. In respect of both 'high' culture (art, literature, theatre and music) and 'popular' culture (Hollywood film, television, popular music and literature), America led the way, exporting its cultural works and the values that underpinned them to countries dependent on its support. The same applied to those cultural movements in America that challenged the prevailing ideas and attitudes of the time, as can be seen in the enduring influence of the 'Beat' generation of the 1950s on the hippy culture that flourished in America and elsewhere in the Western world, including Britain, in the 1960s.

In Britain, however, the development of counter-cultural movements in the 1960s could also be attributed to the effects of the social changes that took place in the preceding decade. There emerged an unfocused sense of restlessness and rebelliousness among young people in Britain at that time, who found themselves with unprecedented disposable income and spending power, and greater educational opportunities, but without a clear sense of their future role in British society. Other domestic factors that paved the way for the emergence of counter-cultural movements in Britain were the general erosion in class deference, and a decline in confidence in politics and politicians. The creation of the Welfare State and the egalitarian impulses that informed it brought into question the hitherto accepted class structure, while recurring political scandals and large-scale events like the Suez crisis confirmed Britain's postimperial decline. One of the most significant cultural manifestations of the loss of faith in the political system was the 'satire boom' of the late 1950s and early 1960s. Stage shows such as *Beyond the Fringe*, magazines like *Private Eye*, and topical TV programmes in the vein of *That Was the Week that Was* specialised in lampooning public figures and treating established authorities with irreverence, setting the tone for a decade in which alternative political, social and cultural perspectives found more scope for expression.

The term 'counter-culture' may be somewhat misleading in suggesting a more cohesive sense of common purpose than actually existed between the proliferation of disparate movements that reacted against conventional society in the 1960s. While most such movements were to some degree politically leftist, many located themselves outside traditional politics, in, for example, Eastern religions, psychology and psychotherapy, communal structures that rejected the traditional family unit, or in experimentation with mind-altering drugs. In the lifestyles and personal relationships which they pursued, and the fashions and cultural activities by which they defined themselves, adherents of counter-cultural movements sought to challenge and subvert authority in all its forms, though not often through direct confrontation. It was rather the case that significant social change emerged gradually, as in the development of more relaxed attitudes to sex and sexuality that characterised the so-called 'permissive society' of the 1960s, or the greater freedom of expression that resulted from shifts in perceptions about what constituted 'high' art and its relationship with popular culture.

There were, however, also major events in the 1960s that politicised the counter-culture and galvanised its many individual subgenres into more organised opposition to authority. The continuing fear of nuclear war was one such factor, and led in Britain to the growth and influence of CND, but the single most significant political issue of the 1960s was the Vietnam War. Opposition to the American presence in Vietnam became the main focal point for counter-cultural political activity, with worldwide protest marches and demonstrations throughout the late 1960s. Elsewhere in Europe, other events also brought radical young people onto the streets in protest, most notably in Paris in 1968, when for a time it seemed that revolution was imminent. Student demonstrations led to escalating violence and rioting, and similar clashes in other French cities. Students and factory workers made common cause and the French government was almost brought down by a national strike. The events had a resounding impact beyond France, and seized the imagination of many British writers and dramatists, many of whom were fired by the prospect of revolution, but also reflected in their work the disillusionment that set in after the revolutionary moment passed.

The consequences of the emergence and growth of counter-cultural movements for British literature were numerous, contributing greatly to the diminishment of the consensus about what constituted literature and the literary that characterises the post-Second World War period. The audience for literature in the 1960s grew due to the continuing expansion of the university sector and the popularity of English as a subject for study at university level at this time. The more diverse social mix that made up the student population was also a factor in bringing about challenges to the traditional syllabus to reflect the experience of readers more accurately. The growth in complexity and cultural significance of rock music lyrics by artists such as the Beatles and Bob Dylan, led to a widening of interest in poetry and an increased emphasis on the performative element of the genre, as demonstrated by the Poetry Festival held at the Albert Hall in 1965, when an audience of around 7,000 came to see Underground and Beat poets reading, chanting and sometimes singing their work. Poets such as Roger McGough, Brian

Patten and Adrian Henri, benefiting from the cultural authority the Beatles had bestowed on their home city of Liverpool, achieved considerable commercial success with their anthology *The Mersey Sound* (1967). The colloquial and accessible style of their poems struck a chord with a young, culturally aware readership that saw more relevance in their work than in supposedly canonical literature.

Other literary genres also underwent radical developments, influenced by counter-cultural values and attitudes. In drama, a new generation of left-wing playwrights began to rise to prominence in the late 1960s and early 1970s, initially through alternative theatre companies like the Joint Stock Company and John McGrath's 7:84. Other dramatists, such as Joe Orton, took advantage of more liberated attitudes towards sex and sexuality to satirise conventional sexual attitudes, helping to bring about the eventual removal of the theatre censorship laws that had constrained playwrights until the late 1960s. The novel also reflected the progressive attitudes and greater freedom of expression of the period. Modernist influences came to the fore again, after being largely rejected by the new writers of the 1950s, and novelists like John Berger, Clive Sinclair and B. S. Johnson began to focus as much attention on experimenting with narrative forms as with subject-matter, though commercial and critical success often eluded these writers. Johnson, for example, produced a series of experimental novels in the 1960s, culminating in 1969 with *The Unfortunates*, his 'novel-in-a-box', which consisted of 27 separate sections that could be read in any order. His work failed to receive widespread recognition, however, and Johnson committed suicide in 1973. Only in the early years of the 21st century did his work begin to attract critical attention, with the reprinting of his novels and Jonathan Coe's acclaimed biography, *Like a Fiery Elephant* (2004).

See also   *Contexts*: Cold War, Political protest, Popular culture, Sex and sexuality, Youth culture; *Texts*: Alternative theatre, Modernism, legacy of, Performance poetry, Political commitment, Underground poetry.

Further reading

Roszak, Theodore, *The Making of a Counter-Culture: Reflections on the Technocratic Society and its Youthful Opposition* (London: Faber & Faber, 1970).

Feminism and the role of women

During the Second World War the demands of the war effort on the home front, and the absence of a substantial proportion of the male population in the armed forces, led to increased work opportunities for women in Britain, especially in factories and in agriculture. Their work was often of a routine or low-level nature, albeit of crucial importance, and there was a general assumption that in peacetime the majority of working women would readily return to the home, while men would take up what was perceived to be their rightful role as breadwinners. Added to this was anxiety about the possibility of a decline in the national birth-rate, which reinforced pressures on women to prioritise their roles as wives and mothers after the war. In the event, the birth-rate increased hugely. Over the same period, the existing labour force came to be perceived as inadequate for the urgent task of postwar regeneration. Increased national prosperity brought a consumer boom in the 1950s, and on the domestic front developments in labour-saving devices eased the household burdens on traditional female roles in the home. All these factors combined to bring women, largely willingly, back into the workforce in unprecedented numbers, many of them, admittedly, on a part-time basis and on lower rates of pay than men. At the same time, opportunities were expanding for younger women to gain access to further and higher education, with the prospect of increasing female participation in traditionally male-dominated professions and institutions, such as politics, the law and the civil service. Nevertheless, conservative elements in British society often expressed disquiet at the possible effect such social changes might have on gender roles, and a combination of low-pay, conflicting demands of career and family responsibilities, and uncertainty on the part of women as to their right to academic and professional fulfilment, continued to inhibit their social status and aspirations well into the 1960s.

It was in that decade that some of the most significant advances for women in Britain were facilitated, through a liberalisation of social, sexual and cultural attitudes, and some crucial examples of enlightened legislation. As a result, fundamental changes in gender roles and relationships became genuine possibilities. As early as 1961, with the introduction of the contraceptive pill, women began to assert more control and choice over their own sexuality and sexual behaviour, though the real breakthrough in this respect came when local authorities were compelled to provide free contraception and contraceptive advice under the Family Planning Act of 1967, the same year in which abortion was legalised. Women's legal rights in relation to marriage also underwent some crucial changes for the better in this period, culminating in the Divorce Act of 1969, which stipulated that the irretrievable breakdown of a marriage was the sole grounds for divorce, whether on account of adultery, unreasonable behaviour, desertion or separation.

These improvements to women's social and legal status were greatly to be welcomed, but in other ways restrictions on their personal and professional lives were still limiting their horizons. The counter-culture offered little in the way of genuine liberation, with the sexual revolution still heavily weighted in men's favour. What seemed at first like sexual liberation was soon revealed, for many women, as a continuation of exploitation and objectification in new ways. In America, women politicized by involvement in the civil rights movement began to see that even there the power structures were male-dominated. Their counterparts in Britain had endured similar experiences, confined to subordinate positions in supposedly democratic movements and organisations. As a consequence, women's groups began to spring up all over America, Britain, and elsewhere in Western Europe from the late 1960s onwards. These groups campaigned for equality in various aspects of social, political and professional life, and protested against what they saw as the inherently patriarchal nature of modern societies that perpetuated gender discrimination. The subsequent emergence of a radical feminist movement that addressed most areas of social, political, personal and cultural life has been one of the most significant agents of change in the post-Second World War period.

In Britain, feminist campaigns helped to bring about legislation against sexual discrimination in the 1970s, and the period also saw an increasing female presence in education and in the professional world, though equality in pay was still the exception rather than the norm, and there were still relatively few women at the very top of most professions. Nevertheless, women's aspirations continued to rise, along with their financial and personal independence. Women in general became more socially assertive and politically active, as can be seen in the impact of the women's peace camp at Greenham Common throughout the 1980s, and the crucial role played by miners' wives support groups in the strike of 1984–5. By the 1990s many women were making even greater professional progress, and were making their mark in official politics in greater numbers than ever before, with around 120 female Members of Parliament after the 1997 election. At the other end of the scale, however, there was an increase in single mothers living on benefits in economically deprived inner-city areas that had suffered social disintegration since the 1980s. By the turn of the 21st century it was clear that the women's movement had made a huge contribution to the advancement of women, though full equality was still to be achieved.

The impact of feminist ideology on British society since the late 1960s was accompanied by an equally far-reaching and transformative effect on academic and cultural practices. In relation to literature, the canonical marginalization of female writers, that had barely been questioned before the 1960s, was held up to scrutiny by feminist critics, and the rise of feminist scholarship brought renewed attention on forgotten or neglected women writers, aided by the emergence of women's presses such as Virago, founded in 1973. The rise of feminist theory in academic circles has provided new analytical perspectives through which canonical and non-canonical literary texts can be studied, based on the idea that gender considerations can fundamentally affect interpretation. The novel proved to be a particularly effective form through which the feminist imagination could be explored, and much of the most innovative and vital fiction of the period has originated from women writers who have addressed gender relationships and female experience from perspectives that transcend conventional realism. In the 1960s and 1970s, women novelists such as Doris Lessing and Angela Carter revived and reclaimed modernist techniques that had fallen into disuse, and combined them with elements of fantasy or Gothic to create imaginative worlds that transcend the patriarchal order. Their lead has been followed by another generation of women writers like Jeanette Winterson, who, in novels including *Written on the Body* (1992), has taken full advantage of the greater freedom writers have been afforded in the late 20th century, to address issues of sexual identity. The legacy of modernist experimentation emerges strongly in Winterson's fiction, as it does in the work of two contemporary Scottish writers, A. L. Kennedy and Ali Smith. Kennedy's work, ranging from short story collections like *Original Bliss* (1999) to novels including *So I Am Glad* (1995) and *Paradise* (2004) is charged with dark eroticism and characteristically explored themes of longing and desire. Smith first came to prominence for *Hotel World* (2001), a novel that draws on modernist and postmodernist techniques of fragmentation and self-reflexivity to chart the intertwined stories of five characters linked by their shared connections to the Global Hotel alluded to in the title. Smith's experimental narrative strategies are also shown to considerable effect in *The Accidental* (2005), a novel that examines the impact of an unexpected visitor on the various members of a disintegrating family unit.

In poetry and drama, traditionally male-dominated spheres, women have generally found it harder to establish themselves. In the early postwar period, Elizabeth Jennings was the only female representative among the Movement poets of the 1950s, and Sylvia Plath was a rare female voice in the early 1960s, while Stevie Smith, born early in the 20th century, did not receive her due critical attention until after her death in 1971. It is true that there are a far greater number of British women poets in print at the beginning of the 21st century than at any time in the past. However, the numerous mixed-sex anthologies of contemporary poetry that have appeared regularly in Britain since the 1960s, still tend to feature the work of considerably more male than female poets; that there remains a perceived need for women-only anthologies, like Linda France's *Sixty Women Poets* (1993) and Maura Dooley's *Making for Planet Alice* (1997), to redress this balance is clearly significant.

For much of the postwar period there have been relatively few women playwrights in Britain: Shelagh Delaney's *A Taste of Honey* (1958) and Ann Jellicoe's *The Sport of my Mad Mother* (1958) and *The Knack* (1962) were among the few plays by women to emerge in the new wave of British drama that began in the late 1950s. Delaney's play was first performed by Joan Littlewood's Theatre Workshop, a company that prefigured the concerns and strategies of the alternative theatre movement. In the 1970s, Caryl Churchill, with the plays *Vinegar Tom* (1976), for the Monstrous Regiment women's theatre group, and *Cloud Nine* (1979), for David Hare's Joint Stock company, and Pam Gems, with *Dusa, Fish, Stas and Vi* (1976) and *Piaf* (1978), first came to prominence, and went on to become arguably the leading British female playwrights of the late 20th century. Their impact was matched only by that of Sarah Kane, whose plays, including *Blasted* (1995), *Phaedra's Love* (1996) and *4.48 Psychosis* (staged posthumously in 2000, after Kane's suicide the previous year), were as radical and shocking as anything produced on the British stage. As with the mixture of positive change and the need for further advancement for women in contemporary Britain as a whole, British literature of the period has been marked by an increasingly influential female presence that has done much to challenge canonical assumptions, but remains largely dominated by male writers in most areas.

See also   *Contexts*: Counter-culture, Political protest, Sex and sexuality; *Texts*: Alternative theatre, Gay and lesbian writing, Magic realism, Modernism, legacy of, Women's writing; *Criticism*: Feminist criticism, Gender criticism, Psychoanalytic criticism.

Further reading

Boles, Janet K., Diane Long Hoeveler and Rebecca Bardwell, *Historical Dictionary of Feminism* (London: Scarecrow Press, 1996).
Freedman, Estelle B., *No Turning Back: The History of Feminism and the Future of Women* (London: Profile, 2002).

Holocaust

By the end of the Second World War the Nazi regime had been responsible for the deaths of 6 million European Jews in gas chambers at concentration camps in Germany and Poland, the culmination of a systematic programme of persecution that was designed to serve Adolf Hitler's quest for a racially pure German race. To that end, other groups were also persecuted on a massive scale, with 5.5 million gypsies, Jehovah's Witnesses, Polish nationals, homosexuals, disabled people and political criminals also slaughtered over the period of Nazi rule. European Jewry was, however, the main target for extermination by the Nazis.

The persecution and oppression of Jews had begun in Germany with Hitler's rise to power in 1933, but the event that has often been cited as denoting the beginning of the Holocaust took place in November 1938. In response to the killing of a German official by a Jewish youth, a pogrom was instigated by the Gestapo against German Jews. The events of *Kristallnacht* on 9 November saw 7,500 Jewish businesses and over 100 synagogues destroyed, many Jews killed and thousands more arrested and sent to concentration camps. In the same year, 15,000 Jews were rounded up and sent to Poland, where a ghetto was created in Warsaw. Many of the main concentration camps were also located in Poland, including Auschwitz–Birkenau, Treblinka, Maidanek and Sobibor; these names, along with others such as Dachau, Buchenwald and Belsen, became imprinted on the public imagination when the full extent of the Holocaust became known after the Second World War.

Throughout the war the deportation of Jews continued, and in 1942 the Nazis announced their 'Final Solution' to the Jewish question: the complete annihilation of all European Jews. To that end, the movement of Jews to the various camps intensified, with all those held in Germany being sent to Auschwitz–Birkenau, where mass exterminations took place on a regular basis. The highest total of Jews killed at Auschwitz on a single day was 46,000, in 1944. On the same day, Russian troops liberated the Maidanek death camp, where an estimated 1.6 million people had been murdered. By this time the Nazi regime was disintegrating, and as camps were abandoned, their leaders ordered the destruction of the evidence, in order to conceal the extent of the genocide. With the liberation of other death camps in Buchenwald and Auschwitz, where 5,000 starving survivors were found, the enormity of the Nazi programme of extermination was revealed for the first time, though public perception struggled to encompass the horrific scale of the genocide perpetrated in the death camps. In the aftermath of the war, many of those responsible for the organisation of the death camps were brought before the Nuremberg trials and sentenced to death. Others escaped justice but were brought to trial later, such as Adolf Eichmann, the head of the Gestapo's Jewish Office, who fled from an American camp to Argentina but was finally captured, tried and executed in Israel in 1962.

By the time of Eichmann's arrest public imagination was starting to come to terms with the scale of atrocity represented in the Holocaust; indeed, the term itself was rarely invoked before the early 1960s. The sense of emotional and physical exhaustion that characterised attitudes towards the events of the Second World War in its immediate aftermath gave way to a compulsion to confront the enormity of the Holocaust's impact. In common with other artists, writers began to devote attention to the moral consequences and implications of the Holocaust, following the lead set by survivors. The Jewish-Italian writer Primo Levi's auto-biographical works *If This is a Man* (1958) and *The Truth* (1963), which drew on his experiences in Auschwitz, were among the earliest and most influential examples of Holocaust writings, while Paul Celan's 'Todesfuge' (1952) is the earliest major treatment of the Holocaust in poetry. Poets without first-hand experience of the events of the Holocaust have nevertheless addressed its key themes, most notably Geoffrey Hill, in poems such as 'September Song', and Tony Harrison, in 'The Morning After' and numerous other poems. Late 20th-century fictional explorations of the intractable moral questions raised by the Holocaust have included Martin Amis's *Time's Arrow* (1991), Ian McEwan's *Black Dogs* (1992) and the Canadian novelist Anne Michaels' *Fugitive Pieces* (1997).

See also   *Contexts*: War; *Texts*: History, Holocaust literature.

Further reading

Engel, David, *The Holocaust: A History of the Third Reich and the Jews* (Harlow: Longman, 2000).
Schwarz, Daniel R., *Imagining the Holocaust* (Basingstoke: Palgrave Macmillan, 2000).

Migrant experience and multiculturalism

The main problem that faced national reconstruction in Britain after the Second World War was an acute shortage of labour. The solution was to appeal to Britain's Commonwealth territories to fill the gaps in the work-force, and as a consequence the first wave of immigration began to arrive in Britain in the late 1940s, largely from the Caribbean, where unemployment levels were high and wage rates low. There was an expectation among the first postwar immigrants that they would be welcomed into the 'mother country', but although most found it rela-tively easy to get employment, albeit in menial capacities, in other respects they faced ignorance, bigotry and discrimination. Housing was a particular problem, and as a result concentrations of immigrants built up in older housing stock in socially deprived inner-city areas, which became a breeding ground for racial tensions. In 1958, those tensions spilled over into race riots almost simultaneously in the Notting Hill area of London and the St Ann's district of Nottingham. Disillusioned by the failure of the police to offer adequate protection, many immigrant communities set up their own associations as an assertion of solidarity and identity, and a mistrust of police attitudes towards immigrants began to emerge, reaching a peak in the 1970s and then again at the end of the 20th century, after the inquiry into the murder of black teenager Stephen Lawrence found evidence of institutionalised racism in the Metropolitan Police Force.

Immigration continued to be a key feature of British social change into the 1960s, with Indian and Pakistani migrants arriving in increasing numbers, and encountering the same levels of racism and discrimination as their Caribbean predecessors. Successive governments came under pressure to revise immigration laws, and a series of restrictive measures were enacted, beginning with the Conservative government's legislation in 1962, that imposed a voucher system prioritising skilled workers and those with guaranteed employment. Although the system was condemned by opposition parties, the government's actions met with approval from large sections of the population, including trade unionists who perceived immigration as a threat to their members' jobs. It was clear that much needed to be done to encourage more enlightened attitudes towards immigration, and in 1966 the Race Relations Board was founded to further this aim, but by the late 1960s violence in black and mixed race communities was in danger of becoming endemic. At the same time, far-right racist groups were coalescing, resulting in the formation of the National Front in 1967, which openly sought to incite racial hatred, especially among young, white working-class men. Skinheads and football hooligans in particular became widely associated with racist attitudes and behaviour, and the late 1960s witnessed a rise in racial violence in urban areas, usually targeted against Asian families.

In 1968 the Conservative politician Enoch Powell made a series of inflammatory speeches on the race question, in which he predicted an escalation of violence and called for the repatriation of immigrants. Powell was widely condemned on all sides in parliament, but received support from extreme right-wing elements in the political establishment and from many people in working-class communities, including East End dock workers, who demonstrated in favour of his proposals. Faced with the prospect of growing racial conflict, coinciding with an expected influx of Kenyan Asians fleeing a change of regime, the Labour government further tightened up the immigration laws, imposing a quota system and limiting entry to those with ties with existing British residents. Racial prejudice and violence intensified in the 1970s as the British economy declined. Unemployment increased, particularly amongst black and Asian communities, social and material conditions in many inner-city areas worsened, and relations between the immigrant population and the police deteriorated still further. The summer of 1981 proved to be a flashpoint for race relations as violence flared up yet again, with rioting in a number of inner-city areas, most notably in Brixton, south London and the districts of Toxteth and Moss Side, in Liverpool and Manchester respectively. An inquiry, chaired by Lord Scarman, was instigated as a consequence of these events, which revealed the extent to which black youths – males in particular – without employment and prospects, and frequently subjected to police harassment, were becoming increasingly alienated from their communities and from society as a whole. Scarman's report advocated reform and there followed a programme of inner-city redevelopment that achieved some limited success, though conditions in many areas continued to decline.

There were positive signs, however, for those prepared to embrace the prospect and strengths of a multicultural society as the immigrant population expanded into a second and third generation by the start of the 21st century. Although racial prejudice had by no means been eradicated in Britain by this time, with far-right parties gaining a foothold in local politics in some inner-city constituencies, racially motivated assaults, and rising tensions as a consequence of the growth of religious fundamentalism and continuing British involvement in Iraq, there was also plenty of evidence of the benefits of multiculturalism. Black and Asian Britons were making their presence felt in many areas of cultural life, politics, entertainment and sport. The black British presence in athletics, football and boxing was particularly noticeable, with figures such as Linford Christie, Kelly Holmes, Ian Wright, Frank Bruno and Naseem Hamed becoming household names. Asian British experience has been widely addressed in literature, television and film. The actress and writer Meera Syal has been involved in film and TV versions of her novels *Anita and Me* (1996) and *Life Isn't All Ha Ha Hee Hee* (1999), and other films depicting British Asian themes and experience, such as *East is East* (1999), directed by Damien O'Donnell and based on Ayub Khan-Din's play, and Gurinda Chadhar's *Bend It Like Beckham* (2002) have attracted commercial success and critical acclaim. Some of the most innovative, socially conscious and challenging popular music of the early 21st century has been produced by black British artists like Nitin

Sawhney, whose work transcends musical and cultural boundaries, and Ms Dynamite, who has become a significant and rare British female presence in the field of rap.

In literature, the migrant experience has provided a new perspective for exploring contemporary social, cultural and political themes, especially that of the outsider or exile either attempting to assimilate into British society, or struggling to assert a sense of cultural identity within that society, a recurrent motif in black British writing from Sam Selvon's *The Lonely Londoners* (1956) to Zadie Smith's *White Teeth* (2000), and in poems such as Linton Kwesi Johnson's 'Inglan is a Bitch' (1981). Johnson's speaker in this poem is a first-generation immigrant from the Caribbean, whose 'struggle fi mek enz meet' by decades of working in low-paid menial jobs ends in redundancy at the age of 55. Black British poets like Johnson, James Berry and Grace Nichols reject conventional literary language and traditional forms in favour of dialect voices and poetic rhythms that reflect their own indigenous cultures and values. The rise of black British writing in the postwar era has posited another challenge to canonical values that has much common ground with wider developments in postcolonial writing over the same period, but focuses much more closely on their experiences within British society.

See also   *Contexts*: British Empire, decline and loss, Religion; *Texts*: Black British literature, Empire, end of, London, literary representations of, Magic realism, Postcolonial literature; *Criticism*: Postcolonial criticism.

Further reading

Baumann, Gerd, *The Multicultural Riddle: Rethinking National, Ethnic and Religious Identities* (London: Routledge, 1999).
Winder, Robert, *Bloody Foreigners: The Story of Immigration to Britain* (London: Little, Brown, 2004).

Northern Irish 'troubles'

Northern Ireland has been in a state of open sectarian and political conflict since the late 1960s. A period of more than 40 years of relative if uneasy calm, established by the Government of Ireland Act of 1920, in which the Protestant community was in the ascendancy, drew to a close after the formation of a Catholic civil rights movement, founded to draw attention to social grievances, particularly relating to housing and unemployment. The birth of new parties such as the SDLP provided a political platform for these concerns, while Unionist unrest over the perceived liberalism of Captain Terence O'Neill's government led to the establishment of extremist Protestant groups seeking to protect the status quo. The escalation of violence led to government intervention from Britain, with the Downing Street Declaration of 1969 being the first of numerous attempts to find a solution to the modern 'Irish problem'. Despite some degree of constitutional progress, conflict continued, resulting in the British government's imposition of an army presence on the streets of Northern Ireland. The Catholic population quickly came to regard these troops as an 'army of occupation' sent to prevent the possibility of a united Ireland. Major incidents such as the events of 'Bloody Sunday' in 1973, when 13 civilians were killed by British soldiers, exacerbated the bitterness of opposition towards the government and its armed forces. Protestant Unionists, on the other hand, decried what they saw as the failure of the army to maintain law and order. In March 1972 the Northern Irish government was suspended and direct rule from Westminster was imposed. Throughout the 1970s various measures such as power-sharing agreements between the Unionists and the SDLP, attempts to establish a constitutional assembly, and moves towards the lifting of internment met with little success. Non-political interventions, such as the 'Peace Movement' begun by two Catholic Belfast women, Betty Williams and Mairead Corrigan (for which they received the Nobel Peace Prize in 1977), were ultimately no more effective. The Thatcher years brought little significant progress and it was not until the second Downing Street Declaration of 1993, brokered by John Major and the Irish Prime Minister Albert Reynolds, that further serious attempts to address constitutional grievances were made. Secret negotiations with Sinn Fein led to an IRA ceasefire that brought two years of relative tranquillity, but further headway could not be made under Major's premiership. Labour's return to power in 1997 brought with it a revival of the peace process but continuing violence hampered these efforts, even after the Good Friday agreement of 1998 and the founding of a Northern Irish Assembly. Over the next few years the question of IRA decommissioning of arms dominated negotiations and the Assembly was periodically suspended and restored. In 2005, the IRA declared an end to its armed campaign, raising hopes that an end to the troubles were finally in sight, though at that point much remained to be done in terms of negotiations on all sides to turn optimism about peace into reality.

The sense of upheaval caused by ongoing sectarian conflict and political intransigence over the later decades of the 20th century had a striking and significant impact on the literary culture of Northern Ireland, which has undergone a marked renaissance since the late 1960s. This was a consequence of what Seamus Heaney, perhaps the period's dominant literary influence, has called the compulsion to 'bear witness' to the historical and political moment. A similar impulse can be detected in the literature of other nations and states where citizens live under oppressive regimes or with a persistent sense of physical, psychological or emotional threat. For Eastern European writers such as Miroslav Holub, Czesław Miłosz and Ivan Klima, the question 'What is literature for?' is one that assumes greater significance and urgency. Often it can be dangerous for writers to address contemporary social and political themes in such times and places, and it requires the adoption of oblique or allegorical strategies which enable writers to comment on their situation while seeming to comment on something else altogether. There are valid parallels to be drawn between the role of the writer in such regimes and that of the Northern Irish writer compelled to write about the contemporary situation since the outbreak of the modern 'troubles'. For poets like Heaney, Tom Paulin and Michael Longley, literature can rarely, if ever, be written, read or fully understood without reference to the social world and context in which it was written, and the very compulsion to 'bear witness' can itself be a burden as well as a source of debate. This is demonstrated in Longley's poem, 'Wounds', for example, where a meditation on the poet's father's wartime experiences on the Somme, 'Going over the top with "Fuck the Pope!"' becomes conflated with accounts of victims of the 'troubles' that balance the horror of violence with mundane detail: the three young British soldiers, 'bellies full of / Bullets and Irish beer', and a bus conductor, murdered in his own home 'By a shivering boy who wandered in / Before they could turn the television down', who mumbles shamefaced apologies to the man's wife and children.

See also *Contexts*: Religion; *Texts*: History, Irish literature, Political commitment.

Further reading

McKittrick, David and David McVea, *Making Sense of the Troubles: The Story of the Conflict in Northern Ireland* (Chicago: New Amsterdam Books, 2002).

Political protest

One of the characteristic features of the political landscape of Britain since 1945 has been a marked decline of trust in politicians and parliamentary politics. The period began with a determination on the part of the electorate to give a mandate for wholesale social and political change. To that end, a Labour government was elected that was committed to national reconstruction on more egalitarian lines, through the creation of a Welfare State that would improve material conditions for those most in need. In its six-year reign the government laid the foundations of the Welfare State, but the optimism of 1945 was short-lived, and the process of disillusionment with 'official' politics began. The Conservatives came to power in 1951 and remained there for 13 years. Although the economy was relatively buoyant during much of this time, bringing improved standards of living for many, there was also evidence of political dissatisfaction, exacerbated by events such as the Suez crisis, and the government's insistence on developing the country's nuclear capability. This led to the emergence of what became known as the 'New Left' at the end of the 1950s: a movement intellectually spearheaded by figures such as Raymond Williams and E. P. Thompson who advocated a radical socialist alternative to the postwar consensus that had failed to deliver on many of its aspirations, and who wanted to extend their ideological vision to the main social and cultural aspects of British life. The 'New Left' found common cause with single-issue pressure groups that were also emerging at the time, such as the Campaign for Nuclear Disarmament, and exerted a growing influence on academia, the education system, social sciences and the arts over the next decade. For a time, after Labour's return to power in 1964 the proposed radicalism of Harold Wilson's administration promised the sort of socialist programme that the 'New Left' sought, but by the late 1960s disillusionment had again set in, with many of the original aims that the Welfare State was set up to achieve remaining unfulfilled.

The 1950s were characterised by an unfocused sense of dissidence among elements of British society, typified by Jimmy Porter, the 'angry young man' of John Osborne's *Look Back in Anger* (1956), who railed against class hierarchies and the political establishment but offered little in the way of organised protest. CND provided the only substantial platform for specifically targeted dissent, with demonstrations against the build-up of nuclear weaponry and annual marches to the British nuclear weapons site at Aldermaston attracting huge numbers. However, CND's influence declined in the 1960s and it was not until the later years of the decade that political demonstrations and protest events became a more common occurrence. American involvement in the conflict with North Vietnam which had begun in 1965 and was to continue until 1973, was the catalyst that provided a focal point for anti-establishment feeling not only in the United States, but throughout Western Europe, including Britain, where the Vietnam Solidarity Committee organised a mass protest march on the American Embassy in London in 1968. At the forefront of late 1960s protest movements was a newly politicised student population: anti-authoritarian demonstrations became a feature of campus life in America, Britain and France in particular. In Britain, there were student revolts at the London School of Economics, and the Universities of Warwick and East Anglia among others, but there was nothing on the scale of the events in Paris in May 1968 that brought students and workers together in a concerted strike action that almost succeeded in bringing down the French government.

Paris '68 was undoubtedly the culmination of student unrest in the 1960s. In Britain in the following decade, as the economy went into decline and livelihoods were threatened, the focus of political protest shifted to recurrent conflicts between government and trade unions. A national miners' strike for improved wages brought the country to a halt in the winter of 1972, with power shortages restricting the supply of electricity to millions of homes, forcing the Conservative Prime Minister Edward Heath to introduce a three-day working week, as a means of conserving energy supplies. The miners' victory in their pay claim played a significant part in the fall of the Heath government two years later, and set the tone for a decade of industrial unrest in which unions strongly defended their members' interests. One of the first objectives of the Conservative government elected under Margaret Thatcher in 1979 was to curb trade union power, and a series of measures were introduced to facilitate this aim. With many sectors of British industry in decline, there was considerable scope for continuing unrest, but in the 1980s the government largely gained the upper hand in its struggles with the unions. The most significant event in this period was the miners' strike of 1984–5. Mindful of the impact of the 1972 strike on the Heath government, the Thatcher administration was anxious to avoid a repeat of the outcome. The dispute was prolonged and bitter, with recurring outbreaks of violence in clashes between police and pickets, and public demonstrations in support of the miners. The government eventually prevailed, and the miners returned to work, having gained no significant concessions. The impact on pit communities over the course of the strike had been devastating, and many never recovered.

Organised union protest activity became rarer and less effective after the Thatcher government implemented legislation to restrict union power. Since the late 1980s political protest has tended to be focused on specific issues that have brought together a wider social and demographic range of participants. CND underwent a resurgence of support in the 1980s as Britain was drawn more closely into America's nuclear weapons and defence programmes, with the locating of Cruise missiles on British soil sparking waves of protest, including the establishment of a women's peace camp at Greenham Common. Public opinion was galvanised at the end of the 1980s in opposition to the government's proposals for a 'community charge', commonly referred to as a 'poll tax', to replace the existing rating system. The new system took insufficient account of the individual's ability to pay and sparked protests after its implementation in 1990, with often violent demonstrations taking place all over Britain. The community charge proved the most unpopular measure of the Thatcher government and was reformed substantially under the subsequent administration of John Major.

Political protests also began to take on a more international dimension around the turn of the 21st century, with worldwide anti-capitalism demonstrations that drew together environmentalists, trade unionists, members and supporters of left-wing political parties, anarchists and pressure groups. The expansion of the internet has done much to facilitate the organisation of political protest on a global scale, and international events now attract a greater response. Anti-capitalist protests aside, perhaps the largest articulation of political dissent of the early years of the 21st century was the expression of opposition to the decision by the United States, supported by the British government, to go to war with Iraq in 2003. Demonstrations took place throughout the world, including most major cities in Britain, where protesters of most political persuasions and many religious faiths came together to register their anger at the decision to go to war.

The role of literature as a vehicle of political protest is one that has long been the subject of intense debate, and many writers since the Second World War have made that debate a fundamental theme of their work, wrestling with W. H. Auden's contention that 'Poetry makes nothing happen'. Poetry's status as an exclusive and elevated discourse often creates difficulties for poets who wish to confront political issues, whereas dramatists and novelists are often more easily able to engage directly or indirectly with the political events of their time, as was the case for the generation of political playwrights, including David Edgar, David Hare, Howard Barker and Trevor Griffiths, which came to the fore in the 1970s. Writers have also often been closely involved with protest movements. Most of the so-called 'angry young men' of the 1950s were prominent members of CND, and more recently writers of later generations, like Ian McEwan and Tony Harrison, have spoken out about issues such as international terrorism and the Iraq war. In common with writers in most societies, British authors are often looked to for responses to contemporary political events, and many find themselves compelled to answer that call.

See also   *Contexts*: Class structure, Cold War, Counter-culture, War, Youth culture; *Texts*: Alternative theatre, 'Angry Young Men', Class, Epic theatre, 'Kitchen-sink' drama, Political commitment, Underground poetry; *Criticism*: Cultural materialism, Marxist criticism, New Historicism.

Further reading

Andrain, Charles F. and David E. Apter, *Political Protest and Social Change: Analysing Politics* (Basingstoke: Macmillan, 1995).

Peterson, Abby, *Contemporary Political Protest: Essays on Political Militancy* (Aldershot: Ashgate, 2001).

Popular culture

The concept of 'culture' has become increasingly difficult to define in the period since the end of the Second World War. Once used almost exclusively to refer to art forms and artifacts that appealed to the taste of an educated elite, the term 'culture' is now used in a wider frame of reference, with a distinction drawn between the limited and exclusive earlier meaning – now usually referred to as 'high' culture – and the vast range of pastimes, leisure activities, different kinds of printed and broadcast media, fashions and consumables that reflect the tastes, interests and experience of the majority of the public. The general trend in British society towards fewer and freer class distinctions and increasing challenges to social and cultural authorities has led to a blurring of the boundaries between high and popular culture, to the extent that it is often difficult to separate the two.

In common with most Western societies, British popular culture was subject to a process of 'Americanization' as the United States' economic and political dominance in the post-Second World War world order facilitated its cultural pre-eminence. American movies, popular music, television programmes, fashions and even food and drink (the ubiquitous Mcdonald's fast-food chain, Coca-Cola, and Starbucks coffee houses, for example) have become fixtures on the British popular cultural landscape, in an era of mass communications and consumerism that ensured the dissemination of American goods and cultural practices. It has often been the more subversive elements of American popular culture, however, such as the various popular musical forms that have developed out of American rock and roll, which have been appropriated and adapted by those in Britain who have sought to locate themselves in opposition to dominant values and attitudes. At times, America's popular cultural dominance has been threatened by the emergence of new phenomena from beyond its boundaries that have had a substantial impact on American cultural sensibilities. The rise of the Beatles in the early 1960s, who took American rock and roll and transformed it into a musical style that was to define fundamentally the direction of popular music for subsequent decades, heralded a period – often described as 'the swinging sixties' – in which Britain led the world in pop music, fashion and other aspects of popular culture. British dominance was short-lived, however, and for much of the postwar period, Americanization has been the dominant trend in popular cultural developments, leaving critics such as Richard Hoggart, in *The Uses of Literacy* (1957), to mourn the decline of traditional working-class culture in Britain.

Other significant factors in the shaping of mass or popular culture in the period involve the rise of mass communication, in particular the pervasive influence of television, and more recently, the internet. Still something of a rarity in British homes in the early 1950s, television became perhaps the single biggest vehicle for mediating popular culture in the later 20th century. As television sets became cheaper and more widely available a mass audience was created; the advent of commercial television in 1954 and a second BBC channel 10 years later gave viewers more choice, and the invention of colour television made the medium even more attractive. Towards the end of the 20th century the addition of two more terrestrial channels and the growth of satellite, digital and cable television gave viewers unprecedented choice and brought immediate access to news, sporting events and entertainment from across the world. The information technology revolution, and especially the internet, has increased the sense of the world as a global village, to positive and negative effect: while new cultural vistas were being opened out and made available to large numbers of people, the new communications technology was not always used to its most enriching potential, and the increased emphasis on an American-dominated global perspective has had damaging consequences for national identity and cultural identification.

Popular culture in its various forms has had a major impact on the arts and literature of the period. Television was perceived as a significant threat to theatre in particular, which came to seem exclusive and elitist in comparison to the mass audience that television drama could command. Television drama also focused on representing the kind of experiences familiar to the majority of its audiences. Single plays, drama series and soap operas often took working-class life as their central theme, using the resources of film to take dramatic realism beyond the boundaries of conventional live theatre. There were positive consequences for the contemporary theatre, however, as many writers and directors, unable to match television's technological advantages in creating an illusion of reality, moved towards more experimental and impressionistic styles. For those playwrights who wanted their work to be a reflection of their political commitment, television also offered a larger and more democratic platform, and many were quick to exploit the medium.

Literature in general has appropriated and interacted with elements of popular culture to an increasing extent over the period, as culture itself has taken on a wider frame of reference. The work of critics such as Raymond Williams tended towards a recasting of culture as a broader reflection of the tastes of the population as a whole, rather than that of an educated, affluent elite. Culture in its wider forms became recognized as a valid source of academic and intellectual enquiry as a result, as demonstrated in the rise of Cultural Studies, pioneered by Williams among others. Postmodern writing and criticism has encouraged inter-action between 'high' and popular culture: by the end of the 20th century, poets as diverse as Peter Reading and Carol Ann Duffy, novelists such as Will Self and Jonathan Coe, and newly emerging playwrights including Jonathan Harvey and Mark Ravenhill were producing work steeped in popular cultural references, often creating grotesque and blackly comic poetic, fictional or dramatic worlds. Coe's *The Rotters' Club* (2001), for example, evokes the sights and sounds, the music, fashions and cultural landmarks of the 1970s, as seen through the eyes of a group of Birmingham schoolchildren moving from adolescence to young adulthood. The novel's comic properties are permeated with more serious elements, closely delineating social attitudes of the time, and addressing themes such as racial prejudice, the effect of the Irish 'Troubles' on the British mainland – the Birmingham pub bombing of 1974 has a devastating effect on the novel's central characters – and the worsening industrial relations of the period. The academic attention that Coe's comic political fiction has attracted is typical in many ways of how the boundaries between the literary and non-literary have become less distinct. Other popular genres, such as science fiction, the detective novel and children's literature are being studied at university level with growing frequency, clearly demonstrating the massive increase in the range of texts considered worthy of critical study at the turn of the 21st century.

See also *Contexts*: Counter-culture, Science and technological innovation, Youth culture; *Texts*: Alternative theatre, Genre fiction, Postmodern literature; *Criticism*: Dialogic theory, Leavisite Criticism, Postmodernist theory.

Further reading

Epstein, Dan, *Twentieth-Century Pop Culture* (London: Carlton, 1999).

Religion

By the second half of the 20th century there was persuasive evidence that organised religion in Britain was continuing a decline that had begun around 100 years earlier, and had accelerated in the aftermath of the First World War. The scale and devastation of that conflict brought many of the old certainties – moral, religious, social, cultural and political – into question. Religion, which in Britain at the time largely meant Christianity, had failed to regain its central role in national life between the wars; in the post-Second World War era of increasing democratisation, lessening respect for authority, and social, cultural and ideological change, the Church of England and the Catholic Church in Britain struggled to appear relevant to the lives of the majority of people: only about 10 per cent of the population attended church regularly in the early 1960s. The large-scale destructive events of the war years – the Holocaust and the bombings of Hiroshima and Nagasaki – had demonstrated the extent of humankind's capacity for inhumanity and led many to question what religious faith had to offer as a response. Some within the church saw the need for modernisation of the message of Christianity: the Bishop of Woolwich, John Robinson, courted controversy with his book *Honest to God* (1962), in which he raised questions about some of the key aspects of Christian belief. Later in the same decade, as counter-cultures flourished, alternative religions enjoyed brief phases of popularity, especially among the young; Eastern mysticism was in vogue for a time, following the Beatles' high-profile support for Transcendental Meditation, and immigration brought other faiths into the religious landscape of late 20th-century Britain. For the most part, though, the tendency was for people to locate their faith and define themselves in relation to more secular belief systems, such as psychoanalysis or political ideology. On the whole, although religious observance was a more prominent aspect in the lives of the immigrant population, for indigenous British people established religion had little appeal for the majority in the post-Second World War period.

Periodically, in the later 20th and early 21st century, the established Church found a role as a vehicle of social criticism, highlighting poverty, inner-city decay and racial tension in the 1980s and 1990s, but more often it has continued to appear outdated and resistant to progressive measures: the prolonged debates about the ordination of women priests and the admission of homosexual priests, as well as the Catholic Church's opposition to issues such as divorce, abortion and contraception, all of which were addressed by radical legislation in the postwar period, have often given the impression of British religious institutions as insular and backward-looking. More seriously, religion has also been seen as having a disruptive and divisive impact, as illustrated by decades of sectarian conflict in Northern Ireland, and by the tensions and occasional outbreaks of violence that have arisen in multi-faith communities, especially since the rise of religious fundamentalism on an international basis.

Religion as a theme in contemporary writing has been less prominent over this period, reflecting its declining role in British society as a whole; few writers have addressed that decline directly, though some, especially Catholic writers such as Graham Greene and Muriel Spark, incorporated an often implicit religious perspective into their explorations of morality and concepts of good and evil. Among contemporary poets, the decline in spirituality and religious observance was inevitably a theme that recurred in the work of the Welsh poet-priest R. S. Thomas, and was addressed frequently by Elizabeth Jennings and John Heath-Stubbs, among others, while a more sceptical and questioning approach to religious faith and experience has often emerged in the poetry of Geoffrey Hill. In Northern Ireland, writers did not shirk from interrogating the conflicts of the time, but largely from a neutral position, promoting neither a Protestant nor a Catholic view and tending to comment from outside the situation they described. Literary language was also affected by the less prominent role played by religion, as familiarity with the Bible, a rich source of imagery, metaphor and subject-matter for writers for centuries, could no longer be assumed. Religious references and allusions were far less pervasive and in any case had lost their cultural and rhetorical force. Nevertheless, for all its diminishing significance, religion as a literary theme could still provoke controversy, especially in a world in which fundamentalism was on the rise, as Muslim-born writer Salman Rushdie discovered when his novel *The Satanic Verses* (1988) was deemed blasphemous against Islam, leading to the imposition of a fatwa by Ayatollah Khomeini of Iran that forced the author into hiding. British literature, long dominated by a Christian perspective, was increasingly permeated and influenced, albeit indirectly and at a relatively lower level, by multiple faith perspectives from the second half of the 20th century onwards, another indication of the growing cultural pluralism informing the writing of the period.

See also *Contexts*: Censorship, Migrant experience and multiculturalism, Northern Irish 'troubles', War; *Texts*: Irish literature, Postcolonial literature.

Further reading

Badham, Paul, *Religion, State and Society in Modern Britain* (Lampeter: Edwin Mellen Press, 1989).

Science and technological innovation

Although British scientists have at times made significant contributions to research and technological innovation, the period since 1945 can be described as one in which many opportunities were missed to establish Britain as a leading scientific nation, with negative consequences for industries old and new. Government initiatives have often promised more than has been delivered in scientific and technological progress, since the first postwar Labour administration in 1945 set up organisations to further the cause of research and development. Initially, this impulse towards encouraging scientific progress led to major advances in medicine, nuclear physics and genetics being made by British scientists, not least the discovery of the structure of DNA by the British-American team of Crick and Watson in 1953. From these promising beginnings, however, there was little evidence in the rest of the decade of the pioneering spirit that characterised British science in the late 1940s. This failure to capitalise on scientific advances led the Cambridge physicist and novelist C. P. Snow to a pessimistic conclusion in his controversial Rede lecture, 'The Two Cultures and the Scientific Revolution', in 1959. For Snow, British intellectual life consisted of two distinct groups: the literary and the scientific, and there was little if any common ground between the two. Furthermore, it was with the literary intelligentsia that cultural authority resided, in spite of what Snow perceived as its insularity and refusal to engage with technological and scientific progress. For this reason, scientific development received far less attention and was, according to Snow, distinctly undervalued, with adverse repercussions for a nation still trying to find its role in the new world order.

The picture was not entirely as bleak as Snow painted it, however, and even in a period of relative stagnation, advances were made in areas such as atomic energy, nuclear power, aircraft development and computing. Nevertheless, by the early 1960s, Britain was falling behind its main industrial rivals, such as the United States and West Germany. In 1964 Labour returned to power under Harold Wilson, with the intention of increasing investment in scientific research, to take advantage of what he perceived as the 'white heat of the technological revolution'.[4] Labour exploited the newly formed Ministry of Technology to facilitate their aims, and sought to raise the profile of scientific subjects in the university system, but many of the proposed projects and initiatives to further scientific advancement remained unfulfilled, and British science failed to realise its potential throughout the 1970s. Worse was to follow in the 1980s, with the decline of manufacturing industries, as Britain lacked the technological capacity to compete with other industrialised nations. Nevertheless, although Britain was rarely at the forefront of scientific research and development throughout the second half of the 20th century, British society benefited from most of the advances in global technology that brought radical changes to social and cultural life. From the rise of television as a major cultural phenomenon at the start of the period, to the all-pervasive influence of the internet by the century's end, high technology has had a profound impact on people's lives, as have developments in labour-saving devices and household white goods. It is also true that scientific developments have had more negative effects, in the development of ever more powerful weaponry, including the nuclear proliferation of the Cold War era, and the environmental damage caused by various forms of pollution.

It is perhaps surprising that the permeation of scientific and technological innovation into all aspects of human experience has not had a more substantial effect on British writing over the same period. Technology has undoubtedly had a revolutionary effect on the publishing industry, enabling smaller print-runs to become cost effective, and thus allowing wider exposure for a greater number of writers. Some poets have explored the possibility of the internet and other media as alternatives to print: the London-based, Canadian-born poet John Cayley is one of the pioneering figures in the field of digital kinetic poetry, a development of the concerns and strategies of concrete and other forms of avant-garde poetry. Kinetic poems like Cayley's sequence 'Riverisland' bring together text, sound and visual image, often in short filmed pieces structured in the form of a loop, so that the poem can be repeated as often as the reader, or rather viewer, wishes. Cayley has collaborated with the British experimental poet Caroline Bergvall, among others, but the field of kinetic poetry has been largely dominated by American poets. For many British writers, it seems that C. P. Snow's earlier distinction between the literary and scientific intelligentsia may still carry some validity, as little contemporary literature seems to have fully or willingly engaged with scientific development as a literary theme, with the obvious exception of science fiction writing. Novelists such as J. G.Ballard and Michael Moorcock are among the most prominent practitioners of a genre that has attracted increasing critical and academic attention since the late 20th century.

See also *Contexts*: Cold War, Popular culture; *Texts*: Concrete poetry, Marketing of literature; *Criticism*: Cultural materialism, New Historicism.

Further reading

Best, Steven and Douglas Kellner, *The Postmodern Adventure: Science, Technology and Cultural Studies at the Third Millennium* (London: Routledge, 2001).

Sex and sexuality

In a period in which many aspects of human experience have undergone fundamental change, arguably the most radical changes have occurred in relation to sexual identity, behaviour and attitudes. In the late 1940s, conventional morality still regarded sex before or outside marriage with strong disapproval, and both divorce and illegitimacy carried a heavy weight of social stigma. There were, however, signs of increasing sexual experimentation, if not promiscuity, among younger people. By the 1960s, although the sense of stigmatisation was still prominent, divorce was becoming increasingly prevalent, though it still had severe financial as well as moral implications for women, given that they were at this time still legally defined as economically dependent on men. Rising divorce rates were just one indication that the 1960s was bringing in what has been described as a sexual revolution, the impact of which on British social and cultural life has been profound and far-reaching. The so-called 'permissive society' of 1960s Britain had several defining characteristics: greater sexual experimentation; a relaxation of attitudes towards premarital sex; an increase in one-parent families; the decline of marriage as an institution; more tolerant public attitudes towards homosexuality; and a general promotion of sensual and sexual indulgence of all kinds. A number of important factors contributed to the liberalisation of attitudes towards sex and sexuality. One of the earliest and most significant was the wider availability of contraception, and particularly the invention of the contraceptive pill, which was first made available in Britain in 1961, though only to married women at that stage. It was not until 1967 that the full impact of the pill was realised, when the National Health Service (Family Planning) Act compelled local authorities to provide free contraception and contraceptive advice, giving women greater control and autonomy over their sexual lives. Despite this, in retrospect, the 1960s did not offer as much sexual freedom to women as it did to men. For all the empowerment the 'pill' provided, it still placed the onus for contraception on women; male sexual attitudes still often objectified women and the new openness in personal relationships failed to eradicate sexual double standards. Furthermore, it was not until the end of the 1960s that changes in divorce legislation gave women greater independence, and it was around the same time that the feminist movement began to react against patriarchal values that had clearly survived the sexual revolution.

Nevertheless, there was much positive change in matters affecting gender roles and sexual relationships in the 1960s, and 1967, the year of the Family Planning Act was particularly significant. Two other pieces of crucial legislation were passed: the Abortion Reform Act and the Sexual

Offences Act. The former legalised abortion, which could be permitted on psychological or medical grounds with the approval of two doctors, and could be performed on the NHS, putting an end to the practice of 'back-street abortions', the termination of unwanted pregnancies by unqualified individuals in unsafe and dangerous conditions. The second act decriminalised homosexual acts between consenting adults, a move that had been proposed some ten years earlier by the Wolfenden Report. The change in the climate of public opinion towards issues of sexual identity meant that the proposals could finally be made law by the end of the 1960s, which in turn facilitated the more open discussion of homosexuality, and a growing confidence among homosexuals in asserting their sexuality, illustrated in the 1970s by the founding of the Gay Liberation movement, the increased circulation of magazines like *Gay News*, and the success of theatre groups such as Gay Sweatshop on the alternative drama scene.

The trend of liberalisation in matters of sex and sexuality in post-Second World War Britain has continued largely unabated throughout the period, though the advent of AIDS (acquired immuno-deficiency syndrome) in the 1980s led to significant changes in sexual behaviour. The condition first emerged in the 1960s, but it was not until the 1980s that it reached epidemic proportions in the West, having a particularly heavy impact on the gay community and those with multiple sexual partners, whether heterosexual or homosexual. Medical advances made a substantial contribution to bringing AIDS under control in the developed world by the end of the 20th century, but it has remained a major cause of death in parts of Africa and the Indian subcontinent into the present century. One of the major consequences of the AIDS epidemic has been an increase in awareness of the need for 'safe sex', for protection against disease as well as against pregnancy, and this has done much to temper the sexual freedom associated with the 1960s. However, British society was considerably more liberal and tolerant about sex and sexual identity by the end of the 20th century than it had been at its mid-point.

Shifts in cultural attitudes also contributed towards the rise of a more liberal sexual outlook in the period, not least the relaxation of censorship in the 1960s. The failure of the prosecution of Penguin Books for obscenity in publishing a paperback edition of D. H. Lawrence's *Lady Chatterley's Lover* in 1960 was indicative of the way in which attitudes were already changing. Writers took advantage of an atmosphere of greater tolerance to adopt more explicit approaches to the description of sexual intimacy and the discussion of sexual identity, both homosexual and heterosexual, as vital aspects of human experience. Women writers especially seemed concerned to explore issues of sexuality and sexual identity in this period, as feminist ideology revealed to them the extent to which the so-called sexual revolution had in many ways sanctioned the continuing objectification of women. Dramatists were given greater freedom of expression by the abolition of the Lord Chamberlain's powers of censorship. This was particularly the case in respect of the depiction of homosexuality, which, in spite of shifts in public opinion since the 1950s, had been forced to remain implicit. Indeed, it was not until 1958 that the censor relented to the extent of even allowing homosexual characters to be represented on stage at all. In general, a greater willingness to explicitly address sexual themes is characteristic of much contemporary writing, in the treatments of lesbian and gay experience in the novels of Jeanette Winterson and Alan Hollinghurst, the explorations of female sexuality by women poets including Fleur Adcock, Penelope Shuttle and Grace Nichols, and the demolishing of sexual taboos by dramatists of the period from Joe Orton in the 1960s to Mark Ravenhill at the end of the century.

See also   *Contexts*: Censorship, Counter-culture, Feminism and the role of women; *Texts*: Gay and lesbian writing, Women's writing; *Criticism*: Feminist criticism, Gender criticism.

Further reading

Grant, Linda, *Sexing the Millennium: A Political History of the Revolution* (London: HarperCollins, 1993).

War

In spite of the relative absence of actual conflicts involving British forces, war – specifically the Second World War – has had a pervasive symbolic impact on the social and cultural consciousness of the British people. Until the declaration of war against Iraq by the United States and Britain in 2003, British military engagement had been confined to the short-lived conflict with Argentina over the Falkland Islands in 1982, support for American and United Nations action in Korea in the 1950s, the first Gulf War in 1991, and the crises in the former Yugoslavia in the 1990s. None of these have superseded the influence of the Second World War on the public imagination. The privations endured by both soldiers and civilians over the six-year duration of the war were intense, and nurtured demands for political change and improved material conditions, giving rise to the creation of the Welfare State. This was accompanied by a desire among the British Left for a social transformation that would reflect the sense of common purpose and unity that was perceived to have existed during the war. For the Right, too, the war symbolised a major British achievement, which constituted a moment of greatness in national history, and owed much to the leadership of Winston Churchill, a figure repeatedly invoked in heroic and patriotic terms by his successors, including Margaret Thatcher. Both Left and Right were to be disillusioned in the decades that followed the Second World War. The Welfare State did indeed succeed to some extent in ameliorating social inequalities, and Britain undoubtedly became more democratic as class hierarchies became less rigidly stratified, but the Left's hoped-for social revolution failed to materialise. Similarly, the idea of Britain as a major world power, that the Right clung to in the aftermath of the war, was hugely undermined by the reality of imperial decline.

Nevertheless, the Second World War's pervasive influence on the public imagination has continued into the 21st century, often in negative ways, as people attempted to come to terms with some of the most traumatic events of the war years. The full horror of the Nazi programme of mass genocide was not comprehended at the time, and it was not until the 1960s that the events were fully assimilated into the public consciousness. For much of the early postwar period, austerity measures due to shortages of essential goods, and a general sense of postwar exhaustion, cast a sense of disillusionment over many areas of British society, even as material improvements were taking place and greater opportunities for advancement were being extended to more people. It was not until the 1960s that Britain began to regain its national self-confidence, and it was also around the same time that British writers, with the benefit of distance, began to engage imaginatively with the Second World War, its consequences and its implications.

British poetry, drama and fiction were all characterised by a withdrawal from engagement with the war in its immediate aftermath. There was considerable anxiety about the capacity of poetry and poetic language to address the major atrocities of the war, and British poets tended to avoid engagement with large-scale themes until some, like Ted Hughes and Geoffrey Hill, responded to A. Alvarez's call for poets to address what he called 'the forces of disintegration which destroy the old standards of civilization', and which were embodied in the century's world wars, the magnitude of the Holocaust, and the possibility of nuclear annihilation that seemed all-pervasive at the start of the 1960s.[5] Alvarez saw a need for British poets to follow the lead of prominent American poets of the time like John Berryman and Robert Lowell, whose pursuit of a confessional mode in their writing enabled them to confront psychological and actual fears and desires, attempting in the effort to make sense of their experience and the events that had shaped the contemporary world in which they lived. In subsequent decades, themes such as the Holocaust began to feature more prominently in British poetry, and poets have continued to debate poetry's validity as a vehicle for addressing the nature of war and its implications for humanity, though the level of British poets' engagement with such themes is markedly less than that of poets from areas such as Eastern Europe, who experienced some of the main political consequences of the war at closer quarters.

Drama of the postwar period initially avoided direct confrontation with issues arising out of the Second World War, tending to offer escapism through identification with themes and settings familiar from before the war. In the 1950s, however, two disparate new strands of drama, the contemporary 'kitchen sink' realism of British playwrights like John Osborne and Arnold Wesker, and the Theatre of the Absurd, that had its initial impact through Samuel Beckett's ground-breaking play *Waiting for Godot*, first performed in Britain in 1955, fundamentally altered British theatre's reflection of the issues facing the contemporary world. Absurdist theatre was more allusive in its treatment of the state of postwar humanity, with Beckett in particular at pains to deny the existence of contemporary resonances in his work. The trend towards naturalism and recognisably modern, usually working-class settings among the 'kitchen sink' realists, on the other hand, strongly implied a desire on the part of these writers to anatomise what the war had done to Britain's national identity and international standing. Many of the political playwrights of the 1970s harked back to the possibilities that the communal war effort had thrown up for a more egalitarian society, even as they mourned the failure of that society to emerge out of the Welfare State ethos.

In fiction, too, writers needed a period of reflection before directly addressing the ramifications of the war. Questions of morality and the validity of categories of good and evil were key elements in the work of writers such as William Golding, Iris Murdoch and Anthony Burgess, from the 1950s to the 1980s. More recently, both world wars have continued to fire the imagination of novelists: Pat Barker's *The Regeneration Trilogy*, comprising *Regeneration* (1991), *The Eye in the Door* (1993), and *The Ghost Road* (1995), while set in the First World War, addresses themes common to all wars, including masculinity and the psychological effects of warfare on its participants. Sebastian Faulks, in the critically acclaimed novels *Birdsong* (1993) and *Charlotte Gray* (1998), addressed First and Second World War experience respectively, while Louis de Bernières' *Captain Corelli's Mandolin* (1994), a huge commercial success both in print and on film, explored the effects of the Second World War from a wider perspective, dealing with the consequences of German occupation on a small Greek island.

In more general terms, the sense of historical discontinuity and the destruction of old certainties that were consequences of the Second World War, and that were exacerbated by the climate of fear generated by the Cold War, were translated into the self-questioning, fragmentary nature of postmodern narrative strategies. The all-pervasive influence of the Second World War on contemporary literature since 1945 can be felt at the level of both formal and thematic developments in the various literary genres, whether or not the texts address the war and its consequences directly.

See also   *Contexts*: British Empire, decline and loss, Class structure, Cold War, 'Holocaust', Political protest; *Texts*: Absurdist Theatre, Empire, end of, Holocaust literature, Postmodern literature.

Further reading

Calder, Angus, *The People's War: Britain, 1939–1945* (London: Pimlico, 1992).
Smith, Harold L., *War and Social Change: British Society in the Second World War* (Manchester: Manchester University Press, 1986).

Youth culture

In the 1950s, the emergence of a constituency of teenagers and young adults with unprecedented spending power coincided with the expansion of the consumer society, as postwar austerity gave way to increased economic confidence. For the first time, youth culture became a distinct and discrete phenomenon in British society. Over the second half of the 20th century young people developed their own styles, fashions, musical tastes, leisure activities and attitudes, which were increasingly at variance with social, cultural and political orthodoxy. Other factors also contributed to the development of youth culture and identity over this period. The expansion in educational opportunity helped to produce a larger proportion of better-educated and articulate young people from a wider demographic range, many of whom were well equipped to make their own lifestyle choices and formulate their own social attitudes. The postwar 'baby boom' had created a larger population of young adults by the 1960s, who were coming of age at a time of relative material and economic comfort, with technological advance increasing the leisure opportunities available to them. Attitudes towards sexual identity and sexuality were becoming much more liberal and a greater sense of optimism and freedom from the constraints of establishment values was prevalent. The abolition of National Service for young British males in the early 1960s meant that they no longer had to spend two years of their young adulthood in a situation of enforced subjugation to authority. From the 1970s onwards, the optimism and extension of opportunity that 1960s youth enjoyed was less in evidence, as economic downturn and rising unemployment limited the earning and spending capacities of succeeding generations. Nevertheless, the concept of youth culture was by this time fully embedded in Britain's social structure, and young people continued to identify with particular styles of dress, music, self-image and, less frequently but often to marked effect, with oppositional political ideologies or counter-cultural values.

As in many other areas of British life in the post-Second World War era, Americanisation played a large part in dictating the cultural interests of young people, not least in the growth of significance of popular music over the period, and the tribal allegiances it spawned. Rock and roll music, with its more explicit sexual content, and its emphasis on the experience of youth, was one of the most influential popular cultural forms to arrive in Britain from America, and was immediately taken up by the Teddy Boy cult, arguably the first British youth movement, who were seen as a threat to social cohesion by older commentators, due to their reputation for violence. Despite some evidence of racist attitudes among this section of youth – they were cited as bearing some responsibility for racial riots in the late 1950s – the Teddy boys, like most youth 'tribes', had little direct interest in political issues or bringing about social change.

By the early 1960s, youth was increasingly making its presence felt, with a fashion industry springing up and developing around the latest trends for longer hair or shorter skirts. Britain began to free itself of American influence, not least in the rise of pop groups like the Beatles and the Rolling Stones, who adopted American musical idioms, adapted them and sold them back to America and the rest of the Western world. Riding on this wave of influence and innovation, Britain became a leading nation in dictating the cultural agenda in areas such as popular music, style and fashion for much of the 1960s. New youth tribes continued to emerge, and rivalry between them often led to violent confrontations: the antipathy between 'mods' and 'rockers' frequently flared up into pitched battles at seaside resorts on Bank Holidays in the early 1960s. Later in the decade, American counter-cultural values began to reassert their influence as the hippy movement, with its message of peace and love brought into play a new, less violent set of oppositional attitudes, with a greater emphasis on perception-altering drugs. LSD and cannabis in particular became much more widely used by young people, though on the whole it was not until the 1970s and 1980s that harder and more addictive drugs began to circulate in Britain.

Through most of the 1960s the various British youth movements had exhibited little in the way of direct political involvement: official politics was seen mostly as just another aspect of traditional authority to be rejected. In America and parts of Western Europe, however, political activism was rising among university students. Student rebellion came to Britain eventually, however, as young people were galvanised by opposition to the Vietnam War. Furthermore, the near-revolution in Paris in 1968 briefly gave a focus to student disaffection in Britain, and inspired demonstrations and occupations at several academic institutions, though student protest had reached its high point by the end of the 1960s.

From the 1970s onwards youth culture became increasingly more fragmented and the idealism of the 1960s rapidly faded away, to be replaced by the nihilistic values associated with punk rock in the late 1970s, and, perhaps more troublingly, by the football hooliganism and racism that were frequently associated with the skinhead movement, seen by far-right groups such as the National Front as a fertile recruiting ground. It should also be recognised, however, that a coalition of youth movements, along with young black Britons, had considerable success in opposing racism through organisations such as the Anti-Nazi League and Rock against Racism in the late 1970s and early 1980s. Among more politicised elements of British youth there was anger at the policies of Margaret Thatcher's Conservative administrations throughout the 1980s, though by the end of that decade political involvement by young people was in decline, and younger voters have been among the most apathetic in every election since 1992. With increasing globalisation and growing multiculturalism, tribal youth movements are less prevalent in the early 21st century, but the creation of a youth constituency with its own sense of identity in the post-Second World War period is undeniable. Writers from Colin Macinnes in the 1950s, chronicling the rise of the teenager in *Absolute Beginners* (1959), to Irvine Welsh depicting the lives of disaffected and disenfranchised drug addicts in Scotland, in novels such as *Trainspotting* (1993), have used youth experience as a barometer of social and cultural change in Britain over the period. Poetry has also benefited from interaction with aspects of youth culture, such as popular music: in the 1960s the distinction between poetry and rock music lyrics became increasingly blurred as the latter grew in sophistication, and performance became a more crucial element of poetry, dictating shifts in form and rhythmic emphasis. From the 1970s black British poets like Linton Kwesi Johnson and Benjamin Zephaniah, turned increasingly towards modern popular musical genres for inspiration. Both Johnson, with albums including *Forces of Victory* (1979) and *Tings and Times* (1991), and Zephaniah, whose *Rasta* (1983) featured Bob Marley's backing band, the Wailers, have recorded with reggae musicians. Punk rock, too, produced its own poets, such as John Cooper Clarke, who was more likely to be found performing at punk clubs than in the more refined venues usually associated with poetry readings, and whose fast-talking, belligerent delivery echoed the intensity and urgency of the punk bands of the late 1970s. The overlapping categories of youth culture, popular culture and counter-culture have all, in their different ways, permeated themes, forms and language associated with contemporary literature, especially in areas such as sexual identity, gender relations, multiculturalism, drug culture and the consumer society.

See also   *Contexts*: Class structure, Counter-culture, Political protest, Popular culture; *Texts*: Class, Performance poetry, Political commitment, Underground poetry.

Further reading

Springhall, John, *Youth, Popular Culture and Moral Panics: Penny Gaffs to Gangsta-Rap, 1830–1996* (Basingstoke: Macmillan, 1998).

2 Texts: Themes, Issues, Concepts

Introduction

The key social, political and cultural changes in Britain since the Second World War, which brought about a reassessment of attitudes towards gender, class, racial identity and sexuality, also had a profound impact on the literature of the period. Established notions of the literary were challenged from a range of previously marginalised perspectives: feminism inspired women writers to foreground their gender experience; the formerly colonised reclaimed their own histories and identities; writers from working-class backgrounds widened the thematic and linguistic range of literature; and a more liberal cultural climate gave greater freedom in the representation of sexuality and sexual orientation. This introductory essay will chart some of the main developments in the specific genres of poetry, prose fiction and drama, and identify some of the key texts and themes that exemplify the period.

In postwar fiction, responses to the process of social change varied from literary generation to generation. Anthony Powell's 12-volume novel sequence, *A Dance to the Music of Time* (1951–75), chronicled British social life from the perspective of an upper middle class that saw its dominant position coming under increasing threat. Younger novelists, including John Braine and Alan Sillitoe, addressed the effects of social transformation on the working class. The protagonists of novels such as Braine's *Room at the Top* (1957) and Sillitoe's *Saturday Night and Sunday Morning* (1958) railed against class hierarchies in a forthright yet articulate manner. In less vituperative mode, Jim Dixon, the central character in Kingsley Amis's *Lucky Jim* (1954), expressed dissatisfaction with the postwar social climate, but exhibited little evident desire to change the system. That desire found greater literary expression in the more liberal atmosphere of the next decade.

In the 1960s, although novelists still explored the ramifications of upheavals in the class structure, greater attention was paid to other aspects of postwar life. Historical distance also enabled writers to respond more fully to the Second World War and the Holocaust, the full horror and import of which was only beginning to be absorbed by the public and creative imagination, while the intensification of the Cold War between the USSR and the West focused literary attention on the possibility of nuclear annihilation. The need to 'bear witness' to recent history led novelists like William Golding and Iris Murdoch to explore the nature of evil and questions of moral choice. At the same time, the liberalisation of social, political and cultural attitudes brought a renewal of writers' interest in formal experimentation, as realist conventions and character-driven plots gave way to a growing preoccupation with the process of narrative construction, in the work of writers as various as John Fowles, John Berger and B. S. Johnson.

By the early 1970s the departure from traditional narrative modes was accelerating, nowhere more rapidly than in women's writing, as feminist challenges to conventional gender roles transformed the literary landscape. The sexual revolution of the 1960s had in some ways proved illusory for women, with traditional double standards still in evidence, but the possibilities for more explicit representations of sexuality were particularly taken up by female authors. As feminism gathered momentum, women's writing rigorously examined the contradiction between increased professional and personal opportunities for women and conventional expectations about their maternal and familial responsibilities. The shift away from traditional realism led to an emphasis on fantasy. Magic realist techniques, associated with male South American writers, in particular Gabriel Garcia Marquez, were appropriated alongside generic traits from Gothic and fairy tale in novels such as Angela Carter's *Nights at the Circus* (1984), that sought imaginatively to transcend social worlds dominated by patriarchal values.

The trend towards fantasy and magic realism, in male as well as female writing – Salman Rushdie was only one of a number of male novelists to adopt magic realist techniques – and the increasing adoption of fragmentary, non-linear narrative structures continued throughout the 1970s and 1980s, mirroring the period's gradual breakdown of political and cultural consensus. Mass genocide and the still-present nuclear threat led writers to reassess the validity of what postmodern theorists called 'grand narratives', stories or myths that offer a single, coherent view of the world. Narrative time itself was addressed in innovative ways, made to run backwards, for example, in Martin Amis's *Time's Arrow* (1991), which dealt with the Holocaust through the perspective of one of its perpetrators. Such self-reflexive narrative strategies are characteristic of late 20th-century fiction. Rushdie, in *Midnight's Children* (1981), used the moment of India's independence as the fulcrum of a narrative based around a typically unreliable narrator born at that exact moment. The postcolonial perspective explored by Rushdie and others was prefigured in the fiction of earlier writers such as Sam Selvon, whose novel *The Lonely Londoners* (1956) was one of the first to address the migrant experience. Selvon recorded the disillusion of those drawn to the 'mother country' in the first waves of postwar immigration. Alienation and displacement were key themes of many of the earliest postcolonial texts, giving way to a more confident assertion of identity in recent decades, by writers who have established themselves within the culture and society of the former coloniser. Novels such as Zadie Smith's *White Teeth* (2000) and Monica Ali's *Brick Lane* (2003) address the pitfalls and potentialities of the multicultural society, drawing on and refashioning Western forms and subverting the language of the coloniser to their own ends.

British poetry in the immediate aftermath of the Second World War was largely characterised by a sense of withdrawal from public and political engagement. The poetry of Philip Larkin was typical, and influential, in this respect. Formally conventional, understated in tone and diction, with a note of muted despondency and a pervasive sense of nostalgia, Larkin's work could be seen as emblematic of a crisis of confidence in national identity in a postimperial world, while his evident distrust of modernist techniques manifested itself in a conscious attempt to reconnect with a tradition of English poetry that had ended with Thomas Hardy in the early 20th century. Robert Conquest, in his anthology *New Lines* (1956), elevated Larkin's thematic and poetic concerns to defining principles for a school of British poetry that became known as 'the Movement', and which included Kingsley Amis, Donald Davie, Thom Gunn and Elizabeth Jennings, though the connections between these writers were perhaps never more than tenuous.

By the early 1960s dissenting voices were beginning to question 'Movement' values and techniques. A. Alvarez, in the introduction to his 1962 anthology *The New Poetry*, castigated the 'gentility principle' in British poetry and demanded greater emotional and political engagement, a call that was answered in the muscular, sensuous poetry of Ted Hughes, with its unsentimental and elemental depictions of nature. Alvarez also championed the American poets John Berryman, Robert Lowell and Sylvia Plath, whose naked confessional styles struck a chord with the 1960s preoccupation with self-expression, as did the free verse and sensual abandon of the American 'beat' poets. Allen Ginsberg, in particular, was an immensely influential figure to those in British counter-cultural movements of the time. In a similar vein, the increasing lyrical complexity of rock musicians such as Bob Dylan and the Beatles widened the potential audience for poetry. Anthologies such as

Michael Horovitz's *Children of Albion: Poetry of the 'Underground' in Britain* (1969) captured the spirit of the era, as did the more populist 'Liverpool poets', Adrian Henri, Roger McGough and Brian Patten.

By the 1960s political and social issues were back on the poetic agenda. National and cultural identity, war and atrocity, were among the themes writers addressed, albeit often obliquely. At the same time, modernist principles also renewed their influence on British poetry, not least in one of the seminal works of the decade, Basil Bunting's *Briggflatts* (1966). In its formal strategies the poem owed much to T. S. Eliot and Ezra Pound, while its Northumbrian setting prefigured the concern with regional identity that came to the fore in British poetry of the 1970s.

In the late 1970s, yet another change of direction emerged, demonstrated in Blake Morrison and Andrew Motion's *The Penguin Book of Contemporary British Poetry* (1981). This anthology focused on poetry from outside the traditional metropolitan English centre, with a particular emphasis on the response of Northern Irish poets to the renewal of religious and political conflict. As poetry from the 'margins' assumed greater importance, issues of national and cultural identity were explored and definitions of poetic language changed dramatically. The assertion of the dialect voice in the work of poets as diverse as Seamus Heaney, Tony Harrison, Tom Leonard and Linton Kwesi Johnson helped to bring about a democratisation of poetic discourse. The work of these poets has helped to create a more receptive climate for others located outside the traditional spheres of influence. Some of the most urgent and compelling, and most linguistically innovative work of the period emerged, for instance, from Caribbean and black British poets, including Jean 'Binta' Breeze, John Agard and Benjamin Zephaniah. Women poets such as Carol Rumens, Jo Shapcott and Pauline Stainer explore contemporary issues that both incorporate and transcend female experience. A concern with regional and national identity can be traced in the work of poets from the constituent nations of the United Kingdom, including generations of Scottish poets from Edwin Morgan to Jackie Kay, Northern Irish poets like Tom Paulin and Eavan Boland, and Welsh poets with a strong sense of national cultural history including R.S. Thomas and Gillian Clarke, not to mention the intense regional English emphases in the work of Ian McMillan and Peter Didsbury, among others.

For much of the 20th century, women poets' traditional confinement to the canonical periphery persisted. However, the impact of feminism in the 1970s brought greater recognition, aided by the emergence and proliferation of women's presses and anthologies of women's poetry.

Sylvia Plath, whose suicide in 1962 predated the rise of feminism, was an enduring influence on late 20th-century women poets. Plath's explorations of women's experience under patriarchy, and her preoccupations with female sexuality and the body, were later taken up by women poets as diverse as Penelope Shuttle, Fleur Adcock and Grace Nichols. Humour, irony and parody, the hallmarks of Stevie Smith's poetry earlier in the period, are key elements in the work of, for example, Scottish poets Carol Ann Duffy and Liz Lochhead, who manipulate poetic tradition and the vernacular voice to challenge conventional patriarchal assumptions about poetry, culture and society.

Towards the end of the 20th century, the articulation of previously marginalised forms of experience had become so prevalent as to instigate a shift, to the extent that debates about language and subject-matter, place and identity, no longer seemed as contentious as they had in the late 1970s and early 1980s. Poets such as Simon Armitage developed a facility for bringing together colloquial diction and poetic form, to facilitate the exploration of a wider range of social and cultural experience than had traditionally been associated with poetic discourse. Over the same period, other poets, less concerned with adapting or renewing poetic forms and conventions, focused on the uncertainties and ambiguities of language itself. Poets including Jeremy Prynne and Tom Raworth exhibited a concern with disrupting syntax and meaning in order to draw attention to the politicisation of language and the fragmentary nature of perception, using techniques and free verse forms that had something in common with contemporary American avant-garde poets like John Ashbery and the earlier 'open field' practices of Charles Olson and the Black Mountain poets.

British drama had arguably the most direct engagement with social and political issues since the Second World War, though there was little indication of what was to come in the early 1950s, when the theatre was dominated by plays focusing on middle-class manners and drawing-room settings, exemplified in the works of Noël Coward and Terence Rattigan. The mid-1950s saw a radical break with this tradition, a break that owed much to three key events. In May 1956, John Osborne's play *Look Back in Anger* was first performed at the Royal Court Theatre in London. The central character, Jimmy Porter, embodied the 'angry young man', a label attached to Osborne and contemporaries such as fellow playwright Arnold Wesker, as well as novelists including Braine and Sillitoe. The targets of Porter's invective struck a chord with contemporary political attitudes at a time when British imperial decline, encapsulated in the Suez crisis of the same year, was entering its terminal stages, and the optimism of the Welfare State ethos was beginning to fade. Equally important in *Look Back in Anger* was the play's depiction of a recognisably working-class domestic interior, which helped to spawn a new and influential genre, the 'kitchen sink' drama. Apart from its setting, Osborne's play was formally conservative, but there were other forces at work on British theatrical practice that had a greater impact on technical innovation.

In the same year that Osborne's play was premiered the Berliner Ensemble theatre company visited Britain to perform three works by its founder, Bertolt Brecht. Brecht had died earlier that year, but his work and his ideas about the role and function of theatre were to have a lasting impact on British playwrights and directors. For Brecht, drama could become an instrument of political instruction if it succeeded in encouraging an objective audience response to the events and action depicted on the stage. His theory of 'epic theatre' incorporated 'alienation effects' that aimed to destroy the comfortable sense of illusion encouraged by traditional theatrical techniques, and create a distance between the play and its spectators. Much British political drama of the next two decades responded positively to Brechtian ideas, which strongly informed plays such as John Arden's *Sergeant Musgrave's Dance* (1959) and Edward Bond's *Lear* (1971).

Samuel Beckett's *Waiting for Godot*, which made its first appearance on the British stage the year before both Osborne's play and the visit of the Berliner Ensemble, was also hugely influential. Initially associated with the Theatre of the Absurd, along with Eugene Ionesco and Jean Genet, Beckett eschewed naturalistic setting and language in favour of a minimalist, impressionistic approach that sought to reflect the existentialist anxieties of the age. While overtly political playwrights developed the 'kitchen sink' dramatic style in the 1960s and 1970s, others owed more to the influence of Beckett. The work of one prominent dramatist of the period, Harold Pinter, straddled both camps. In early works such as *The Birthday Party* (1958), and *The Caretaker* (1960), Pinter achieved a synthesis of the realist and the absurd, placing characters in recognisable settings and contexts, and using everyday, colloquial language, but presenting situations and dialogues that were ambiguous in meaning, demonstrating the potency of language as an instrument of power. Similar concerns and techniques recur throughout Pinter's work, though later plays, like *One for the Road* (1984), and *Mountain Language* (1988), demonstrate a more explicit degree of political commentary and commitment.

The influence of Beckett and Pinter can also be clearly recognised in the early work of another leading postwar dramatist, Tom Stoppard. His *Rosencrantz and Guildenstern are Dead* (1966) used similar devices of minimalism, linguistic repetition and fragmentation to those found in *Godot* and some of Pinter's early plays, but from these derivative beginnings Stoppard established a characteristic style, and a concern with the slipperiness of language, temporal shifts and complex philosophical ideas that sets him apart from his Beckettian- or Brechtian-influenced contemporaries.

From the late 1950s until well into the 1970s, British drama was largely characterised by the leftist inclinations of its leading practitioners, which was also reflected in the ideological slant of the Royal Court Theatre, the institution that arguably did most to give exposure to new playwrights and directors. Over the same period there was a rapid expansion in the independent theatre sector, with the help of substantial Arts Council funding. More theatres attracted larger and more diverse audiences, and drama became a popular and often populist art form. Some of the themes explored by the 'angry young men', such as class and imperial decline, remained pertinent throughout this period in the work of Pinter, Bond, David Mercer and Peter Barnes, but as with poetry and the novel, wider concerns gathered momentum, aided by the abolition of the Lord Chamberlain's powers of censorship in 1968. Sexual liberation, for example, was explored in the plays of Joe Orton, with their celebrations of promiscuity and critiques of traditional moral values. The 1960s also witnessed a huge rise in alternative theatre, often centred on non-traditional performance spaces, in a consciously political attempt to reach a wider audience. However, that alternative status also entailed limitations on the political impact that could be achieved, and many writers and directors moved increasingly towards collaboration with established national theatres, in order to bring their radical vision to the mainstream. The 'shock tactics' employed in plays such as Howard Brenton's *The Romans in Britain* (1980) certainly attracted attention, though the controversy surrounding the play's depiction of male rape may have detracted from its incisive critique of imperialism, still a key theme in contemporary drama of the time.

Other dramatists, including John McGrath, Howard Barker and John Arden, stayed more loyal to the political values of alternative theatre, continuing to seek to extend the demographic range of their audiences. However, many alternative companies fell victim to cuts in Arts Council spending instigated by Conservative governments in the 1980s. Financial problems also affected larger theatres and companies, which had to rely on business partnerships and sponsors, with damaging consequences for new writing, especially that critical of the prevailing political ideology of the period. That is not to say that playwrights abandoned political commitment completely, but rather that the more overtly polemical approach gave way to more subtle interventions. Caryl Churchill, for example, demonstrated this in her explorations of the effect of Thatcherism on gender roles in *Top Girls* (1982), and on the social consequences of monetarism in *Serious Money* (1987). Social and political issues were also explored in more uncompromising and often shocking terms by playwrights over this period who courted controversy with explicit representations of sex and violence. Sarah Kane's *Blasted* (1995) graphically depicted rape and murder to draw parallels with the contemporary situation in Bosnia, while Mark Ravenhill's *Shopping and Fucking* (1996) attacked consumerism and social alienation in a play that was as explicit as its title. Ravenhill's depictions of gay sex demonstrated the way in which taboos had been exploded and boundaries pushed back in the three decades since the abolition of theatre censorship. Other emergent new dramatists of the period, though less controversial in their treatment of contemporary concerns than Ravenhill and Kane (the latter of whom committed suicide in 1999 at the age of 28), helped to reinvigorate British drama at a time when financial constraints discouraged innovation and experiment. Plays such as Patrick Marber's *Closer* (1997), and *Howard Katz* (2001), which addressed issues of masculinity and male sexuality, and Jonathan Harvey's explorations of homosexual experience and identity in a succession of plays from *Beautiful Thing* (1993) to *Out in the Open* (2001) were typical products of the late 20th-century revival of drama's role as an effective vehicle for reflecting the changing structures of British culture and society over the postwar period.

Further reading

General

McRae, John and Ron Carter (eds), *Routledge Guide to Modern English Writing* (London: Routledge, 2004).

Sinfield, Alan, *Literature, Politics and Culture in Postwar Britain*, 2nd edn (London: Athlone Press, 1997).

Stevenson, Randall, *The Oxford English Literary History*, vol. 12: *1960–2000: The Last of England?* (Oxford: Oxford University Press, 2004).

Waugh, Patricia, *Harvest of the Sixties: English Literature and its Background, 1960–1990* (Oxford: Oxford University Press, 1995).

Fiction

Childs, Peter, *Contemporary Novelists: British Fiction since 1970* (Basingstoke: Palgrave Macmillan, 2005).

Head, Dominic, *The Cambridge Introduction to Contemporary Fiction* (Cambridge: Polity Press, 1999).

Mengham, Rod (ed.), *An Introduction to Contemporary Fiction* (Cambridge: Polity Press, 1999).

Taylor, D. J., *After the War: The Novel and England since 1945* (London: Flamingo, 1994).

Poetry

Acheson, James and Romana Huk (eds), *Contemporary British Poetry: Essays in Theory and Criticism* (New York: State University of New York Press, 1996).

Day, Gary and Brian Docherty (eds), *British Poetry from the 1950s to the 1990s: Politics and Art* (Basingstoke: Macmillan, 1997).

Hampson, Robert and Peter Barry (eds), *New British Poetries: The Scope of the Possible* (Manchester: Manchester University Press, 1993).

O'Brien, Sean, *The Deregulated Muse: Essays in Contemporary British and Irish Poetry* (Newcastle: Bloodaxe, 1998).

Drama

Berney, Kate (ed.), *Contemporary British Dramatists* (London: St James Press, 1994).

Dromgoole, Dominic, *The Full Room: An A–Z of Contemporary Playwriting* (London: Methuen, 2000).

Shank, Theodore (ed.), *Contemporary British Theatre* (Basingstoke: Macmillan, 1996).

Shellard, Dominic, *British Theatre since the War* (New Haven, CT, and London: Yale University Press, 1999).

Absurdist theatre

The concept of the absurd that flourished in European drama in the 1950s and early 1960s also had some degree of influence on British theatre over the same period. The movement drew heavily on the philosophical definition of 'absurdity' associated with existentialist thinkers such as Albert Camus. For Camus, human beings were adrift in the chaos of an empty and meaningless universe, in which the comforting illusions of faith and reason could no longer offer consolation. Absurdity in this context derived out of humanity's yearning for those consolations, and it was absurdity that defined the human condition at this point in history. In this analysis, human beings were isolated and alienated from the world around them; the Theatre of the Absurd sought to dramatise this condition.

The plays of absurdist theatre's main exponents, Eugene Ionesco, Samuel Beckett and Jean Genet, reflected the absurdity of human existence in the form as well as the content of their plays, rejecting dramatic conventions of plot cohesion, naturalistic settings, psychologically consistent characterisation and rational dialogue. Ionesco's *The Bald Prima Donna* (1958) and Beckett's hugely influential *Waiting for Godot* (1953) featured repetitive, inexplicable action and dialogue, demonstrating a lack of connection between characters that verged at times on the nonsensical, evoking a lost and bewildered state of humanity. Vladimir and Estragon, the two tramps who are the main protagonists of *Waiting for Godot*, for example, are unsure of whom they are waiting for and why, and even how long they have been waiting. The play's two acts contain many similarities, though the tramps give few indications that they are aware of this, despite encountering the same characters in both acts. Beckett's play clearly reveals the influence of popular forms of comic entertainment, such as mime, slapstick and circus-clown-style antics on absurdist drama, but the fundamental existential despair underlying the characters' words and actions reveal the greater tragic dimension of the genre (*Godot*'s subtitle is 'A Tragicomedy in Two Acts').

In addition to existentialist influences, absurdist drama also drew on the artistic and literary movements of surrealism and expressionism from before the Second World War, and owed a particular debt to the fiction of Franz Kafka. The Theatre of the Absurd was largely a continental European movement, with its key figures based for the most part in Paris, including the Irishman Beckett, who wrote in French and translated his work into English. By the end of the 1950s, absurdist influences had permeated British theatre thanks to the mixture of critical acclaim and confusion with which *Godot* was received. Only one major British playwright of the period, Harold Pinter, however, was generally regarded as having deeply absorbed absurdist influences, in plays such as *The Caretaker* (1960) and *The Homecoming* (1965). Yet Pinter's work differed substantially from that of Beckett and Ionesco, in that he juxtaposed absurdist incongruity and inexplicable character action with naturalistic, if somewhat skewed, domestic settings and recognisably everyday speech patterns. The effects created by Pinter's marriage of the ordinary and the illogical were as disquieting, if not more so, than the more overtly surrealist techniques of other absurdist writers, and had arguably a more profound impact on the development of British drama over subsequent decades. Tom Stoppard, similarly, drew heavily on Beckettian and absurdist strategies in early plays like *Rosencrantz and Guildenstern are Dead* (1967), later transcending these models to develop a distinctive and innovative dramaturgical style that, like Pinter's, has had a wide-ranging and lasting impact on contemporary drama in Britain. The cultural authority attained by both Pinter and Stoppard argues at the very least that absurdist theatre has had a significant indirect impact on British drama of the period, with many of its characteristic techniques later entering the theatrical mainstream.

See also *Texts*: Alternative theatre, Modernism, legacy of.

Further reading

Esslin, Martin, *The Theatre of the Absurd*, new edn (London: Methuen, 2001).

Alternative theatre

One of the most influential of the counter-cultural art forms that flourished in the 1960s, and one of the few that continued to have a lasting impact in subsequent decades, was that of alternative or fringe theatre: plays and other dramatic events that were often the result of collaboration between members of a small-scale company, usually containing a strong political message, and performed in smaller theatre spaces or other, sometimes non-theatrical, locations. Alternative theatre companies began to emerge in the mid-1960s as writers, directors and actors, frustrated by the limitations of mainstream theatre, both in terms of its preferred themes and performance strategies, sought to transform drama into an instrument of political articulation and instruction. These companies were to a large extent dependent on Arts Council funding, which until the economic downturn of the mid-1970s was relatively plentiful. Theatre companies sprang up that aimed to focus on specific issues, or represent interest groups, that were ignored or marginalised in the traditional theatrical repertoire. The early 1970s saw the development of feminist theatre companies such as Monstrous Regiment, who often employed all-female casts, and the Gay Sweatshop collective, which was set up to address issues affecting homosexual experience.

The continuing expansion of fringe theatre companies brought with it a growing need for new venues. Some companies deliberately sought to perform in non-theatrical locations such as workplaces, community centres, schools and colleges, in order to reach a wider audience, while others took advantage of the proliferation of smaller theatres in the 1970s. These theatres provided more intimate performance spaces than the traditional proscenium arch, bringing audience and actors into closer proximity and rejecting naturalism in favour of more experimental styles that both transcended dramatic realism and captured some of the close-up intensity of television drama.

The dramatic strategies of Bertolt Brecht were particularly influential in the alternative theatre movement. The desire to deliver a political message required a different relationship between performers and spectators, so that those watching would respond with greater objectivity. Minimalist stage sets that made no attempt to disguise the theatrical nature of the experience were highly effective in this respect, as were other Brechtian techniques such as direct addresses by actors to the audience, the use of song and music, and episodic structures that broke up the narrative flow in order to focus attention on the play's central themes.

The alternative theatre scene gave initial exposure to many of the playwrights who became leading figures in British contemporary drama in the 1970s and 1980s. David Hare, for example, first came to attention for his work with two alternative theatre companies: Portable Theatre, founded in 1968, in which he collaborated with Howard Brenton, and Joint Stock, which in the 1970s featured work by Caryl Churchill, who was later to gain critical acclaim for plays such as *Top Girls* (1982) and *Serious Money* (1987). Although many of the playwrights who dominated British theatre in the 1970s, including David Edgar, Trevor Griffiths and Howard Barker, followed the trajectory of Hare, Brenton and Churchill, moving from alternative companies to work for the major national and provincial theatres, there were others who moved in the opposite direction. John McGrath had worked for the Royal Court Theatre before forming, in 1971, one of the most critically successful alternative theatre groups of the period, 7:84 (the name of the company refers to the statistic of the time, that 7 per cent of the population owned 84 per cent of the nation's wealth). McGrath was inspired by the idea of taking theatre out of its traditional environment into less conventional locations, often in working-class areas, where it might attract a more demographically diverse audience. Throughout the 1970s, 7:84 enjoyed considerable success with its touring productions of plays including McGrath's *Sergeant Musgrave Dances On* (1972), a reworking of John Arden's 1959 drama, but like many other alternative companies, it became a victim of the worsening economic circumstances of the 1980s, as its financial lifeline was severed by government cuts in Arts Council funding. The rise of Thatcherism led many of the generation of playwrights spawned by the alternative theatre movement to question the effectiveness and impact of their work, disillusioned as they were by the failure to achieve political change of the kind that had been envisaged in the more idealistic atmosphere of the 1960s. Nevertheless, many of the changes in the staging, direction and acting that have taken place in the post-Second World War era owe much to the innovations implemented on the margins by alternative theatre groups.

See also *Contexts*: Counter-culture, Feminism and the role of women, Political protest, Popular culture; *Texts*: Absurdist theatre, Class, Epic Theatre, Gay and lesbian writing, Political commitment, Women's writing; *Criticism*: Marxist criticism.

Further reading

Itzin, Catherine, *Stages in the Revolution: Political Theatre in Britain since 1968* (London: Eyre Methuen, 1980).

Kershaw, Baz, *The Politics of Performance: Radical Theatre as Cultural Intervention* (London: Routledge, 1992).
McGrath, John, *A Good Night Out: Popular Theatre: Audience, Class and Form* (London: Methuen, 1981).

Anglo-Welsh literature

The definition of Anglo-Welsh literature has been the subject of much debate since the early 20th century, but is now generally taken to refer to literature written in English by writers born in Wales, on themes that relate to Welsh history, culture or contemporary experience. Writers of different geographical origins who have spent a considerable amount of time in, and have written extensively about, Wales, such as the English-born poet Jeremy Hooker, are also often included within this definition. A distinction needs to be drawn between Anglophone Welsh writers and Anglo-Welsh writers, however. Anglo-Welsh literature characteristically examines the social and political implications of national and cultural identity, and derives out of two sometimes conflicting traditional communities: the rural and the industrial. Dylan Thomas, for example, though a major poet of the 20th century, paid little attention to questions of national identity and culture, and is not generally regarded as an Anglo-Welsh writer. R. S. Thomas, on the other hand, a Welsh-born poet whose published work spanned the second half of the 20th century, and focused on themes such as rural Welsh life, politics and religion, is widely regarded as one of the most significant figures in Anglo-Welsh poetry.

R. S. Thomas first came to prominence in the 1960s as a politically committed poet who brought a critical focus to bear on issues such as the decline of the Welsh language, the quest for Welsh autonomy from the British political system and the growing Anglicisation of Welsh culture. Thomas, a priest as well as a poet, was also inspired by his strong Christian consciousness: his poetry often celebrated the religious impulse at the heart of Welsh rural life and reflected a sense of lost communality. Gillian Clarke, in works like her long poem 'Letter from a Far Country' (1985), also attempted to re-establish a connection with her rural ancestry, while also reflecting the rise of feminist consciousness and its implications for female experience within a largely masculinist society and culture. Other poets, including Hooker, Robert Minhinnick and Anthony Conran, saw the conventional symbols of Welsh cultural identity and the emphasis on rural life as outdated, focusing instead on industrialised urban communities. Minhinnick's poetry in particular addresses the damaging effects of industrial decline that decimated those communities in the South Wales valleys dependent on steel and coalmining for their economic survival and cultural identity.

Anglo-Welsh fiction flourished with a sense of purpose earlier in the post-Second World War period: the novels of Emyr Humphreys, like the poetry of his contemporary R. S. Thomas, centred on rural experience and the process of social change, while Glyn Jones, who began publishing poetry and short stories in the 1930s, later turned to the novel. His fictional works included *The Valley, the City, the Village* (1956), an exploration of the life in the industrialised communities of the South Wales Valleys. As in the poetry of R. S. Thomas, religion played a large role in the work of two of the most prolific Anglo-Welsh novelists of the late 20th century: Alice Thomas Ellis and Bernice Rubens. Welsh-born, but of Russian Jewish descent, Rubens published over 20 novels from the early 1960s until her death in 2004, including the 1970 Booker Prize winner, *The Elected Member* (1969). Rubens's work characteristically explored themes such as Jewish history and culture, and illness, both mental and physical, and drew heavily on her own Welsh background. Ellis, by contrast, was a staunch Catholic. Many of her novels had Welsh settings and, as well as exploring religious themes, she addressed Celtic myth and history in *The Inn at the Edge of the World* (1990) and contemporary urban life in *Pillars of Gold* (1992). The death of Ellis in 2005, and of Rubens some months earlier in 2004, deprived Anglo-Welsh fiction of two of its most distinctive voices.

For Anglo-Welsh writers, themes and issues centred on national identity, society, politics and culture are rendered particularly problematic by the changes and challenges to traditional ways of life that have affected modern Wales. Welsh culture is largely defined by its duality: the conflicts between its two different languages, one of which was in decline for a considerable period of time, and between the values of rural and industrial society, problematised still further in the postindustrial era since the 1980s. However, since the decline of traditional rural and urban industries a process of regeneration has begun in many parts of Wales, which has led to an increasing self-confidence about national identity, aided by greater political independence from Westminster. This more positive outlook offers new potentialities and possibilities for Anglo-Welsh literature in the 21st century.

See also   *Texts*: Englishness, Irish literature, Nature, Regional identity, Scottish literature.

Further reading

Conran, Anthony, *Frontiers in Anglo-Welsh Poetry* (Cardiff: University of Wales Press, 1997).
Humfrey, Belinda (ed.), *'Fire Green as Grass': Studies of the Creative Impulse in Anglo-Welsh Poetry and Short Stories of the 20th Century* (Llandysul: Gomer, 1995).
Jones, Glyn, *The Dragon has Two Tongues: Essays on Anglo-Welsh Writers and Writing* (Cardiff: University of Wales Press, 2001).

'Angry young men'

Jimmy Porter, the protagonist of John Osborne's play *Look Back in Anger*, which was widely regarded as heralding a major thematic shift in British drama when it was first performed in 1956, has been described as the embodiment of the term 'angry young man', a phrase which was often used to describe some of the main dramatists and novelists who were coming to prominence in the late 1950s. Porter represented a social phenomenon that was becoming more prevalent in the period: a young working-class man, university-educated due to the postwar extension of higher education, but disaffected and disillusioned by bourgeois society and a hierarchical class system that was proving resistant to the social changes taking place in the period. Osborne's play featured numerous vituperative verbal assaults by Porter on various establishment targets. These were all the more effective in a climate of British imperial decline and growing frustration at the limited progress of the Welfare State. The concerns expressed by Osborne's Porter were also reflected in the work of contemporaries of the stage such as Arnold Wesker, whose trilogy of plays, *Chicken Soup with Barley* (1958), *Roots* (1959) and *I'm Talking about Jerusalem* (1960), explored the struggles of an East London Jewish socialist family, as they tried to maintain their political idealism in the face of economic reality, and the decline of postwar optimism about the possibilities for radical social change.

The new generation of novelists emerging at this time also contained writers, usually from working-class provincial backgrounds, who engaged closely with issues of class and politics. John Braine's *Room at the Top* (1958) depicted the rise of his socially-mobile anti-hero Joe Lampton to a position of status and authority in local government, through often ruthless and cynical tactics. Alan Sillitoe's factory worker, Arthur Seaton, the central character of *Saturday Night and Sunday Morning* (1958), lacked the educational or professional opportunities of Osborne's or Braine's characters, but his class anger and flouting of authority are similar in their iconoclastic effect to Porter's tirades against the contemporary social world. That said, many of the writers and characters associated with the label 'angry young man', with the exception of Wesker, lacked a coherent sense of how genuine change and social reform might be brought about. Porter bemoans the absence of 'good, brave causes', but in doing so only demonstrates how the rebellious mood amongst writers of this generation was largely unfocused. Many of the writers associated with the 'angry young men', such as Osborne, Kingsley Amis, John Wain and John Braine came to reject their earlier radicalism in later decades, as they became more established as part of the literary and cultural mainstream, turning from socialist idealism to reactionary conservatism in some cases, and finding little to inspire them in the more challenging counter-cultural ethos of the 1960s. The legacy of the so-called 'angry young men' lies in their insistence on representing aspects of social experience, from a working-class perspective that literature had largely ignored before the Second World War. The settings of their plays and novels were indicative of important social and cultural shifts in the aftermath of the war, and their use of naturalistic language and realist narrative techniques also offered a challenge to literary conventions that had become established between the wars. Their work also made a huge contribution to a renaissance in British film, with many of the novels and plays being adapted for the big screen, and the 'kitchen sink' realism they helped to create was also critically influential on television drama of the period. Their work offered less in terms of formal innovation, however, and in this respect they were part of a general resistance to modernist techniques that had dominated earlier in the century, and were to reassert their influence in the more liberal decade to follow.

See also   *Contexts*: Class structure, Political protest; *Texts*: Campus novel, Class, Empire, end of, 'Kitchen sink' drama, Movement, the, Political commitment, Realism.

Further reading

Allsop, Kenneth, *The Angry Decade: A Survey of the Cultural Revolt of the Nineteen-Fifties* (Wendover: Goodchild, 1985).

Rebellato, Dan, *1956 and All That: The Making of Modern British Drama* (London: Routledge, 1999).

Avant-garde poetry

Since the early 20th century, British poetry has been increasingly open to the possibilities of experimentation with traditional forms and modes of expression. The enduring impact of modernism, apart from brief periods in the 1930s and 1950s, has influenced generations of British poets who have sought to transcend the limitations of poetic convention. Parallels can also be drawn between prominent developments in the more experimental branches of American poetry. The strategies employed by established British avant-garde poets like J. H. Prynne, Tom Raworth and Lee Harwood are to some extent informed by the 'open field' practices of Charles Olson and the Black Mountain poets, as mediated by the American poet Ed Dorn, who collaborated with a number of poets in England in the 1960s. Olson and his followers were concerned with reflecting the immediacy of perception, rejecting traditional metres, rhythms and syntax, in favour of free verse forms based on the natural rhythms of breathing and speech. The work of poets such as Prynne reflects a similar dedication to fluidity of line and stanza, though with a more meticulous approach to syntax and punctuation, for example. The formal and thematic concerns of the 'Language' school of poetry, developed by Charles Bernstein and others in the mid-1980s, have closely informed the experimental work of contemporary Scottish poets Robert Crawford and W. N. Herbert.

Avant-garde British poets have also mirrored the dissemination strategies of their American counterparts, using magazines and small independent presses based outside the metropolitan mainstream, in places like Cambridge and Brighton, as well as in London. These dissemination strategies have been partly forced on them by the reluctance of larger publishers to invest time and resources in poetry that challenges convention and subverts expectation. Other poets have deliberately chosen the independent press and magazine sector to maintain greater control over their work and avoid the risk of compromising their aims and intentions. Only rarely have these writers received wider exposure in the form of anthologies published by larger concerns: Carcanet's collection *A Various Art* (1987), edited by Andrew Crozier, and Iain Sinclair's *Conductors of Chaos* (1996), published by Picador, are two notable exceptions.

Avant-garde poetry is characterised by an emphasis on free verse, rather than traditional metres and established poetic devices, such as rhyme and regular stanzaic structure. Typographical arrangement of words on the page assumes primary importance in many types of avant-garde or experimental poetry, especially in subgenres like concrete poetry, in which the visual appearance of the poem contributes centrally to its meaning. Linguistic innovation, explored through syntactic experimentation and the juxtaposition of incongruous concepts and images, is also a prominent concern among many British avant-garde poets. The aim of such techniques is to defamiliarise language and render meaning open to continual reinterpretation and re-evaluation. These poets also often seek to escape the constraints of the printed page as a medium for their work; performance of various kinds is crucial to the full realisation and effect of works by poets such as Caroline Bergvall, who specialises in installations and other kinds of performance art.

The roots of the thematic and formal approaches favoured by contemporary British avant-garde poets can be traced back to the revival of interest in modernist strategies in the 1960s, and the emergence of the Underground poetry movement that flourished in that period, in response to the conservatism of the Movement poets who had dominated the previous decade. The emphasis on the performative elements of poetry in the 1960s, following the principle of spontaneous creation embedded in the work of 'Beat' poets like Allen Ginsberg, shifted attention away from conventional metrics and rigorous poetic formality. The avant-garde and experimental poets who began to write in the following decade largely rejected the lures of spontaneity and confessionalism, associated with the 'Beats', in favour of the more considered approaches of, for example, Olson and William Carlos Williams.

For many critics, avant-garde and experimental poetry comes nearest in its themes and techniques to reflecting and offering a critique of the fragmentation and social alienation that have been seen as key characteristics of the postmodern era. Avant-garde poetry also reflects post-structuralist scepticism about the stability and reliability of meaning. Prynne's poetry, for example, resists easy interpretation by offering putative but always provisional connections of images, giving his poetry an impressionistic sense of momentary and shifting perception that evokes comparison with modernist stream-of-consciousness techniques. But in Prynne's work, these self-referential and potentially inward-looking strategies are put to the service of revealing the social implications of language use, and commenting, albeit obliquely, on the corruption of language in a postmodern era dominated by commercial and media interests.

See also *Texts*: Concrete poetry, Language poetry, Modernism, legacy of, Performance poetry, Postmodern literature, Underground poetry.

Further reading

Duncan, Andrew, *The Failure of Conservatism in Modern British Poetry* (Cambridge: Salt Publishing, 2003).
Jackson, K. David, Eric Vos and Johanna Drucker (eds), *Experimental – Visual – Concrete: Avant-Garde Poetry Since the 1960s* (Amsterdam and Atlanta, GA: Rodopi, 1996).
Prynne, J. H., *Stars, Tigers and the Shape of Words: The William Matthews Lectures* (London: Birkbeck College, 1993).

Black British literature

Some of the most original and creative literary work in Britain since the end of the Second World War has been produced by successive generations of black British writers. The immediate postwar era brought an influx of immigration from the Commonwealth territories of the West Indies, India, Pakistan and Africa to ease a serious labour shortage that was hindering reconstruction. Many of these first-wave immigrants experienced severe disillusionment when they encountered a hostile reception from some sections of the white British population. A number of writers were among those who arrived in Britain in the late 1940s and early 1950s; the novelist Sam Selvon was one. In early works such as *The Lonely Londoners* (1956), Selvon explored the theme of the migrant experience, which was to become one of the characteristic concerns of black British writing in the contemporary period. Selvon's work was marked by his pervasive use of a Trinidadian Creole linguistic register, not just in the dialogue, but also in the narrative voices of his novels. In this respect Selvon anticipates the work of later writers, who also sought to assert a sense of black British identity, by drawing on their own indigenous linguistic characteristics and literary forms. Two particularly influential figures, who helped black British writers to find a voice through which their own social, cultural and political concerns could be expressed, were the West Indian poets Edward Kamau Brathwaite, educated at Cambridge, and Derek Walcott, who did not take the migrant trail to Britain. Both came to prominence in the 1960s, bringing Caribbean writing to international attention. Brathwaite is widely credited with coining the term 'nation language' to describe the creolised English in which he wrote. He also rejected traditional Western literary forms, as demonstrated in his much quoted assertion 'the hurricane does not roar in pentameters',[1] which encapsulates his reaction against the imposition of colonial cultural values on Caribbean peoples, an imposition that proved inadequate or inappropriate for addressing their experience. Walcott's approach was less radical; he, too, often adopted creolised diction and speech rhythms, but incorporated these alongside more standard linguistic registers and established poetic forms and conventions. The hybridity of Walcott's style manipulates and celebrates the positive aspects of both Western and Caribbean culture and literary tradition. Although they differed widely in their ideological outlooks and poetic techniques, both Braithwaite and Walcott gave authority to the exploration of West Indian dialects as appropriate idioms for poetic discourse, and in doing so endorsed the primacy and validity of the oral tradition.

For black British writers in the late 20th century, reconnection with the oral tradition became one of the key strategies informing their work, alongside the development of a language appropriate to the articulation of a black perspective on British culture and society, and the widest possible dissemination of work that was deeply engaged with public and political concerns. These intentions permeate the poetry of Linton Kwesi Johnson, whose characteristic theme was the disaffection of black urban British youth. Johnson's collection *Dread Beat and Blood* (1975) did much to establish black British writing as an effective vehicle for political protest and social commentary. Just as Brathwaite had rejected the forms and rhythms of Western poetry, so Johnson eschewed traditional metres and conventional poetic language in favour of musical rather than poetic rhythms (many of his poems have been recorded with the backing of reggae musicians), and the deployment of Caribbean speech idioms and black British patois. The articulation of Johnson's political consciousness – a blend of Marxist dialectics and Rastafarianism – through linguistically radical and rhythmically innovative poetry, allied to a forceful performance style, made his work popular with a young black audience not normally receptive to poetic discourse. Johnson's work also connected with a wider audience at a time when various manifestations of youth protest – punk rock, black and gay rights activism, and anti-fascist coalitions – were at their height.

Contemporary black British writing addressed alienation and displacement on various levels, as its concern with the migrant experience gave way to an exploration of racial tension and the effect of social and economic deprivation in the 1970s and 1980s. Throughout this period, the work of black British writers was also often characterised by a related sense of duality, as writers addressed both their geographical origins and the site of their displacement. The poet James Berry explored this theme in his 'Lucy's Letters' sequence, where warmly evocative manifestations of Caribbean life are juxtaposed with coldly prosaic depictions of British society. Black women writers such as Grace Nichols have also dealt with this kind of experience, depicting female characters that were far from the passively suffering, abused stereotype of common perception. Nichols focuses rather on the strength and life-enhancing spirit of black women, and this celebratory tone is one that has emerged increasingly in black British writing in recent decades, demonstrating the wider sense in which black identity has become more confidently assertive in an increasingly multicultural society, as reflected in turn-of-the century texts like Zadie Smith's *White Teeth* (2000). That is not to underestimate the difficulties still faced by black British citizens, which continue to be addressed by writers such as Kwesi Johnson. However, what black British writers share is a commitment to articulating their central concerns, through modes of discourse that reflect their own social and cultural values, rejecting where necessary the language and forms of those who once colonised them, or appropriating, manipulating or subverting that language and those forms to their own ends.

See also *Contexts*: Migrant experience and multiculturalism; *Texts*: Empire, end of, Englishness, London, literary representations of, Performance poetry, Political commitment, Postcolonial literature, Urban experience; *Criticism*: Postcolonial criticism.

Further reading

Dabydeen, David (ed.), *The Black Presence in English Literature* (Manchester: Manchester University Press, 1985).

Dabydeen, David and Nana Wilson-Tagoe, *A Reader's Guide to West Indian and Black British Literature*, 2nd edn (London: Hansib, 1997).

Lee, A. Robert (ed.), *Other Britain, Other British: Contemporary Multicultural Fiction* (London: Pluto Press, 1995).

Campus novel

The emergence of campus fiction in 1950s Britain coincided with the expansion of the university sector and the widening of higher educational opportunities in the immediate post-Second World War era. As more students from more diverse social and economic backgrounds entered university, and many stayed within academia for career purposes, the result was a more demographically varied university population by the mid 1950s. This had distinct imaginative possibilities for British fiction at the time, particularly given the preoccupation many writers had with issues of class in the Welfare State era. The university campus provided one of the few settings in which the interaction of people from different class backgrounds could feasibly be represented, and writers such as Kingsley Amis, Malcolm Bradbury and David Lodge developed the campus novel in directions that enabled them to address changes and trends in academia and the social structure.

The environment usually explored in campus fiction is that of the newer provincial redbrick university, rather than the Oxbridge settings featured in Evelyn Waugh's *Brideshead Revisited* (1945), for example, probably because of the greater demographic range of those institutions. The first British campus novel is generally held to be Kingsley Amis's comic satire *Lucky Jim* (1954). The novel's central protagonist, Jim Dixon, is a university lecturer from a lower middle-class background, whose irreverent attitude towards the university hierarchy and anti-establishment views were enough to ensure Amis was labelled among the 'angry young men' of 1950s literary culture, though the novel's comic emphases and conventional ending tended to dilute its subversive possibilities. Nevertheless, *Lucky Jim* provided some acute social observations and helped to establish the campus novel as a fertile genre for the exploration of postwar social change. Other major practitioners of the form include Malcolm Bradbury, whose first campus novel was *Eating People is Wrong* (1959), and who continued to chart social and political developments in the university sector in later works. *The History Man* (1975) satirises radical political activism at a time when the intense but short-lived period of student rebellion in British universities in the late 1960s was still a recent memory. David Lodge, like Bradbury, combined an academic role with a career as a novelist, frequently using the campus setting, most notably in the trilogy comprising *Changing Places* (1975), *Small World* (1984) and *Nice Work* (1988). Lodge's main satirical target in these novels was the rapid growth and development of literary theory, which had come to dominate English studies from the 1970s. In spite of the abstruse subject-matter, the novels were commercially and critically successful, largely due to the predominant comic tone which is a characteristic element of the British campus novel. American versions of the campus novel, such as Don DeLillo's *White Noise* (1984) and Philip Roth's *The Human Stain* (2000), tend towards darker humour and set their narrative events more closely in the context of external social and political forces.

The 1980s saw the beginning of a prolonged period in which British universities often found themselves at odds with government educational policies and constrained by financial and economic difficulties. Since this time, the campus novel has diminished somewhat in its appeal to contemporary writers, though Lodge was able to combine satire against academia with an exploration of British industrial practices under Thatcherism in *Nice Work*. On the whole, however, the essentially comic, often farcical tone of the traditional British campus novel was far less effective when applied to a university sector in a continuing state of crisis.

See also   *Contexts*: Class structure; *Texts*: 'Angry Young men', Class, Movement, the.

Further reading

Carter, Ian, *Ancient Cultures of Conceit: British University Fiction in the Postwar Years* (London: Routledge, 1990).
Showalter, Elaine, *Faculty Towers: The Academic Novel and its Discontents* (Oxford: Oxford University Press, 2005).

Class

For much of the period since the Second World War, class has been a central theme in contemporary British literature, particularly among the increasing numbers of writers from lower middle-class and working-class backgrounds, who have emerged during an era predominantly characterised by social and cultural democratisation. British literature until the end of the war had been dominated by upper- or middle-class settings and preoccupations; even those who focused on political issues from a class perspective and were sympathetic to the situation of the working class, such as George Orwell and W. H. Auden, were themselves from relatively privileged backgrounds. It was not until the 1950s that the extension of educational provision began to produce a substantial cohort of writers who could plausibly address working-class experience from first-hand knowledge. So-called 'provincial' novels, such as Alan Sillitoe's *Saturday Night and Sunday Morning* (1958) and David Storey's *This Sporting Life* (1960), while formally conservative in their narrative strategies, could claim to represent radical shifts in theme and subject-matter, depicting complex and fully rounded working-class characters chafing against social hierarchies in their everyday lives. Others, like Raymond Williams in *Border Country* (1961), addressed a recurrent theme of the period: the conflicts experienced by working-class characters who, through the acquisition of education, have transcended their origins and background, but find themselves unable either to fully assimilate themselves into their new social strata, or to reconnect with the values of their class and family. The same theme preoccupied poets like Tony Harrison, whose sonnet sequence *From the School of Eloquence*, begun in the early 1970s, has explored the theme almost obsessively. Seamus Heaney, too, especially in early poems such as 'Digging' (1966), engaged with the intractable difficulties of this position. The fact that both Heaney and Harrison have chosen to address class issues in poetry, conventionally regarded as the most exclusive of genres, adds further layers of paradox to their position, and the strategies they have used, especially Harrison's combination of dialect voice and traditional metres and verse forms, have enacted the conflict within the formal constraints that define the genre. Edwin Morgan's 'Glasgow Sonnets', in *From Glasgow to Saturn* (1973), also play off colloquial and idiomatic language against poetic convention, acting as a telling intervention in a long-running debate in Scottish literature about the validity of Scots dialect as a means of articulating issues of class and national identity.

British and Irish poets have increasingly challenged received ideas of what should constitute poetic language and the thematic concerns appropriate to poetry, often but not exclusively from a class perspective, as can be seen in the work of many black British poets, but it is arguably in British drama that the most sustained engagement with class experience has been enacted in the contemporary period. The turning-point for British theatre in this respect was John Osborne's *Look Back in Anger* (1956), with its departure from the anachronistic middle-class setting and concerns that had dominated the British stage until this point. The theatrical style of 'kitchen sink' realism that Osborne's play did much to pioneer lent itself to working-class drama. One of the first plays to take advantage of this was Shelagh Delaney's *A Taste of Honey* (1958), which not only addressed working-class experience, but did so through the perspective of an adolescent girl. Class as a literary theme has tended to be the preserve of male writers, with notable exceptions such as Maureen Duffy, Christina Stead, Nell Dunn, and in Pat Barker's early work. Delaney's play also featured an interracial sexual relationship and an overtly homosexual character at a time when theatre censorship still exerted severe constraints on what could and could not be depicted on stage.

Throughout the 1960s, working-class characters and concerns continued to feature with increasing regularity in British drama. Arnold Wesker, who had first announced his concern with issues of class and politics in a trilogy of plays at the end of the 1950s – *Chicken Soup with Barley* (1958), *Roots* (1959) and *I'm Talking about Jerusalem* (1960) – continued to highlight the conflicted relationship between class experience, political idealism and social reality in plays including *Chips with Everything* (1962), and *Their Very Own and Golden City* (1966). Playwrights such as Harold Pinter and Edward Bond made much of the defamiliarising effect of working-class speech patterns in dramatic settings, in their often unsettling and oblique social and political commentaries. The growth and development of alternative theatre gave greater scope for writers not only to address class as a theme, but also to take their plays to non-theatrical venues in order to attempt to reach a working-class audience. This proved a formative experience for many involved in the alternative theatre scene, who later became prominent figures in British drama in the 1970s and 1980s: David Mercer, Trevor Griffiths and Howard Barker were among the key figures of this period, whose later work continued to explore issues of class and social change.

The optimism of the 1950s and 1960s, concerning the possibility of significant social transformation, had largely disappeared by the late 1970s, in spite of the general trend towards increased social mobility and democratisation, leaving many writers on the Left disillusioned about the validity of their earlier work. This was particularly the case among the leading dramatists of the period, and there were signs that engagement with political issues, especially class, was in decline, a situation exacerbated by government cuts in Arts Council funding that forced many alternative theatre groups to curtail their activities, and curbed the willingness of mainstream theatres to take chances with new writing.

In the 1980s, rising unemployment and industrial decline had a particularly severe impact on material conditions in working-class communities and inner-city areas. The effects of Thatcherite social and economic policies became a recurrent theme in much of the writing of the period. In 1985 British poetry produced two polemical state-of-the-nation works: Peter Reading's *Ukulele Music* blended a range of narrative perspectives, verse forms and linguistic registers into a bleak and despairing portrait of inner-city deprivation, while Tony Harrison's *v.* combined an unruly obscenity-strewn demotic voice with a traditional verse form, in a fierce condemnation of the hopelessness and disaffection faced by working-class youth in the mid-1980s. Other writers, such as Martin Amis in his novel *Money* (1984), and Caryl Churchill in the play *Serious Money* (1987), responded to the social effects of the increasing division between the haves and have-nots, in a society where affluence for those who benefited from Thatcherism's monetarist policies contrasted starkly with the plight of a rapidly expanding underclass. Pat Barker is another writer who highlighted class concerns in her fiction of the 1980s. Her first novel, *Union Street* (1982), focused specifically on female working-class experience in the north-east of England, while *The Century's Daughter* (1986) addressed the same confluence of class and gender against a wider chronological background.

Clearly, with the rise of multiculturalism and greater social mobility, society is organised less clearly according to traditional class hierarchies than it was at the start of the postwar period, though class can still provide a useful perspective for the reflection of modern society in contemporary writing, given continued evidence of social inequality. Towards the end of the 20th century, English novelists have generally been less directly concerned with class as a theme, but Scottish and Irish writers in particular, reflecting the impact of increased poverty and unemployment in their respective nations, have continued to address working-class experience. The fiction of the Scottish novelist and short story writer James Kelman frequently takes as its theme the travails of working-class figures in his home town of Glasgow, while his contemporary Jeff Torrington looked back to the recent past of the Gorbals slums of the 1960s, in his bleakly comic first novel, *Swing Hammer Swing* (1992). The Irish novelist Roddy Doyle's *Barrytown* trilogy, *The Commitments* (1988), *The Snapper* (1990) and *The Van* (1991), engages with similar thematic areas to those explored by Kelman and Torrington, though Doyle's work is generally more accessible. His depictions of the struggles of modern day Dubliners to escape economic deprivation are notable for the wit and authenticity of his protagonists' voices, in novels that have achieved considerable success – all three have been adapted for the cinema – demonstrating that class can still provide a useful perspective for the delineation of modern society in contemporary writing.

See also   *Contexts*: Class structure, Political protest, Youth culture; *Texts*: Alternative theatre, 'Angry young men', Campus novel, Englishness, History, 'Kitchen-sink' drama, Political commitment, Realism, Regional identity, Urban experience; *Criticism*: Cultural materialism, Marxist criticism, New Historicism.

Further reading

Eagleton, Mary and David Pierce, *Attitudes to Class in the English Novel: From Walter Scott to David Storey* (London: Thames & Hudson, 1979).

Hawthorn, Jeremy (ed.), *The British Working-Class Novel in the 20th Century* (London: Edward Arnold, 1984).

Haywood, Ian, *Working-Class Fiction: From Chartism to 'Trainspotting'* (Plymouth: Northcote House, 1997).

Klaus, H. Gustav and Stephen Thomas Knight (eds), *British Industrial Fictions* (Cardiff: University of Wales Press, 2000).

Concrete poetry

The term 'concrete poetry' was first used in the 1950s to describe an experimental form in which visual rather than linguistic concerns dominate, and verbal meaning of the type normally associated with poetic writing is subordinated to an emphasis on the typographical and spatial arrangement of words and other symbols or images. Concrete poems are often made up of words or phrases reproduced in particular patterns, that work by implication to make oblique connections or juxtapositions between language and the visual object depicted. Ian Hamilton Finlay's 'Poster Poem' (1964) is one such example: its typographical arrangement suggests a traditional circus poster, while its textual content both describes and evokes the paraphernalia of a sea-fishing expedition.

Concrete poetry flourished throughout the 1960s as one element of the alternative or underground poetry scene. Its practitioners tended to avoid negotiation with the mainstream publishing market, taking advantage of the availability of cheaper and simpler printing processes to disseminate their work through small presses and magazines that were more receptive to experimental work. In its use of modern technology and rejection of traditional poetic forms and structures, concrete poetry is firmly rooted in the contemporary avant-garde. However, many of its strategies are comparable with the pattern poems of George Herbert in the 17th century, the relationship between words and visual images in William Blake's poetry, 20th-century precursors such as the Russian poet Vladimir Mayakovsky, and American practitioners of typographical experimentation, most famously, perhaps, e. e. cummings.

In addition to leading practitioners such as Hamilton Finlay and Bob

Cobbing, a number of more established poets were also drawn to the liberation from traditional form offered by concrete poetry. Edwin Morgan's 'Message Clear' (1968), for example, one of a series of what he termed 'emergent poems', repeats fragments of the phrase 'I am the resurrection and the life', spelling out a series of different phrases that create a disturbing, fragmented narrative. Concrete poetry does not yield its meaning easily to conventional forms of critical reading; in fact, it often cannot be read at all in the normal sense of the word, but is generally regarded as an innovative aesthetic practice that invites reassessment of the nature and function of poetry in contemporary literary discourse.

See also *Contexts*: Science and technological innovation; *Texts*: Avant-garde poetry, Modernism, legacy of, Postmodern literature, Underground poetry.

Further reading

Cobbing, Bob, *Changing Forms in English Visual Poetry: The Influence of Tools and Machines* (London: Writers' Forum, 1988).
Mottram, Eric, *Towards Design in Poetry* (London: Writers' Forum, 1988).

Empire, end of

Although the dismantling of the British Empire largely took place in the post-Second World War era, literary engagement with imperial decline, and critiques of imperialism, began to emerge between the wars. Novels such as E. M. Forster's *A Passage to India* (1924) and George Orwell's *Burmese Days* (1934) tentatively looked forward to the end of British dominance over its colonial territories and attacked the ideology behind Western assumptions of superiority over the colonised. When the dissolution of the British Empire became a reality, starting with the granting of Indian independence in 1947, however, the majority of British writers at first failed to respond directly to the issues facing Britain in the postimperial world order, reflecting, perhaps, the limited extent to which the empire impinged on the wider public consciousness.

Nevertheless, the diminishment of Britain's status as a world power became increasingly apparent in the 1950s, a fact brought forcibly home by the humiliations of the Suez crisis in 1956. It was clear that the loss of its imperial role was a major contributing factor in the discernible crisis of national identity and self-confidence that came to characterise the decade. John Osborne's *Look Back in Anger*, first performed in the same year as the Suez crisis, was one of the first plays to question explicitly the values that had informed the imperialist project for centuries; the British Empire was just one of the many targets of the invective of the play's main protagonist, Jimmy Porter. John Arden's *Sergeant Musgrave's Dance* (1959) mounted a more explicit attack on imperialist values, demonstrating the enduring potency of the ideas that underpinned British actions abroad by setting the play in an unspecified period between 1860 and 1880, but drawing implicit parallels between the real and threatened violence in the play, and events in Cyprus in 1958, when British soldiers killed a number of Cypriot nationals in reprisal for the murder of a British military wife. The play's changing reception, from its first performance in the late 1950s, to the 1980s, is instructive of the way attitudes towards British imperialism shifted. At first, Arden's play was poorly received by audiences and critics, apparently unwilling at this time to embrace its anti-war and anti-imperialist rhetoric. By the middle of the following decade the play had grown in popularity, being performed frequently, and its message struck a chord with a generation more critical of the political and imperialist values of the past. In 1981 the play was revived again by the National Theatre, made relevant by the presence of British troops in Northern Ireland, and its highly positive reception reflected the extent to which British theatre had become an effective vehicle for the expression of oppositional political values.

Other plays and novels by so-called 'angry young men' of the period like Alan Sillitoe, also made passing reference to Britain's present decline and the attitudes that had underpinned its former dominance, but for the most part end of empire was, up until the 1970s, more of a subtext to the literature of the period than a central theme. Philip Larkin's poetry, for example, has often been said to characterise a general mood of postimperial despair; the air of wistful nostalgia that permeates poems such as 'MCMXIV' (1960), with its description of volunteers queuing to enlist for the First World War, 'Grinning as if it were all / An August Bank Holiday lark', and its poignant conclusion, 'Never such innocence again', may not refer directly to Britain's decline as a world power, but the poem evokes a sense that the symbols and characteristics that defined national identity are no longer to be relied upon. Similarly, the dreary, decaying urban perspectives that recur in, for example, 'Mr Bleaney'(1955) and 'Ambulances' (1961) can be interpreted as an implicit recognition that the postwar and postimperial world was one of reduced horizons and lowered expectations. Ted Hughes's poetry, very different in theme and setting from Larkin's, with its focus on a brutal and visceral natural world, seems again to offer little overt commentary on Britain's postimperial role, but the predatory lifeforms that inhabit his landscapes can be read as symbolising imperialist values. The eponymous speaker of Hughes's poem, 'Hawk Roosting' (1960), provides one such perspective, imposing its will on the world it inhabits:

It took the whole of Creation
To produce my foot, my each feather:
Now I hold Creation in my foot
[...]
I kill where I please because it is all mine.

Historical distance, together with the emergence of postcolonial and multicultural perspectives in contemporary British writing, have brought the theme of end of empire more frequently to the forefront of the literary imagination. Paul Scott's experiences in the British army in India informed an extensive body of work, culminating in his Booker Prize-winning novel, *Staying On* (1977), which deals with the difficulties facing the few Britons who remained in India after independence, and their struggle to come to terms with the radically changing social and political landscape around them. More frequently, however, the perspective represented in writing of the postimperial era is that of the formerly colonised. Salman Rushdie, Indian-born but British-educated, has repeatedly addressed the Indian postcolonial experience, structuring his novel *Midnight's Children* (1981) around the lives of characters born at the moment of Indian independence in 1947. Rushdie's use of fantasy and magic realist strategies, one soon realises, are vastly different from those of Scott, demonstrating the extent of cultural change in the postcolonial world, and the growing emergence and confidence of postimperial writing.

See also *Contexts*: British Empire, decline and loss, Migrant experience and multiculturalism, War; *Texts*: 'Angry young men', Black British literature, Englishness, History, Movement, the, Nature, Postcolonial literature; *Criticism*: Postcolonial criticism.

Further reading

Darby, Philip, *The Fiction of Imperialism: Reading between International Relations and Postcolonialism* (London: Cassell, 1998).
Giddings, Robert (ed.), *Literature and Imperialism* (London: Macmillan, 1990).
Sauerberg, Lars Ole, *Intercultural Voices in Contemporary British Literature: The Implosion of Empire* (Basingstoke: Palgrave Macmillan, 2001).

Englishness

One of the most enduring preoccupations in English literature since the early 20th century has been with the connotations and implications of national identity, and their literary representations. Conceptions of Englishness have changed and evolved over the period, and have become increasingly problematic in the post-Second World War era of imperial decline. Many of the characteristics long associated with English national identity either disappeared or underwent radical transformation after the war. The rapid rise of Americanisation over the same period obliterated many other aspects of traditional English culture, though the sense of crisis that this has engendered seems stronger and more profound in the case of English national identity, than in the other constituent nations of the United Kingdom, or indeed among second- and third- generation immigrant communities.

The increasing significance of Englishness as a literary concept is inextricably bound up with the growth and development of English literature as a subject for academic study at university level since the early 20th century. As a consequence, literature came to be seen as a potential ideological force for promoting national unity and confirming and strengthening social hierarchies. The relationship between English literature and Englishness became more problematic as social hierarchies were challenged after the Second World War. Increasingly, too, canonical literary assumptions began to be questioned from a range of marginal perspectives that often raised implications for nationhood and national identity. Nevertheless, many of the established characteristics of Englishness proved surprisingly resistant to these challenges. Englishness continued to evoke particular images in the creative imagination. These often still centred on pastoral settings and imagery, in spite of England's longstanding status as a predominantly industrialised nation. The consequence of this was to exclude a substantial proportion of the population – the urban working class – from identification with what was conceived as the English national character. Englishness tended to be associated with the characteristics of those who held social and political power, essentially the middle and upper classes, a state of affairs that led George Orwell, in 1941, to point to the existence of at least two 'Englands' – the England of the rich and the England of the poor. Orwell's analogy of England at that time, as 'a family with the wrong members in control',[2] was one which the postwar Welfare State consensus sought to eradicate, though with only limited success.

In the aftermath of the war, representations of Englishness in the literature of the period were often imbued with a sense of loss and nostalgia, as well as trepidation about what imperial decline on the one hand, and possible social transformation on the other, might mean for those used to having social, cultural and economic power. The poetry of Philip Larkin seems in many ways to embody the sense of national identity in crisis in the immediate postwar era. Much of Larkin's work adopted a defensive attitude towards the process of change as social and moral certainties began to erode. Larkin's poetry invests heavily in symbols of an England that no longer existed at the time he was writing, if indeed it ever had. Traditional communal rituals – rural village shows and Whitsuntide wedding parties – seem to take on an almost sacramental status in Larkin's poems, summed up by the almost fervent invocation, 'Let it always be there', that concludes his poem 'Show Saturday' (1973). But Larkin's is no straightforward nostalgic yearning for a better world: often, the pastoral idylls he invokes belong to a world that Larkin was too young to have experienced directly, and his celebration of the communal is undercut by the archetypal narrative persona of many of his poems. The Larkinesque observer is invariably a detached figure, often viewing the literal and metaphorical social landscape through windows, or in other ways physically separated from the scenes he describes, denying the possibility of connection. In mourning national decline and articulating a weary disillusionment with the contemporary world, Larkin presents a vision of a lost England that is tellingly devoid of human occupation in 'Going, Going' (1971):

> And that will be England gone,
> The shadows, the meadows, the lanes,
> The guildhalls, the carved choirs.

In the same poem, the crowded motorway café, filled with 'kids . . . screaming for more', is presented by Larkin as a hellish vision compared with the potency he invests in disappearing pastoral emblems.

Larkin's Englishness, like other versions, is revealingly partial and exclusive, as instructive for what it leaves out as for what it includes. Writers such as Anthony Powell and Evelyn Waugh, for all the vast narrative sweep of their novels, focused on a relatively narrow social world, bringing in characters from other milieus to show the perceived dangers of transgressing class boundaries. As writers from more diverse social backgrounds rose to prominence, different aspects of England and Englishness were increasingly represented in literary discourse, and the emergence of black British writers like Hanif Kureishi brought a new perspective to bear on issues of national identity. Karim Amir, the mixed-race protagonist of Kureishi's *The Buddha of Suburbia* (1990), introduces himself as 'an Englishman born and bred, almost . . . a funny kind of Englishman, a new breed as it were, having emerged from two old histories', demonstrating the extent to which the rise of multiculturalism has problematised Englishness. The outsider perspective on Englishness has assumed growing significance in the post-Second World War period. The early experiences of Caribbean migrants has been a theme that has captured the literary imagination since the 1950s. Novels like George Lamming's *The Emigrants* (1954), and Sam Selvon's *The Lonely Londoners* (1956) demonstrated the extent of antipathy shown to immigrants by the indigenous white population of Britain, a theme that has been frequently revisited throughout the period, for example in Andrea Levy's Orange Prize-winning novel *Small Island* (2004).

Migrants from other geographical areas expanded the range of multicultural experience. Other novels that, like Kureishi's *The Buddha of Suburbia*, have addressed Asian-British experience include Meera Syal's *Anita and Me* (1996), while Timothy Mo, in *Sour Sweet* (1982), depicted the difficulties of assimilation that faced the expanding Chinese community in London. The journey of self-discovery that the protagonists of such novels undergo illustrate the cultural shifts and social issues of the period. Often, these characters' experiences are ultimately affirmative, suggesting that English national identity can have much to gain from a greater openness to wider cultural influence, but also illustrating how much more difficult the concept of Englishness has become over the post-Second World War period.

See also   *Contexts*: British Empire, decline and loss; *Texts*: Anglo-Welsh literature, Black British literature, Class, Empire, end of, London, literary representations of, Movement, the, Nature, Regional identity, Scottish literature, Urban experience.

Further reading

Baucom, Ian, *Out of Place: Englishness, Empire and the Locations of Identity* (Princeton, NJ: Princeton University Press, 1999).
Doyle, Brian, *English and Englishness* (London: Routledge, 1989).
Gervais, David, *Literary Englands: Versions of 'Englishness' in Modern Writing* (Cambridge: Cambridge University Press, 1993).
Spiering, M., *Englishness: Foreigners and Images of National Identity in Postwar Literature* (Amsterdam: Rodopi, 1992).

Epic theatre

The visit of Bertolt Brecht's theatre company, the Berliner Ensemble, to Britain in 1956, during which three of Brecht's plays were performed in London, had a profound impact on British dramatists. William Gaskill, who later directed Brecht's play *Mother Courage and her Children* (1940), one of the three performed by the Berliner Ensemble, claimed that the Ensemble's performance of the play was the most important production seen in Britain up to that time; John Arden, author of *Sergeant Musgrave's Dance* (1959), which incorporates many Brechtian elements, described *Mother Courage* as the play he would most like to have written. Brecht's theatrical strategies and practices are usually described under the heading 'epic theatre', or dialectical theatre, and are difficult to summarise, not least because Brecht continually developed those theories throughout his career (he died some months before the Berliner Ensemble's London performances). However, the influence of 'epic theatre' is unquestioned, with supporters and critics equally forceful in their responses to the theory, and to its effectiveness in performance.

The term 'epic theatre' was not originally coined by Brecht, but had been current in discussions in Germany for some time before Brecht first used it in a 1930 essay, 'The Modern Theatre is the Epic Theatre'. For Brecht, epic narrative was characterised by objectivity, in that the story was told from a distanced perspective, with the interpolation of authorial comment; Brecht wanted to incorporate such features into his plays, which he saw as potential instruments of political instruction. This was a reaction against traditional theatrical techniques, which he claimed absorbed the audience into a comforting illusion, encouraging them in an emotional engagement with the characters and events on the stage that left them predisposed to accept the world as it was. Brecht, on the other hand, wanted to make his audience think about what they had witnessed; to be aware of the social forces underlying the narrative developments of the play. To this end he conceived a set of specific theatrical devices and techniques, which he described using the term *Verfremdungseffekt*. This has usually been translated into English as 'alienation effect', which perhaps does not give the full flavour of what Brecht was trying to achieve. Rather than alienating his audience, Brecht wanted to create a sense of defamiliarisation that would distance the audience from what they were seeing, and encourage them to take an objective view, questioning why the events unfolding before them were happening. In Brechtian drama, props and scenery were kept to an absolute minimum, and the mechanics of stage production were often deliberately left visible to the audience, in order to dispel the kind of naturalistic illusion that Brecht felt would detract attention from the ideas being expressed. The structure of Brecht's plays was often episodic, consisting of a succession of short scenes, and any sense of theatrical suspense was removed by the use of a titlearum, a device which displayed a plot summary of each scene before the audience witnessed it, so that they could be encouraged to think about the events rather than speculate about what was going to happen next. Songs also often broke up the narrative flow, reinforcing the underlying political message Brecht wanted to convey, and actors were encouraged to step out of their roles and address the audience directly.

'Alienation effects' were widely adopted by politically committed British playwrights. Edward Bond was perhaps Brecht's closest follower, especially in plays like *Saved* (1965), which used extreme examples of violence to challenge audience reaction. Similar tactics were used by another Brechtian acolyte, Howard Brenton, in *The Romans in Britain* (1980), a highly controversial play that was the target of a legal prosecution for indecency. Brecht's influence on post-Second World War drama, particularly in Europe, has been fiercely debated, but the extent to which many of his dramatic strategies have been adopted is evidence of the sustained impact of his ideas, even if critics of Brechtian 'epic theatre' can with some validity claim that turning Brechtian theory into practice can never guarantee that the audience will respond in the way expected of them.

See also *Contexts*: Political protest; *Texts*: Alternative theatre, Class, History, Political commitment, Theatre of Cruelty.

Further reading

Benjamin, Walter, *Understanding Brecht*, trans. Anna Bostock, with an intro. by Stanley Mitchell (London: Verso, 1998; first pub. 1966)
Brecht, Bertolt, *Brecht on Theatre: The Development of an Aesthetic*, ed. and trans. by John Willett, 2nd edn (London: Meuthen, 1974; first pub. 1964).

Gay and lesbian writing

One of the key literary consequences of the radical shift in attitudes towards issues of sexual identity and gender roles since the Second World War has been an increase in, and greater acceptance of, writing about gay and lesbian experience. A number of related developments created the more receptive climate for this kind of writing: the decriminalisation of homosexuality in 1967; the greater sexual freedom of the 1960s; the removal of sanctions against the depiction of gay characters and relationships on the stage; and a greater acceptance of sexual explicitness in literature. Earlier in the period, gay and lesbian writers had to resort to more circumspect approaches to their subject matter, but by the late 20th century homosexual writing had largely gained acceptance in the literary mainstream. The novels of Alan Hollinghurst, from *The Swimming Pool Library* (1988) to the Booker Prize-winning *The Line of Beauty* (2004), have been among the most critically acclaimed novels about homosexual experience. Hollinghurst's Booker victory would have been inconceivable 50 years earlier, at which time writers like Angus Wilson and Christopher Isherwood had to rely on allusion and allegory to address their chosen themes. The more liberal climate of the late 1960s helped homosexual writing to gain acceptance in the literary mainstream, and writers from earlier in the century, like E. M. Forster, whose long-suppressed novel *Maurice* was finally published in 1971, and Radclyffe Hall, whose banned novel about lesbian experience, *The Well of Loneliness* (1928), was reissued in 1949, were subject to new critical scrutiny. The emergence of gay and lesbian studies as a discipline in many European and American universities also helped to stimulate wider debate about issues relating to homosexual identity.

Gay and lesbian writers were among those most willing to reject traditional literary conventions in favour of experiment and innovation to find appropriate forms and idioms for the representation of homosexual experience. The poet Thom Gunn began writing in the more repressive era of the 1950s; his early work, characterised by formal and metrical rigour, led to his inclusion among the Movement poets. However, in retrospect, the artfully disguised homoerotic subtext of poems such as 'On the Move' and 'Elvis Presley' (1957) placed him apart from his contemporaries' thematic concerns. In 1960, Gunn moved permanently to San Francisco, and in a more liberal environment his poetry became freer and more radical in both form and subject-matter. Gunn was able to express his homosexuality more openly in work that owed more to the confessional tendencies of American 'Beat' poetry than to the English tradition.

Gay and lesbian novelists were also open to influences from other literary cultures: magic realist techniques can be identified in the fiction of Jeanette Winterson, whose first novel, *Oranges Are Not the Only Fruit* (1985), the story of a young woman's assertion of her sexual identity as a lesbian, in defiance of familial and religious condemnation, juxtaposed traditional realism with elements of fairy-tale and other non-naturalistic genres. Sexual identity was a recurrent theme in fiction of the period, often addressed with the use of non-realist strategies, in order to facilitate the assertion of 'otherness'. Brigid Brophy's *In Transit* (1969) posed a fundamental challenge to conventional modes of characterisation and narrative progression: the gender of her central character remains undefined throughout a novel that presents two alternative conclusions, printed side by side on the page in double columns.

In British drama there were, until the late 1960s, more constraints on dramatists who wanted to engage with homosexual issues. Some attempted to stretch the existing boundaries as far as possible: most notably, Joe Orton, in plays such as *Loot* (1965), who presented an often violent, black comic vision in which homosexuality and various forms of perverse behaviour were depicted as the sexual norm. In the 1970s, alternative theatre groups like Gay Sweatshop took advantage of greater freedom of expression on stage to address gay experience in touring productions that took drama to areas and environments where it was not usually found. By the 1990s, the theatrical climate had fundamentally changed, to the extent that plays that explored homosexual identity, such as Jonathan Harvey's *Beautiful Thing* (1994) and Kevin Elyot's *My Night with Reg* (1994), were finding success on the London stage, with the former transferring successfully to the cinema screen. The need to assert the significance of sexual identity, and to focus attention on the prejudice that homosexuals had historically encountered, necessitated the use of innovative stylistic techniques and language, and explicit, often deliberately shocking subject-matter. As attitudes have grown more tolerant, gay and lesbian writing has emerged from the margins and found acceptance on its own terms. There have been setbacks, however, for the cause of gay rights: the shift towards political conservatism in the 1980s threatened to halt some of the advances that had been achieved in previous decades, not least with the implementation of the notorious Clause 28, which sought to ban affirmative references to homosexuality in schools. More serious, and more widespread, was the rise of the AIDS epidemic in the same decade, which had its greatest impact on homosexual lives and lifestyles. AIDS became a central theme for many gay writers, including Thom Gunn, whose collection *The Man with Night Sweats* (1992) catalogued the effect of AIDS on many of the poet's friends and acquaintances, in stark and uncompromising detail. The openness of Gunn's treatment of the theme is indicative of the way in which issues affecting homosexuals have been brought into the literary mainstream; homosexual relationships and concerns are now established themes in literature of the contemporary period.

See also *Contexts*: Feminism and the role of women, Sex and sexuality; *Texts*: Political commitment, Women's writing; *Criticism*: Gender criticism.

Further reading

Haggerty, George E. and Bonnie Zimmerman (eds), *Professions of Desire: Lesbian and Gay Studies in Literature* (New York: Modern Languages Association of America, 1995).

Hutton, Elaine, *Beyond Sex and Romance: The Politics of Contemporary Lesbian Fiction* (London: Women's Press, 1998).

Sedgwick, Eve Kosofsky, *Novel Gazing: Queer Readings in Fiction* (Durham, NC: Duke University Press, 1997).

Summers, Claude J. (ed.), *The Gay and Lesbian Literary Heritage* (New York: Henry Holt, 1995).

Genre fiction

One of the consequences of the critical preoccupation with redefining the concept of literariness in the contemporary period has been to blur the distinctions between literary and popular, or 'genre', fiction. The term 'genre fiction' can be taken to include such forms as popular romance, detective and crime fiction, espionage and science fiction. Such genres had not traditionally attracted academic attention, but in an era that has witnessed greater interaction between 'high' and 'popular' culture and the emergence of postmodern ideas challenging cultural and literary categories, the relationship between literary and genre fiction has become more complex. English literature curricula are expanding to incorporate the study of certain types of genre fiction, especially science fiction and the detective novel. Other factors have added to the decline of elitist perceptions of literariness in the period. The paperback revolution of the 1960s, largely pioneered by Penguin Books, not only made so-called serious literature more widely available at a cheaper price, but also brought those texts into closer contact with more populist titles that made up the bulk of the paperback market, making writers and readers more aware of other types of fiction writing.

For some writers, the freedom to move between genres was a possibility to be exploited even before the cultural democratisation ushered in by the 1960s; throughout his long writing career, Graham Greene had produced spy novels and thrillers alongside his more complex explorations of human experience. Other writers have freely switched between literary and genre fiction: Iain Banks, author of *The Wasp Factory* (1984) and *The Crow Road* (1992), among other examples of contemporary literary fiction, is also a prolific science fiction writer, publishing under the name of Iain M. Banks. Similarly, Julian Barnes, better known for postmodernist novels like *Flaubert's Parrot* (1985), writes crime fiction under the alias of Dan Kavanagh.

As writers from the 1960s onwards displayed a greater willingness to experiment with alternatives to traditional narrative forms, negotiations with the techniques and strategies of genre fiction increased, as demonstrated by Peter Ackroyd's manipulation of the conventions of the detective novel in *Hawksmoor* (1985). The growth of this kind of intertextual borrowing has become a two-way process in recent decades, indicated by the popular success of genre novels such as Helen Fielding's *Bridget Jones's Diary* (1996), a text that owed a structural debt to the tradition of the epistolary novel, and depended for much of its comic effect on parallels drawn with the plot and characters of Jane Austen's *Pride and Prejudice* (1813).

Genre fiction itself has become increasingly sophisticated in its techniques over the contemporary period. The continuing popularity of crime and detective fiction is in no small part due to developments away from the formulaic structure long associated with the genre. Writers such as P. D. James, Ruth Rendell, Ian Rankin and Reginald Hill place greater emphasis on depth of characterisation and narrative complexity, and use themes and settings that reflect contemporary issues and social experience, to a greater extent than many of their predecessors.

Like its literary counterpart, genre fiction can be used to reflect and comment on social, political and cultural processes of change. The popularity of the spy novel from the 1960s to the late 1980s was to a considerable extent a consequence of continuing concerns about the Cold War over that period; sexual explicitness became more prevalent in popular romance as it did in other literary genres; and apocalyptic visions in science fiction novels and thrillers, such as J. G. Ballard's *Crash* (1973) and *Super-Cannes* (2000), implicitly explored modern anxieties and concerns at the end of a century of global conflict, mass genocide and environmental crisis. For these and other reasons, academic literary study in the 21st century addresses a wider and more diverse range of textual practices, taking account of categories other than the so-called literary, and recognising that those categories overlap and intersect to a far greater extent than had been the case earlier in the post-Second World War period.

See also *Contexts*: Cold War, Popular culture; *Texts*: Marketing of literature, Postmodern literature, Realism; *Criticism*: Postmodernist theory.

Further reading

Bennett, Tony (ed.), *Popular Fiction: Technology, Ideology, Production* (London: Routledge, 1990).
Kelly, R. Gordon, *Mystery Fiction and Modern Life* (Jackson: University Press of Mississippi, 1998).
Shippey, T. A. (ed.), *Fictional Space: Essays on Contemporary Science Fiction* (Oxford: Blackwell, 1991).

History

The relationship between literature and history has grown more complex and problematic in the period since the end of the Second World War. Definitions of both terms have undergone increasing challenge with the rise of postmodernism, which has cast doubt on the validity of so-called 'grand narratives' and the concept of objective truth. Many contemporary novelists have held historical narrative up to scrutiny, often through the use of techniques aimed at revealing its inherent subjectivity and perceived unreliability. Julian Barnes's *A History of the World in 10½ Chapters* (1989) is a prime example. Barnes explores various theories of history in the novel, using a range of different literary and non-literary forms, including biography, dream sequences, invented historical documents and letters. The effect of these different modes of discourse contributes to the novel's deliberate lack of linear progression and narrative cohesion, two of the key elements of traditional historical narrative. Adam Thorpe's *Ulverton* (1992) deploys similar techniques in a novel that covers 300 years in the history of an English village, through various narrative forms and perspectives, including film and radio scripts.

Other kinds of engagements with history and historical narrative are also commonplace in contemporary fiction. The two world wars have proved fertile sources for novelists like Pat Barker and Sebastian Faulks, while the 20th century as a whole provided the backdrop to Anthony Burgess's *Earthly Powers* (1980). Other writers have focused on more distant historical periods as a means of commenting obliquely on the present. For example, Barry Unsworth's *The Songs of the Kings* (2002) takes the Trojan War as its setting, but serves also as a commentary on more recent conflicts, while his earlier *Sacred Hunger* (1992) drew implicit parallels between the slave trade and the ideology of Thatcherism that dominated 1980s Britain.

Major historical events, many of them deeply traumatic, have wrought fundamental change on social, moral and political values and attitudes, and have, in Seamus Heaney's phrase, compelled writers to 'bear witness'. Writers in each of the main literary genres – prose fiction, poetry and drama – have responded to recent history in different ways, following a period immediately after the Second World War in which there seemed to be little appetite for engagement with that conflict and its consequences. In Britain, the Movement writers of the 1950s were reluctant to confront the implications and issues arising out of the war. Elsewhere, many writers shared the view of Theodor Adorno that literature, and poetry in particular, was ill equipped to address the enormity of the Holocaust and other examples of mass destruction.

Writers in the 1950s who did address themes deriving out of the war did so largely by implication: William Golding's *Lord of the Flies* (1954), the story of a group of boys stranded on a desert island whose attempt to create a democratic civilisation disintegrates into a reign of terror, can be read as an analogy of the rise of Nazism as well as an exploration of moral issues and the concepts of good and evil. It was only with the distance created by the passing of time that writers felt able to face up to the war directly. J. G. Ballard, who as a young boy was incarcerated by the Japanese during the Second World War, and who made his reputation as a leading science fiction writer, did not feel able to draw on his wartime experiences for almost 40 years, until his novel *Empire of the Sun* (1984). Even then, it was to fiction rather than autobiography or memoir that Ballard turned, allowing him the freedom to oscillate between literal and psychological truth. Ballard was also able to maintain distance and detachment through his use of the child's perspective, rather than the controlling device of the adult narrator viewing events retrospectively, and through a deliberately impassive and unemotional narrative tone. The Second World War has had such a pervasive impact on many aspects of British social and cultural experience that strategies of estrangement and defamiliarisation like those used by Ballard have become crucial devices for writers wishing to demonstrate the moral implications of the events described.

Novelistic discourse, being an account of change over time involving explanation, analysis and narrative, lends itself effectively to the fictionalising of history in autobiographical terms such as those followed by Ballard; other genres differ in their approach to engagement with historical events. Poetic form and language facilitates a more subtle and indirect negotiation with history than both fiction and drama. Poetry's characteristic devices of symbolism, imagery and myth lend themselves to detailed treatment of defining moments, and to exploration of the effect of large-scale events on individuals. Many contemporary poets have felt compelled to take on the Shelleyean role of the 'unacknowledged lesgislator', articulating the grievances of a society and acting as that society's memory and conscience. In some areas of the postwar world, such as Eastern Europe, where political persecution and unrest have been prevalent, the compulsion to bear witness has been more urgent, and often more dangerous where censorship and suppression of free speech were rife. Poets in such environments became adept at using allusion and historical displacement to comment on the issues affecting their societies while avoiding censorship and persecution. British poets have generally suffered fewer such constraints, but being more distanced from the main political and social upheavals since the Second World War, their work has also often lacked the intensity of their Eastern European counterparts.

Geoffrey Hill's concern with history, the corruption of language and the abuse of power mark him as one of Britain's leading public poets. Hill draws widely on historical instances of the misuse of power and authority, charting the persecution of the powerless from the Wars of the Roses in 'Funeral Music' (1968), to the unnamed Holocaust victim in

'September Song' (1968). His long poem *Mercian Hymns* (1971) presents a political and social history of England that intertwines the life of the Anglo-Saxon king of Mercia, Offa, with the author's family history, including his childhood memories of the Second World War.

The impulse to bear witness is not confined to poetry; drama offers the opportunity to address moments in history that poetry's miniaturist approach favours, and the wider-scale treatment of historical events on society in general and individuals in particular. Left-wing playwrights of the 1970s were drawn towards the depiction of historical events, often invoked in order to shed light on contemporary situations: Trevor Griffiths' *Occupations* (1970) used the technique of historical displacement, often a feature of Brechtian epic theatre, to draw analogies between political protests by Italian workers in 1920, and similar struggles taking place in Western Europe in the late 1960s, including the near-revolution in Paris in May 1968. The agit-prop style of Griffiths' play has been superseded by more elliptical and subtle negotiations with the concept of history as narrative in the intervening decades. Caryl Churchill's *Cloud Nine* (1979), a collaboration with the Joint Stock company, addressed both colonialism and sexual identity, through cross-gender and cross-racial casting. The play operates on two time-scales – the Victorian era and a period over a century later – but uses the same characters in each setting. Similar historical disjunctions are a feature of plays as different as Tom Stoppard's *Arcadia* (1993), David Greig's *Victoria* (2000) and Mark Ravenhill's *Mother Clapp's Molly House* (2001). Such plays demonstrate that although postmodern scepticism has questioned the validity of historical narratives, the deployment of imaginative reworkings of time and place can still yield perceptive insights about past and present.

See also *Contexts*: Holocaust, Northern Irish 'troubles'; *Texts*: Class, Empire, end of, Holocaust literature, Irish literature, Political commitment, Postcolonial literature, Women's writing; *Criticism*: Cultural materialism, Marxist criticism, New Historicism.

Further reading

Kermode, Frank, *Poetry, Narrative, History* (Oxford: Blackwell, 1990).

Palmer, Richard H., *The Contemporary British History Play* (Westport, CT and London: Greenwood Press, 1998).

Scanlan, Margaret, *Traces of Another Time: History and Politics in Postwar British Fiction* (Princeton, NJ: Princeton University Press, 1990).

Smith, Stan, *Inviolable Voice: History and 20th-Century Poetry* (Dublin: Gill and Macmillan, 1982).

Holocaust literature

Literary responses to the Holocaust fall into three general categories: the first two categories include first-hand accounts of experiences in the concentration camps – survivors who have written retrospective factual or fictionalised accounts – and those who died but left documentary evidence of their sufferings, in the form of diaries or other kinds of writing. The third category, which includes British and American writers of Holocaust literature, consists of those who have responded imaginatively to an event of unparalleled horror and depravity that has had a lasting impact on human experience. The liberation of the concentration camps in 1945 had first brought the world's attention to the Nazi programme of genocide that accounted for the lives of 6 million Jews, and nearly as many more who were deemed 'undesirables': other racial minorities such as gypsies, homosexuals and disabled people. However, it was not until the early 1960s, when the fugitive Adolf Eichmann was finally apprehended, tried as a war criminal and executed, that the full extent of the Holocaust became apparent. Since that time, the Holocaust has become a recurrent theme in contemporary literature: the ultimate symbol of brutality at a time when such moral absolutes were hard to define.

The theorist and critic Theodor Adorno voiced concerns that many writers echoed in his claim that to conceive of writing lyric poetry after Auschwitz could only be described as barbaric. Adorno's words have been open to misinterpretation: he did not claim that poetry could not or should not be written, but questioned whether it could effectively address atrocities on the scale of the Holocaust. Adorno's words resonated for many contemporary poets, who have nevertheless sought to engage, directly or indirectly, with the Holocaust as a theme. Poets such as Geoffrey Hill, Jon Silkin and Sylvia Plath examined the implications of the Holocaust with persistent intensity. All were writing without direct experience of the concentration camps, and in Hill's case this lent a self-questioning tone to poems such as 'September Song' (1968), in which he imagines the fate of a fictional victim of the gas chambers, born on the same date as himself. Hill's disquiet about his right to write this kind of poem, and poetry's capacity to confront the theme of genocide, is encapsulated in the parenthesised aside, '(I have made / an elegy for myself it / is true)'. The narrator's distance from the experience he describes is also emphasised in the contrast between the Zyklon-B gas used in the camps and the 'smoke / of harmless fires' that touches the narrator's eyes, and the poem's understated and ambiguous conclusion: 'This is plenty. This is more than enough.' Silkin's Jewish background, his fervent belief in poetry as a vehicle of political commitment, and his determination to engage with major historical themes and events fuelled his compulsion to depict the Holocaust as the culmination of centuries of persecution of the Jews, in works such as his long poem sequence 'The People' (1974). Plath's evocations of Jewish suffering, however, have been markedly more contentious: her poem 'Daddy' (1962), for example, draws an analogy between patriarchal subjugation of the female and the victims of the gas chambers that some critics have found morally questionable.

In drama and fiction, too, the Holocaust has featured as a reference point for debating the consequences of human depravity on a previously unimaginable scale. The disjunctions and incongruous juxtapositions of absurdist theatre and the Theatre of Cruelty challenged conventional perceptions of human behaviour and morality, while British playwrights of the 1970s pessimistically analysed the Holocaust's consequences for the future of humanity, in plays such as Peter Barnes's *Laughter* (1978). In fiction, writers seem to have become more and more engaged with the implications of the Holocaust as time has granted them a distance from the events. Towards the end of the 20th century, novelists including Martin Amis and Ian McEwan, neither of whom was born at the time of the Holocaust, attested to its enduring impact and symbolic potency in their respective novels, *Time's Arrow* (1991) and *Black Dogs* (1992). Amis's novel is predicated on the black irony of reversing the order of events so that the crimes against humanity perpetrated by his protagonist, a concentration camp officer, appear almost as the acts of a benefactor: he appears to be bestowing rather than taking lives. The use of such elaborate and startling narrative strategies demonstrates how writers have had to resort to new ways of exploring events that have become indelibly imprinted on the human imagination.

See also   *Contexts*: Holocaust, War; *Texts*: History, Political commitment, Postmodern literature.

Further reading

Friedman, Saul S. (ed.), *Holocaust Literature: A Handbook of Critical, Historical and Literary Writings* (London: Greenwood Press, 1993).
Vice, Sue, *Holocaust Fiction* (London: Routledge, 2000).

Irish literature

In a period in which national and regional identity has assumed a greater centrality as a major theme for literary exploration, Irish literature, and especially the poetry of Northern Ireland, has been particularly prominent. In their 1982 anthology, *The Penguin Book of Contemporary*

British Poetry, Andrew Motion and Blake Morrison paid tribute to the role Northern Irish poetry had played in giving a lead to British poets seeking new directions that would allow them to address contemporary social, political and cultural issues, through more radical explorations of form, language and imagination. For Morrison and Motion, Seamus Heaney was the key figure in this new era, though this was not a role he was prepared to embrace, distancing himself from the anthology's British emphasis. Nevertheless, Heaney's insistence on poetry's engagement with political and historical forces and their impact on language, society and culture helped to set an agenda for other Irish poets and those from Scotland, Wales and the regions of England who shared a preoccupation with exploring national and regional consciousness.

The key theme of the period for Northern Irish poets was provided by the renewal of sectarian conflict in the late 1960s. The need to address, reflect and comment on these events was one that Northern Irish poets were compelled to fulfil, and the theme loomed large in the work of Heaney and contemporaries such as Michael Longley and Derek Mahon throughout the 1970s and 1980s: Longley's 'Wounds' and Mahon's 'Afterlives', for example, evoke the impact of the 'troubles' with a dispassionate tone and a relative lack of judgement; Heaney, in the 'bog poems' that featured prominently in his 1970s work, addresses contemporary conflict more obliquely, through historical displacement. A more explicit engagement with the 'troubles' comes in Heaney's poem 'Casualty' (1979), which focuses on the effects of sectarian conflict on a single individual and the community in which he lived. The protagonist of the poem is a victim of the fall-out from the events of Bloody Sunday in 1973, killed because he refused to allow a curfew to disrupt his regular routine. The individual's story allows Heaney to also demonstrate the strength of Irish communities, by depicting the scene of the man's funeral and the society's determination to exist as normally as possible under extreme circumstances.

A more indirect approach to the 'troubles' can also be found in the work of a later generation of Northern Irish poets, exemplified in the work of Tom Paulin, who shared Heaney's concern with the relationship between Irish dialect and the 'official' language of the English poetic tradition. Others, like Paul Muldoon, were more circumspect about commenting directly on the contemporary Northern Irish situation. Muldoon's work has a wider thematic sweep, and is characterised by the use of postmodernist formal devices, shifting temporal perspectives and multiple narrative personae, though he shares other Irish poets' desire to experiment with diverse linguistic registers and extend the boundaries of poetic language.

Irish and Northern Irish writers in the contemporary period exhibit problematic attitudes to their national literary tradition, that reflect the rapid pace of social change as well as the conflicted political and religious situations in the North. Prolonged spells of economic growth in the South in the 1960s and 1990s, punctuated by a period of decline in the 1980s, brought an expansion of the urban middle class, a shift of emphasis from rural social and cultural values to those of the city, and changes in moral outlook that reflected those in most Western societies over the same period. Many of the changes that resulted went against traditional conceptions of Irish literary and artistic culture. Novels such as Patrick McCabe's *The Dead School* (1995) explored the tensions between traditional Irish culture and modern Ireland, in which attitudes towards nationalism and national identity were being increasingly challenged. An acute sense of locality is a feature of a great deal of contemporary Irish writing, often alongside a preoccupation with issues of language and identity in the face of rapid social change. Brian Friel, in *Translations* (1981), brings these themes into close proximity, using temporal distance as a device for addressing contemporary as well as historical issues. In this play, set in 1833, the renaming of place names from Gaelic into English by the British military conducting an Ordnance Survey is used by Friel as a device which illuminates the relationships between language and identity, and between British colonial attitudes and Irish nationalism.

Ireland's complex relationship to Britain evokes parallels with the experiences of formerly colonised nations in the postcolonial era. For Irish writers, as for postcolonialist writers, concerns with establishing national identity and reclaiming and revising traditional cultural values were major preoccupations. The revival of sectarian conflict and the British government's intercession, leading to the imposition of a military presence on the streets of Northern Ireland, ensured that debates about nationhood were informed by a particular sense of urgency. The different situation obtaining in the South possibly gave writers more scope to engage other themes and issues, reflecting the positive and negative aspects of social and cultural change. The novels of John Banville are wide-ranging in their subject-matter, and transcend geographical boundaries both physically and temporally. Early novels such as *Doctor Copernicus* (1976), *Kepler* (1981) and *The Newton Letter* (1982) focus on the growth of modern science, while later novels like *The Book of Evidence* (1989), *Ghosts* (1993) and *Eclipse* (2000) draw on and refashion the conventions of crime fiction, the castaway novel and the ghost story, respectively. Loss, reconciliation and memory are typical themes in Banville's work, and all three are explored in his Booker Prize-winning novel *The Sea* (2005), as the central protagonist, Max Mordern, makes a pilgrimage to the seaside town where he holidayed in his youth, to make sense of events in both his recent and his distant past. The contemporary moment is more urgently addressed in the work of novelists such as Roddy Doyle, whose Barrytown trilogy charted the lives of modern Dubliners during the recessions of the 1980s, while *The Woman who Walked into Doors* (1996) reflected an emphasis on the experiences of other marginalised constituencies, in this case victims of domestic violence, transcending issues of national identity and culture that had tended to dominate Irish writing throughout the 20th century.

See also *Contexts*: Northern Irish 'troubles', Religion; *Texts*: Anglo-Welsh literature, Class, Englishness, History, Political commitment, Regional identity, Scottish literature.

Further reading

Corcoran, Neil, *The Chosen Ground: Essays on the Contemporary Poetry of Northern Ireland* (Bridgend: Seren, 1992).

Harte, Liam and Michael Parker, *Contemporary Irish Fiction: Themes, Tropes, Theories* (Basingstoke: Palgrave Macmillan, 2000).

Kenneally, Michael (ed.), *Poetry in Contemporary Irish Literature* (Gerrards Cross: Colin Smythe, 1995).

Mahony, Christina Hunt, *Contemporary Irish Literature: Transforming Tradition* (Basingstoke: Macmillan, 1998).

'Kitchen sink' drama

One of the most striking aspects of John Osborne's *Look Back in Anger* (1956), a play that was for many critics a turning-point in British drama, was the fact that the action took place in a domestic setting that clearly denoted a working-class environment, rather than the middle-class drawing room that featured so prominently in the work of the leading playwrights of the immediate post-Second World War period, Terence Rattigan and Noël Coward. The representation of working-class experience in British theatre had been a rarity up until this time, but Osborne's play was only the first of a spate of explorations of this theme in the late 1950s, by writers associated with the phenomenon of the 'angry young man'. It should be noted, though, that one of the most critically and commercially successful of these 'kitchen sink' dramas, as they became known, was *A Taste of Honey* (1958), written by Shelagh Delaney.

Kitchen-sink dramas were characterised not only by their preoccupation with contemporary issues affecting the postwar working class; in performance they sought to represent what Arnold Wesker, a prominent and influential dramatist in the kitchen-sink realist mode, called 'the physical business of living': a naturalistic representation of the minutiae of working-class life. It was this attention to detail, allied to dialogue that accurately reflected working-class speech that enabled Wesker, in plays like *Chicken Soup with Barley* (1958) to dramatise the struggle between the political idealism of his characters, and the social reality in which they were trapped. Kitchen-sink drama's prominence in British theatre was relatively short-lived, being supplanted by the end of the 1950s by Brechtian epic theatre and Beckettian absurdist techniques. However, kitchen-sink realism extended a lasting influence in other literary and cultural directions into the 1960s and beyond.

At the same time that Osborne, Delaney, Wesker and others were pioneering significant changes in British theatre, a new generation of novelists was engaging with similar themes in British fiction, in styles that had many correspondences with kitchen-sink realism. Many of these novels, like Alan Sillitoe's *Saturday Night and Sunday Morning* (1958) and David Storey's *This Sporting Life* (1960), were made into films that tried to adapt kitchen-sink dramatic techniques to the cinema screen. The success of these films in turn inspired other writers and directors to develop similar themes and strategies in the genre of television drama. Soap operas that focused on working-class life, such as *Coronation Street*, were originally styled along the lines of kitchen-sink realism and met with critical acclaim and huge viewing figures, as did one-off television dramas like *Cathy Come Home*, part of the long-running BBC *Play for Today* series that did much to revolutionise television drama in the 1960s. In the theatre, some elements of kitchen-sink realism continued to be used to great effect: Harold Pinter's use of recognisable working-class settings, speech patterns and linguistic registers provided a theatrically disquieting contrast with his use of sinister elliptical dialogue and absurdist techniques, and many of the prominent left-wing agit-prop dramatists on the alternative theatre circuit in the late 1960s and early 1970s synthesised Brechtian alienation devices and kitchen-sink naturalism to equally telling effect.

See also *Contexts*: Class structure, Political protest; *Texts*: 'Angry Young men', Class, Realism.

Further reading

Lacey, Stephen, *British Realist Theatre: The New Wave in its Context, 1956–1965* (London: Routledge, 1995).

Language poetry

Since the early 1980s, Language poetry, a genre associated with American poets including Charles Bernstein, Ron Silliman and Susan Howe, has had a profound and far-reaching impact on British avant-garde or experimental poetry. Language poetry began to flourish in a number of small magazines on the margins of American poetry from around 1971, reaching a wider audience with Bernstein's founding of *L=A=N=G=U=A=G=E* magazine in 1978. As the name implies, the poetry of Bernstein and his contemporaries is characterised by an emphasis on the language of the poem itself. Language poets stress the linguistic processes of the poem, and its status as a poem, drawing attention to its form and structures, which involve a rejection of traditional poetic and metrical practices. Language poetry can be defined as self-referential and self-conscious, placing it clearly in the line of transition from modernism to postmodernism.

More than most contemporary schools of poetry, the concerns and strategies of Language poetry are closely aligned to current ideas in literary and critical theory: its recognition of the inherent instability of language chimes in with developments in poststructuralism, including the deconstructionist agendas of Roland Barthes and Jacques Derrida. Language poems explore often random-seeming juxtapositions of words, which refuse to conform to syntactical expectations, and resist conventional modes of interpretation. The self-referential nature of Language poetry is not, however, intended to represent an insular concern merely with the poem as artefact, and with its linguistic strategies. Language poets share a concern with demonstrating how language and perception are used in support of the dominant political ideologies that control contemporary societies by obscuring or misrepresenting social reality.

Language poetry was in turn influenced by an earlier challenge to the mainstream of American poetry: the 'open field' practices of Charles Olson, the most celebrated of the Black Mountain school of poets of the 1940s and 1950s. Olson regarded the function of poetry as the unmediated expression of instantaneous perception, and believed that traditional forms and metres actively prevented poetry from fulfilling this function. He advocated instead more fluid poetic strategies that would allow the poet's consciousness to move with greater freedom. Language poets developed Olson's notions of open form still further, incorporating linguistic disjunction and fragmentation. Many British avant-garde poets, among them J. H. Prynne, Andrew Crozier and Lee Harwood, have responded to the oppositional tendencies, structural freedoms and fractured syntax and of open form and Language poetics that, in challenging conventional notions of the relationship between language and the world it describes, have made a lasting contribution to postmodernist strategies of writing in the late 20th century and beyond.

See also *Texts*: Avant-garde poetry, Modernism, legacy of, Postmodern literature, Underground poetry.

Further reading

Reinfeld, Linda, *Language Poetry: Writing as Rescue* (Baton Rouge: Louisiana State University Press, 1992).

London, literary representations of

In the work of many contemporary British writers, including Peter Ackroyd, Martin Amis, Hanif Kureishi and, perhaps above all, Iain Sinclair, London has made such an integral contribution to their thematic preoccupations as to transcend mere setting and almost become a character in its own right. The rationale behind the use of London as a location for British post-Second World War fiction has changed over the second half of the 20th century. As the centre of the nation's political and financial power, London has long had a symbolic appeal to the literary imagination, which was reinforced by the city's world-wide cultural pre-eminence for a brief period in the 1960s, when it took a prominent role in dictating trends in the arts, music, fashion and entertainment. Later, as the optimism of the 1960s gave way to the bleaker outlook of the 1970s and the divisiveness of the Thatcherite era, the impersonality of the metropolitan environment became emblematic of the mood of alienation and social disaffection that was reflected in some of the most significant writing of the period.

The social and cultural changes that the capital has experienced since the end of the Second World War reflected, to a heightened degree, those that took place throughout Britain as a whole. The rise of multi-culturalism, for example, arising largely as a consequence of the increase of immigration in the immediate postwar era, has been partic-ularly noticeable in London, impacting on the city's already diverse demographic structure. For many of the early migrant writers, London was not only their destination but the symbol of everything they expected from the 'mother country'. The deflation of those expectations was charted in novels such as Sam Selvon's *The Lonely Londoners* (1956), and in the white perspective on black experience in the capital provided in *City of Spades* (1957) and *Mr Love and Justice* (1960), by Colin Macinnes, who was also one of the first writers to record the significance of the emergence of youth culture in *Absolute Beginners* (1959). That novel anticipated the impact of counter-cultural movements in the 1960s, and the centrality of London's role as a focal point for many of those movements. By the turn of the 21st century, novels like Zadie Smith's *White Teeth* (2000) and Monica Ali's *Brick Lane* (2003) reflected the extent to which London had become a genuinely multicultural city, revealing both the positive and the negative effects on individuals of contemporary urban experience.

In some respects, the prevalent use of London as a setting for the contemporary novel represents a continuation of the trend that emerged in modernist writing of the earlier 20th century, towards locating texts in urban landscapes. The greater sense of impersonality associated with metropolitan locations facilitated the modernist emphasis on social and cultural alienation, which seemed to reflect human experience in the aftermath of the First World War. A similar mood existed after 1945, manifested in a general sense of exhaustion after five years of war, during which London itself suffered enormously, and partly due to the dawning realisation of humankind's capacity for mass genocide and destruction. Later in the 20th century, the increasingly frenetic pace of modern life and the effects of social division were reflected in literary representations of contemporary London, especially in the 1980s, a period in which vast fortunes were being made in the City, while within the same metropolitan area material conditions in the inner city were worsening. Martin Amis made considerable use of London as a location in his novels anatomising this period. *Money* (1984), which shifted its focus between London and New York, exposed the social, cultural and material forces at work in two of the major capitalist cities of the late 20th century, while *London Fields* (1987), through its demographically disparate set of characters, strikingly demonstrated the diversity of the capital, and by extension, of British social experience in general.

Representations of London past and present pervade the fiction and non-fiction of Peter Ackroyd, who, in addition to novels including *Hawksmoor* (1985), *The House of Doctor Dee* (1993) and *The Clerkenwell Tales* (1993), has also written *London: The Biography* (2000), a history of the city that led to a BBC television series in 2003. Ackroyd's fiction characteristically functions on several temporal levels, shifting between present-day and historical perspectives, a technique shared by Iain Sinclair, whose long poem *Lud Heat* (1975), was acknowledged by Ackroyd as an inspiration and key source for *Hawksmoor*. Sinclair's novels *Downriver* (1991), set in late Thatcherite London, but taking in a wider historical sweep, and *Dining on Stones* (2004), further illustrate his all-pervasive concern with the history, geography, society and mythic resonances of the city. As for Ackroyd, London also provided Sinclair with fertile subject-matter for his non-fiction writings: a collection of London-based essays, *Lights Out for the Territory* (1997), and *London Orbital* (2002), a wide-ranging and discursive account of the author's odyssey on foot around the M25.

See also   *Contexts*: Migrant experience and multiculturalism; *Texts*: Black British literature, Englishness, Urban experience.

Further reading

Phillips, Lawrence (ed.), *The Swarming Streets: 20th-Century Literary Representations of London* (Amsterdam: Rodopi, 2004).

Sandhu, Sukhdev, *London Calling: How Black and Asian Writers Imagined a City* (London: Harper Perennial, 2004).

Magic realism

The term 'magic realism' has had various applications since it was first used to describe aspects of the work of the *neue Sachlichkeit* school of German painters in the 1920s, who utilised realistic techniques to portray fantastic or surrealistic images. The art world appropriated the term again in the 1940s when it was used in the title of an exhibition entitled 'American Realists and Magic Realists', featuring the work of Edward Hopper among others, but the label has become most associated with late 20th-century fiction, initially to describe the novels and stories of Latin American writers including Jorge Luis Borges and Gabriel Garcia Marquez, and later to refer to writers of the English-speaking world like Salman Rushdie and Angela Carter. Garcia Marquez's novel *One Hundred Years of Solitude* (1967), the story of seven generations of a family that established a village in the South American jungle, is generally regarded as the classic magic realist text, owing to its combination of realistic descriptive detail, elements of fantasy, dream-like sequences, recurrent narrative motifs and complex, chronologically fractured plot structure. The technique of placing fantastic narrative events in recognisable settings became a characteristic feature of much British writing and other writings in English, aided by the translation of Garcia Marquez and other Latin American writers, at a time when British literature was becoming increasingly open to outside influences.

Magic realism had a particular appeal to those writers of the period who wanted to transcend the constraints of traditional narrative strategies as part of a challenge to the established literary canon, especially from postcolonial or feminist perspectives. The reshaping and manipulation of conventional literary realism to accommodate fantasy, myth, fairy-tale and other non-canonical generic forms expanded the imaginative landscape for writers, enabling them to comment critically on social and political issues. Salman Rushdie's *The Satanic Verses* (1988), for example, depicts among its narrative strands an incisive analysis of racial and urban disaffection in Britain under Thatcherism, as seen through the experiences of two characters, Gibreel Farishta and Saladin Chamcha, who begin the novel by surviving the mid-air explosion of the hijacked jumbo jet in which they had been travelling to England. In the course of the narrative, Chamcha is transmuted into a goat-like figure, while Farishta takes on the appearance of his angelic namesake and seems to acquire supernatural powers. Narrative cohesion is further compromised by shifting narrative perspectives and dream sequences.

For many women writers, magic realist techniques provided one of a number of ways in which patriarchal canonicity could be circumvented. The celebration of female experience, historically marginalised from novelistic discourse, could be made to coexist alongside non-realistic characterisation and subject-matter, drawing on myth and fairy tale to implicitly challenge the assumptions and preoccupations of male canonical literature. Emma Tennant's novel *Wild Nights* (1979) was one of the first British women's novels to fully engage with magic realist techniques and concerns: mixing fiction and memoir, the novel transforms its autobiographical subject-matter into an updated Gothic fantasy. The novels of Angela Carter, including *Nights at the Circus* (1984), with its winged central character, Fevvers, arguably constitute British fiction's fullest engagement with magic realism, synthesising the ordinary and everyday with an often utopian feminist world-view that both subverts and transcends patriarchy and conventional gender politics.

See also   *Contexts*: Feminism and the role of women, Migrant experience and multiculturalism; *Texts*: Modernism, legacy of, Postcolonial literature, Realism, Women's writing.

Further reading

Hegerfeldt, Anne C., *Lies that Tell the Truth: Magic Realism Seen through Contemporary Fiction from Britain* (Amsterdam: Rodopi, 2005).

Zamora, Lois Parkinson and Wendy B. Faris (eds), *Magical Realism: Theory, History, Community* (Durham, NC: Duke University Press, 1995).

Marketing of literature

At periodic intervals since the Second World War critics and commentators have voiced pessimistic concerns about the future of the book.

Developments in mass media, such as television and the internet, and the accelerating pace of daily life, have been perceived as posing a threat to the continued centrality of reading as a cultural activity among the British public. Publishers and booksellers have frequently described the state of the book market as one of crisis, and ways of marketing and disseminating books have changed vastly in the late 20th century, in response to changing social and economic circumstances. The place of the literary text within the book trade has been seen as particularly endangered, with commercial interests increasingly taking precedence over aesthetic considerations.

One of the most transformative developments in publishing and bookselling since the Second World War was the phenomenon of the 'paperback revolution', largely pioneered by Penguin Books. Penguin first entered the paperback market in 1935, but it was not until the late 1950s that the company substantially expanded the range and diversity of its paperback list. This coincided with the emergence, for the first time, according to Raymond Williams, of a majority book-reading public in Britain. The controversial, but generally positive, publicity generated for Penguin by the favourable outcome of the 'Lady Chatterley' trial of 1960 made a huge contribution to the paperback revolution. An increasing number of literary texts were made available in this format throughout the 1960s, facilitating their appeal to a wider audience. At the same time, the expansion of the higher education sector gave rise to a greater number of students reading English, which in turn led to an increase in demand for the kinds of books traditionally found on the university syllabus. The greater demographic diversity of the student population also contributed to the wider dissemination of literature, which was no longer regarded as the preserve of the middle and upper classes. The growth of free lending libraries, provided and funded by local councils throughout Britain, was another factor in the creation of a mass reading public that had become strongly established by the 1960s.

The economic difficulties of the 1970s saw a retrenchment in the publishing and bookselling trades, however, that had a particularly damaging effect on new writing. The number of publishing houses began to decrease, as the costs associated with publishing rose rapidly, and the publishers that survived were less willing to take risks with styles and forms of writing that might not appeal to the wider reading public. Even Penguin cut back its list of available titles in this period. From the late 1970s, market forces took over to a considerable extent, and both publishers and booksellers became more concerned to publish and stock titles and the kinds of writing that they knew would sell.

The impact of market forces on contemporary literature is evident in the rise in significance of the literary prize, and its impact in dictating the critical as well as the commercial success of a text. Novels shortlisted for Britain's largest literary prize, the Man Booker, are invariably guaranteed increased sales, and the winning book in a given year is usually assured significant commercial success. The decision of a small panel of judges can, therefore, have a disproportionate effect on the dissemination and reception of novels. Writers whose books fail to gain recognition can face increased difficulty in reaching an audience, given publishers' and booksellers' need for guaranteed sales. The emergence of large chains of bookstores such as Waterstones and Borders has transformed the processes of selling and buying books; the stores are more customer-friendly, offering a more sophisticated shopping experience, with the establishment of coffee bars and comfortable browsing areas within the shops. However, there is evidence that the range of titles on offer has diminished, with more space allocated to bestsellers and less scope for offering a more esoteric selection of texts.

Poetry has had particular difficulty in creating a space for itself within the new, more aggressive book market. The traditional slim volume with its sober, understated cover design, that was the hallmark of the largest poetry publisher, Faber & Faber, came under increasing challenge from the expansion of publishers such as Carcanet and Bloodaxe, with their more eye-catching designs and more diverse range of authors. Bloodaxe, in particular, underwent a massive expansion from small beginnings in the 1980s, giving exposure to poetry from previously marginalised groups by publishing a significant proportion of women, black British and regional poets, and becoming one of the major success stories in the late 20th-century British book world. Attempts were also made to bring poetry to a wider audience through the creation of a proliferation of poetry prizes, most notably the Forward Prize, and initiatives such as National Poetry Day and Poems on the Underground, which sought to increase poetry's visibility in everyday life. The effect of this has often been to privilege more accessible forms of poetry, however, and innovative and experimental work, as with the novel, has experienced more difficulty in securing a position in the market place. The positive measures that have succeeded in increasing public exposure to poetry have to be tempered by evidence of decline in the contemporary period, as in the decision by Oxford University Press, in 1998, to terminate its commitment to publishing poetry.

Nevertheless, it is clear that some of the more gloomy prognoses of critics, publishers and booksellers had failed to materialise by the turn of the 21st century. Film and television, both perceived as a significant threat to the survival of the book, have proved beneficial to the wider dissemination of literature, through the success of adaptations of modern and classic novels. The emergence and growth of online book-sellers such as Amazon has engendered a revolution in the way books are disseminated, and made a wider range of titles available that has gone some way to counteracting the increasing tendency in the larger bookstore chains to prioritise guaranteed bestsellers. The emphasis on market forces in modern publishing and bookselling has undoubtedly had many negative effects, but the expansion of the reading public has continued in spite of the myriad alternative cultural and leisure activities now available, enabling literary writing to maintain a substantial, if much changed role within the book trade as a whole.

See also   *Contexts*: Science and technological innovation; *Texts*: Genre fiction.

Further reading

Delaney, Paul, *Literature, Money and the Market: From Trollope to Amis* (Basingstoke: Palgrave Macmillan, 2002).

Modernism, legacy of

Critical opinion has long recognised the lasting significance of literary modernism on developments in 20th-century literature, even if there is a lack of consensus about when modernism was at its most influential. Many critics define the first half of the 20th century as the high point of modernism; others trace its roots back to the 1890s, but claim that it flourished only for a relatively short time in the 1920s and 1930s. Whatever the merits of these conflicting claims, it is clear that radical changes took place in literature over a sustained period from some time before the First World War, which were accelerated by wider changes in social and cultural attitudes, as a consequence of the weakening of established values and certainties in the aftermath of war.

By around 1910 it was already becoming clear that conventional liter-ary forms and language were proving inadequate to the demands of reflecting contemporary experience. Writers such as T. S. Eliot, James Joyce and Virginia Woolf were rejecting the forms and conventions associated with 19th-century realism, and starting to formulate more experimental techniques. In modernist fiction, the complex, linear narratives of the Victorian novel gave way to minimalism of plot and a greater emphasis on formal innovation: the aesthetic qualities of the text took precedence over the events and characters it described; narrative became more fragmented, and the mediating figure of the author was replaced by multiple perspectives represented in the stream-of-consciousness technique used to radical effect in novels like Woolf's *Mrs Dalloway* (1923) and Joyce's *Ulysses* (1922). The role and function of the narrative voice in modernist poetry, too, became less clearly defined; shifts in perspective were a feature of major poems like Eliot's *The Waste Land* (1922), implying a fundamental distinction between the author and the various narrative voices in the text. Traditional forms and metres were largely abandoned, as densely layered levels of myth and allusion became more crucial to the formal structures of modernist poetry. Discontinuity of language and ideas, and the deliberate obfuscation of connections, were also features of poetry that sought to reflect the complexity of modern civilisation. Thematically, much modernist writing shared a concern with the alienation of the individual, consequent on the destruction of old certainties and beliefs after the First World War, a concern that was to strike a chord with a similar sense of existential despair in 1945.

The influence of modernism on British literature declined somewhat in the years immediately after the Second World War. The conservatism of form, theme and language that characterised Movement poetry in the 1950s, for example, constituted an attempt to turn back the modernist tide of the interwar years. The provincial novelists of the same period were, on the whole, equally uninterested in narrative experimentation. In drama, on the other hand, the rejection of theatrical naturalism and the innovative techniques associated with Brechtian epic theatre, absurdism and the Theatre of Cruelty could be seen as directly descending from movements in European modernism of the 1930s. A play such as Samuel Beckett's *Endgame* (1957), with its non-naturalistic, ahistorical setting, elliptical and repetitive dialogue, and alienated characters, clearly drew on modernist themes and techniques. The psychologically isolated characters of Harold Pinter's early plays demonstrated some Beckettian characteristics, though Pinter's deceptively simple and colloquial language masked multiple layers of contradictory meaning, highlighting the inherent instability of language, itself a characteristically modernist concern.

Greater receptiveness to innovation and experimentation characterised much of the literature of the 1960s, as might be expected of a decade defined by more liberal creative, cultural and social attitudes. The imaginative scope available to writers expanded, along with the emergence of more diverse thematic possibilities. Traditional narrative structures in the novel gave way to a greater emphasis on self-reflexivity. Texts such as B. S. Johnson's *Albert Angelo* (1964) and John Fowles's *The French Lieutenant's Woman* (1969) drew attention to their status as fictions, rather than trying to create an illusion of reality, even commenting implicitly on the impossibility of such a venture, in ways that antici-pate techniques later associated with postmodernism. Doris Lessing's departure from conventional realist modes, in *The Golden Notebook* (1962), similarly prefigured postmodernist concerns with the tenability of 'grand narratives'. The narrative structure of *The Golden Notebook* moves back and forth between chapters of a novel purportedly written by Lessing's protagonist Anna Wulf, and extracts from notebooks that the character keeps, which relate to different aspects of her identity. The fragmentary nature of the novel was suggestive of the period which it addressed, and the focus on the disparate elements of Anna Wulf's char-acter represented an early engagement with gender identity and sexual politics, issues that would be of central importance to women writers later in the century.

Influences from beyond Britain also had an impact on dictating a shift away from literary realism, with a number of writers responding posi-tively to the French *nouveau roman*, or 'antinovel' movement of the 1950s, pioneered by Alain Robbe-Grillet. The *nouveau roman* fundamen-tally rejected realist conventions of plot, setting and consistent charac-ter development. Robbe-Grillet's leading British disciple was Christine Brooke-Rose, whose three novels of the 1960s, *Out* (1964), *Such* (1966) and *Between* (1968), were influential landmarks in the revival of modernism, and among the first signs of a shift towards what became known as postmodern techniques and strategies which dominated late 20th-century literature.

The self-reflexive modernist impulse in the contemporary novel, from the 1960s onwards, was echoed in poetry of the period that resisted both the insularity of the Movement and the emotional imperatives of the confessional school. Basil Bunting's *Briggflatts* (1966), though adopting a northern British landscape setting, and drawing on elements of autobi-ography, was regarded by some critics as in the modernist tradition of Eliot's *The Waste Land*. The combination of sparse, unsparing diction and dense allusion in Geoffrey Hill's explorations of language and power relationships also owed much to modernist preoccupations. However, it was on the fringes of the poetic avant-garde, amongst poets influenced by American literary movements that had maintained a connection with modernist principles, that modernism's characteristic strategies and techniques were adapted most imaginatively. J. H. Prynne, Lee Harwood and Veronica Forrest-Thompson maintained the sprit of modernist experimentation at its purest in drawing attention with deliberate self-consciousness to the potentialities of poetic form and language.

See also *Contexts*: Counter-culture, Feminism and the role of women; *Texts*: Absurdist theatre, Avant-garde poetry, Concrete poetry, Language poetry, Magic realism, Postmodern literature, Realism, Underground poetry, Urban experience, Women's writing.

Further reading

Mellors, Anthony Matthew, *Late Modernist Poetics: From Pound to Prynne* (Manchester: Manchester University Press, 2005).
Murphy, Richard, *Theorizing the Avant-Garde: Modernism, Expressionism and the Problem of Postmodernity* (Cambridge: Cambridge University Press, 1999).
Nicholls, Peter, *Modernisms: A Literary Guide* (Basingstoke: Macmillan, 1995).

Movement, the

British poetry of the 1950s was dominated by a group of writers who came to prominence at around the same time, including Kingsley Amis, Philip Larkin, Donald Davie, Elizabeth Jennings and Thom Gunn, whose work shared certain formal and thematic characteristics. These writers were labelled collectively as 'the Movement' by J. D. Scott of The *Spectator* in 1954. Their styles, concerns and attitudes soon diverged, but the influence of the Movement on British poetry in the post-Second World War era was profound and wide-ranging, as a force which later generations of writers either responded to or reacted against.

Robert Conquest, in *New Lines* (1956), an anthology that included most of the leading Movement poets, identified one of the key common features of their writing, rather vaguely, as 'little more than a negative determination to avoid bad principles'.[3] What this amounted to was a rejection of the emotionalism and elaborate rhetoric of the neo-romanticist movement of the previous decade, epitomised in the poetry of Dylan Thomas, and of the formal experimentation, mythical allusions and linguistic obscurity of modernist poetry in the tradition of T. S. Eliot and Ezra Pound. Movement poetry, by contrast, relied on conventional stanzaic and metrical structures, that lent themselves to the restrained and straightforward diction characteristic of Davie, and Larkin in particular. Thematically, Movement writing avoided negotiation with political themes, seeking inspiration and affirmation in everyday experience. The reasons for this were probably related to the postwar mood of exhaustion that pervaded British life in the period, and a reluctance to confront the complex moral questions raised by the war's revelation of the baser elements of human nature. There was also a desire among these poets to forge a reconnection with an 'English' line of poetic development that had been effaced earlier in the century by the shift to American and European modernist influences. The English poetic tradition had seemed to reach a conclusion in the work of Thomas Hardy, and many of the

Movement poets resolutely invoked that tradition: Larkin made no secret of his admiration for Hardy and his disdain for modernism, while Davie outlined his poetic influences in his critical study *Thomas Hardy and British Poetry* (1973). The rationality and restraint of Movement writing also incorporated nostalgia for the England that Hardy and earlier poets had known and written about, and for the certainties that had underpinned national identity earlier in the century. It is surely significant that the muted, somewhat defensive and anxious poetry of the Movement was being written in a period of imperial decline and fading national self-confidence, even if Movement poets did not directly address such themes.

The generation of poets that succeeded the Movement showed a greater inclination to address recent history and to confront moral questions about human nature and the wider social and political world. A. Alvarez's anthology *The New Poetry* (1962), though it contained work by a number of leading Movement poets, also rejected the now established modes of wry understatement and conservative formal techniques. Alvarez championed the work of poets like Ted Hughes, whose dark and often violent depictions of the animal and natural world were far removed from the dominant themes of 1950s poetry. Hughes's then wife, Sylvia Plath, was another key figure whose work reacted against Movement principles, conflating personal and political issues through emotive language and imagery. In the more expressive climate of the 1960s the restraint and parochialism of Movement writing began to seem somewhat anachronistic, though, alongside the more experimental and counter-cultural strains of poetry that came to the fore in that period, Movement techniques and strategies still exerted some influence. The accessibility of the Movement poets' plain-spoken diction, and the absence of complex allegory and mythical or classical reference in their work, meant that it retained its appeal and accessibility.

The Movement poets did not retain a coherent identity for long; only Larkin's work largely stayed true to the characteristics Conquest outlined in 1956. Kingsley Amis became better known and more critically acclaimed as a novelist; both Amis and Larkin shifted their political stance from a broadly left-leaning attitude that bordered on the apolitical to a more and more reactionary conservatism. Donald Davie became increasingly open to European and American influences, and more willing to reach an accommodation with modernist techniques. Elizabeth Jennings, the only major woman poet associated with the Movement, turned her focus to intense engagements with personal relationships, with exploring her Catholic beliefs and with her own experiences of mental breakdown. Thom Gunn, whose original link with the other leading Movement writers was arguably the most tenuous, departed furthest from Movement concerns and techniques, moving to America and adopting freer modes of discourse and a more confessional tone, in a body of work that increasingly and more explicitly addressed homosexual experience. The Movement was a short-lived phenomenon, but it exerted considerable influence on poetic developments and directions for much of the remainder of the 20th century.

See also   *Contexts:* British Empire, decline and loss; *Texts:* 'Angry young men', Campus novel, Empire, end of, Englishness, Nature, Realism.

Further reading

Bradley, Jerry, *The Movement: British Poets of the 1950s* (New York: Twayne Publishers, 1993).

Morrison, Blake, *The Movement: English Poetry and Fiction of the 1950s* (Oxford: Oxford University Press, 1980).

Nature

The representation of nature in literature has historically been one of the most prevalent themes in the Western tradition, since the Romantic movement of the eighteenth century, and the subsequent development of a pastoral tradition that remained influential in spite of the increasing trend towards urbanisation in British society. That tradition retained a considerable degree of legitimacy in the 20th century, but apart from a brief revival in the work of a number of Movement poets, has been in decline for much of the post-Second World War period. In poetry, the period has been characterised by rejection or reworking of traditional poetic forms, language and themes, leading to fundamental reconsiderations of the relationship between language and representation. Greater scepticism about the reliability of language and meaning has led writers to question the validity of investing the natural world, or any kind of physical environment, with the transcendental qualities that writers in earlier literary periods sought to attribute to their surroundings.

In the immediate postwar period, British literature was characterised by a rejection of the modernist impulses that had dominated the interwar years, and a reluctance to engage with major social and political themes. Amongst many of the Movement writers, including Philip Larkin and Donald Davie, there was a desire to establish a reconnection with the specifically English tradition exemplified earlier in the 20th century by Thomas Hardy. The idealised pastoral landscapes in the work of these writers were celebrations of a benign natural world that bore little resemblance to any landscape they might have encountered, and was inextricably bound up with conceptions of English national identity that were coming to seem outdated in the less hierarchical postwar era.

The later response against the insularity and gentility of Movement strategies and perspectives was thematically wide-ranging, but included new approaches to representations of the natural world by poets such as Ted Hughes, Peter Redgrove and Ken Smith. Hughes's more elemental depictions of the natural world were permeated with violent imagery intended to show the harsh, unsentimental reality of the animal kingdom in ways that drew parallels with some of the darker episodes in recent human history. The vivid if pessimistic world-view in Hughes's poetry, of an untamed natural world beyond the control of humankind, posited a different relationship between the writer and nature.

A number of leading contemporary poets continued to commemorate aspects of traditional rural life that were fast disappearing: R. S. Thomas's work focused centrally on the customs and values that were in decline in rural Wales, for example, and Seamus Heaney's early work was permeated with meditations on the Irish countryside of his childhood. Newer generations of poets, like Alice Oswald, in her T. S. Eliot Prize-winning 'river poem', *Dart* (2002), and the collection *Woods, etc.* (2005), and John Burnside, in *A Normal Skin* (1997) and *The Light Trap* (2002), explore the relationship between the human and the natural world. That relationship is also at the heart of ecocriticism, an approach to literary study and analysis that is growing in significance in the early 21st century, and sees place as a critical category that could potentially become as significant as class, race and gender, the social determinants that have had a substantial influence on literary theory and criticism in the contemporary period.

See also *Texts*: Anglo-Welsh literature, Empire, end of, Englishness, Irish literature, Movement, the, Regional identity.

Further reading

Kerridge, Richard and Neil Sammells (eds), *Writing the Environment: Ecocriticism and Literature* (London: Zed Books, 1998).
Picot, Edward, *Outcasts from Eden: Ideas of Landscape in British Poetry since 1945* (Liverpool: Liverpool University Press, 1997).

New voices in 21st-century literature

Much of the literary output of newly-emerging writers in Britain around the turn of the 21st century reflects the extent to which British culture has creatively absorbed the diversity of multicultural experience that has come to characterize contemporary society, while allowing individual literary voices to develop and flourish. The problems faced by ethnic minorites in establishing a sense of place and identity in Britain, that preoccupied black and Asian British writers in the second half of the previous century, continue to play a significant role in plays like Kwame Kwei-Armah's *Elmina's Kitchen* (2003), but ethnic identity is increasingly approached from a wider global perspective in plays by other black playwrights, most notably Debbie Tucker Green's *Stoning Mary* (2005), a striking example of the greater internationalist emphasis in British writing at the beginning of the 21st century. This emphasis is further illustrated by the emergence of a new wave of writers born outside Britain who have established their reputations in their adopted country. The rise to prominence in Britain of Japanese-born Kazuo Ishiguro, and Timothy Mo, originally from Hong Kong, paved the way for the emergence of novelists like Tash Aw, who came from his native Malaysia to study in England, and won international acclaim for his first novel, *The Harmony Silk Factory*, in 2005. The novel, set in Malaysia against the backdrop of events leading up to the Second World War, is a love story that draws together East and West, depicting the relationships between Chinese, Malaysian, Japanese and British expatriate cultures. Aw, like Susan Fletcher, whose novel *Eve Green* (2004) won the Whitbread First Novel award in 2005, is a graduate of the celebrated creative writing programme at the University of East Anglia, which has produced a number of major contemporary novelists, including Ishiguro, Ian McEwan and Tracy Chevalier, the American-born novelist, author of *Girl with a Pearl Earring* (1999), which was a massive commercial success, both as a novel and in the filmed version of 2003 starring Scarlett Johansson and Colin Firth.

The widening of the migrant experience that was originally the preserve of Caribbean and Indian writers in the post-Second World War period has extended not only to East Asian writers like Mo, Ishiguro and Aw. The increasing scale of refugee movement from Eastern Europe to Britain since the end of the Second World War began to be reflected in contemporary writing to an increasing extent in the early 21st century. Marina Lewycka's *A Short History of Tractors in Ukrainian* (2005) offered a new perspective on the difficulties of assimilation facing ethnic minorities, drawing on a blend of Western and Slavic narrative strategies in her story of the experiences of two Ukrainian refugee sisters in Peterborough, England.

Other kinds of migrant writers, who have settled to work in Britain voluntarily, rather than out of necessity, are also adding to the formal and thematic diversity of contemporary British literature. Michel Faber, born in Holland and raised in Australia, later took up residence in the Scottish Highlands, and his breadth of cultural experience is apparent in his early short stories, collected in *Some Rain Must Fall* (1999), and in his two novels, *Under the Skin* (2000) and *The Crimson Petal and the White* (2002). The latter is a contemporary reworking of the epic conventions of the 19th-century novel, focusing on the experiences of Sugar, a Victorian prostitute striving to leave her old life behind. *The Crimson Petal and the White* became a major success in both Britain and America, placing Faber as potentially one of the key international figures in early 21st century literature.

Contemporary writers born in Britain share Faber's willingness to draw on literary tradition, but do so with a greater recourse to foreign influences than many of their predecessors. Nineteenth-century literature in the Russian rather than the British tradition informs James Meek's *The People's Act of Love* (2005). Meek's novel takes the Russian Civil War of the early 20th century as its theme and setting, but resonates with issues arising out of more recent conflicts, as might be expected from an author who, in his role as a journalist, spent a considerable amount of time reporting on the Iraq war.

Other British novelists of the turn of the century have sought to find new ways to address some of the dominant themes in fiction since the Second World War. Yet another kind of migration – that which has seen British citizens cross once rigid class barriers in increasing numbers since 1945 – is given a different kind of treatment in the work of writers such as Caron Freeborn, whose dark, erotically charged novels *Three Blind Mice* (2001) and *Prohibitions* (2004) explore class and familial relationships, language and power, and sexual identity and obsession. Freeborn's is a distinctive contemporary voice, which captures the cadences and nuances of vernacular speech through the use of innovative narrative strategies and vividly drawn settings and characters. The eroticism of Freeborn's writing is indicative of the greater freedom available to writers to address issues of sex and sexuality since the 1960s. Gay and lesbian writers have also benefited from the more liberal climate. The lesbian historical fiction of Sarah Waters has attracted considerable mainstream recognition, especially in the case of her novel *Tipping the Velvet* (1998), which made an acclaimed, if controversial, transition to the small screen in 2002.

Contemporary poetry, like the novel, has become more outward-looking in the early 21st century. British avant-garde poets are as likely to reflect the influence of established Australian poets like John Kinsella and John Tranter as previous generations were to cite American contemporaries such as John Ashbery and the Language poets. The range of poetic language, subject-matter and cultural reference available to British poets has expanded since the late 20th century. The ease with which poets like Simon Armitage handle colloquial language and other non-literary registers is reflected in newly emerging poets such as John Stammers and Simon Perill, whose poems betray a wide range of influences, from Britain, America and beyond. High and popular cultural references permeate Stammers' explorations of personal relationships in *Stolen Love Behaviour* (2005), and Perill's more wide-ranging private and public concerns in *Hearing is Itself Suddenly a Kind of Singing* (2005). A similar eclecticism is evident in the work of contemporary Northern Irish writers like Nick Laird in *To a Fault* (2004), and Sinéad Morrissey in *Between Here and There* (2002) and *The State of the Prisons* (2005). Both continue to draw on themes and traditions that shaped the work of previous generations of Irish poets, with inevitable references to the ongoing political situation in Northern Ireland, but not exclusively so. Morrissey's work in particular ranges extensively across time and place, mediated through a consciously internationalist perspective that seems characteristic of some of the most vital writing coming out of Britain and Ireland at the start of the 21st century.

See also   *Tests*: Black British literature, Class, Gay and lesbian writing, Irish literature, Postcolonial literature.

Performance poetry

The role of poetry as a public art form has undergone considerable revision and reassessment in the post-Second World War period, and particularly since the mid-1960s. The rapidly expanding influence and appeal of rock music at this time was one of the most significant factors: the growing lyrical sophistication and complexity of the songs of artists such as Bob Dylan, Leonard Cohen and the Beatles attracted the kind of critical attention traditionally accorded to poetry. Rock music lyrics articulated a powerful message that shaped the values and attitudes of a predominantly young counter-cultural audience; if poetry was to make an appeal to this audience it would have to do so on the same terms. The emergence and growing influence of performance poetry was the consequence of the determination of poets to reach out to this potentially large audience; for a time, at least, poetry became a genuinely popular mode of literary discourse. Roger McGough, Adrian Henri and Brian Patten, collectively known as the Liverpool poets, were among the first poets to connect with this wider readership, as evidenced by the huge sales of their anthology, *The Mersey Sound* (1967), but the first major public breakthrough for performance poetry came two years earlier at the First International Poetry Incarnation at the Royal Albert Hall, which took place before an audience of several thousand spectators. Many of the leading counter-cultural poets of the time performed at the event, including the American 'Beat' poet Allen Ginsberg, a crucial influence on performance poetry of the 1960s. The majority of those taking part saw poetry as a means of disseminating a powerful political message against establishment values, and many of them were later featured in Michael Horovitz's anthology of Underground poetry, *Children of Albion* (1969).

The economic decline of the 1970s brought an era of substantial arts funding to a close, limiting the range and number of opportunities for public performance of poetry, though poets of the avant-garde, such as Caroline Bergvall and Brian Catling, gave primacy to the performative elements of their work throughout this time. In the field of black British poetry, too, performance was a vital aspect of most poets' work. One of the key concerns of these poets, especially those of Caribbean descent, such as Benjamin Zephaniah and Linton Kwesi Johnson, was to establish a reconnection with the oral tradition celebrated by predecessors like Edward Kamau Brathwaite. Johnson is widely regarded as the pioneer of 'dub' poetry, a form developed out of the practice of Jamaican DJs, who chanted and recited over instrumental versions of reggae songs; from the mid-1970s Johnson worked with reggae musicians both in live performance and on record. The rhythms of reggae music, rather than traditional poetic rhythms and metres, inform Johnson's poetic strategies, providing another example of the fruitful relationship between popular music and poetry that did much to extend poetry's potential appeal to a wider audience. The late 1970s threw up other, often unlikely connections between music and poetry: the emergence of rap music, for instance, owed something to the pioneering work of the dub poets; and the rapid fire delivery of performance poets like John Cooper Clarke was profoundly influenced by the frenetic rhythms of punk rock.

From the 1960s onwards, performance became an integral part of the poet's role and responsibilities, both for communicating a political vision to as large an audience as possible, and as a reflection of how literature in general began to compete more aggressively in the market place, forcing poets to publicise their work. This culminated in a resurgence of popular interest in poetry for a brief period in the mid-1990s, with an increase in activity on the performance poetry circuit, funded by money from the National Lottery. In the work of Simon Armitage, Carol

Ann Duffy and others, a more colloquial, conversational tone could be discerned, which was indicative of the widening definition of poetic language in the late 20th century. This was largely a consequence of the greater emphasis on performance that informed many poets' techniques and strategies. Critical opinion is divided on the contribution of performance to developments in contemporary poetry, with some welcoming the ensuing diversity and range of dialect voices and linguistic registers available to the poet, while others detect a decline in formal complexity and the nuances of poetic language.

See also   *Contexts*: Counter-culture, Youth culture; *Texts*: Avant-garde poetry, Black British literature, Political commitment, Underground poetry.

Further reading

Habekost, Christian, *Verbal Riddim: The Politics and Aesthetics of African–Caribbean Dub Poetry* (Amsterdam: Rodopi, 1993).
Oliver, Douglas, *Poetry and Narrative in Performance* (Basingstoke: Macmillan, 1989).

Political commitment

The question of literature's effectiveness as a vehicle for the articulation of political commitment is one that has long held a central position in literary debate, but has been discussed with greater urgency in the 20th century, and especially in the post-Second World War period. Many leading British writers of the 1930s saw their work and their role as politically oriented. Some were compelled by their political principles to participate in and write about the Spanish Civil War, and poets such as W. H. Auden wrote presciently about the threat of Nazism. However, the failure of literature to do anything more than offer a warning about the possibility of war, led to a sense of disillusionment on the part of many, including Auden. 'Poetry makes nothing happen', claimed Auden in his poem 'In Memory of W. B. Yeats' (1940), a poem that heralded his withdrawal from political engagement. After the Second World War, the relationship between literature and political commitment was challenged by Theodor Adorno, who maintained that literature, and particularly poetry, lacked the capacity to comprehend and confront destructive events on the scale of the Holocaust. Jean-Paul Sartre, on the other hand, writing immediately after the war, continued to insist on the validity of politically committed literature. The conflicting views of writers and critics like Adorno, Auden and Sartre have set the terms of debate underlying the attitudes of many contemporary writers towards the literary expression of political commitment.

The relationship between poetry, the most elevated and exclusive of literary discourses, and the imperatives and demands of political commitment is especially problematic. Poetry's formal and linguistic modes of expression, its characteristic qualities of allusiveness and compression, are largely inimical to the polemical and ideological nature of the political statement. Contemporary poets such as Geoffrey Hill, Seamus Heaney and Tony Harrison, among others, are acutely aware of the limitations and contradictions of their chosen genre. Much of their work is characterised by a self-questioning impulse that holds poetry itself up to scrutiny and raises doubts about its status as a public art form and its capacity to address and challenge contemporary social and political forces. Other writers, however, were less troubled by the concerns that inform the poetry of Hill, Harrison and Heaney. Emergent poetic movements of the period, that were staking a claim for voices and experiences previously denied recognition within the traditional forms and thematic concerns of poetry, such as feminist and black British poetry, adopted a more polemical approach. In both cases, their statements of political intent were reinforced by the rejection of conventional forms and metres: black poets like Linton Kwesi Johnson adapted the rhythms of reggae music and Caribbean-British patois, while a generation of women poets in the early-1970s tended towards declamatory free verse styles to liberate themselves from poetic conventions they regarded as inherently patriarchal. As the political impetus and urgency informing their early work receded, more complex engagements with traditional form and language were implemented. Later in the 20th century, poetry tended increasingly to retreat from direct political engagement, relying instead on implication, and explorations of the instability and corruption of language to inform more sophisticated political commentaries.

Similarly oblique strategies informed much of the fiction writing of the period, as modernist and postmodernist imperatives replaced the realist modes that had characterised 1950s fiction. From the 1980s particularly, with the Left struggling to find a coherent response to Thatcherism, there is less evidence of direct political engagement in British literary fiction, which, under the influence of magic realist and postmodernist strategies, was more concerned with formal experimentation and self-reflexive narrative strategies that did not lend themselves to overt political interventions. Some leading Scottish fiction writers, particularly James Kelman and Irvine Welsh, demonstrated that it was possible to combine political commitment with narrative innovation. Both reflected the impact of Thatcherism on their disenfranchised and disaffected characters, through dialect-inflected narrative perspectives. English writers like Martin Amis and Ian McEwan also addressed key political and social concerns of the period, albeit at a more indirect level. The postcolonial perspective of Salman Rushdie's early work too, was, inherently politicised, as was that of feminist magic realist writers like Angela Carter.

Politically committed writing was much more to the fore in British drama of the period, especially between the late 1950s and the early 1990s. The high point of British political drama came with the rise to prominence of a generation of left-wing playwrights that included David Hare, Howard Brenton, David Edgar and others. Most of these dramatists had served their apprenticeship on the alternative or fringe circuit in the late 1960s, and came to dominate the national and provincial drama scenes throughout the next two decades. Energised by the revolutionary potential of the *événements* of May 1968 in Paris, and the possibility of radical social change, these writers gave full expression to their political impulses. However, by the 1980s, many of them were beginning to question the effectiveness of their methods, and their work after that time tended increasingly towards Audenesque pessimism, and a sense of mourning for lost opportunities and lost idealism. Others, however, continued to provide politically charged critiques of the prevailing ideologies of the late 20th century. David Hare, in particular, has continued to deliver incisive state-of-the-nation commentaries for the stage, not least in his critically acclaimed trilogy *Racing Demon* (1990), *Murmuring Judges* (1991) and *The Absence of War* (1993).

The work of politically committed writers often privileges the need to offer a clear and persuasive polemical argument above aesthetic considerations. In the contemporary period, growing scepticism about the capacity of language to offer determinate meaning has caused writers to reconsider the capabilities of literature to perform a political function. Some of the new writings from once marginalised constituencies, however, such as postcolonialism and feminism, are inevitably politicised, and the political tendencies that inform them are inherent in the fabric of the text. In other areas of writing, especially those using modernist or postmodernist strategies, political statements are more likely to be mediated by allusion and implication, highlighting the crucial relationship between language, and political, social and economic power. The polemical approach is less in evidence in contemporary writing, but that is not to say that the literature of the period can be judged as necessarily apolitical; more complex and sophisticated strategies are employed to offer critiques of political issues and attitudes.

See also *Contexts*: Class structure, Cold War, Counter-culture, Northern Irish 'troubles', Political protest, Youth culture; *Texts*: Alternative theatre, 'Angry young men', Black British literature, Class, Epic theatre, Gay and lesbian writing, History, Holocaust literature, Irish literature, Performance poetry, Postcolonial literature, Realism, Underground poetry, Women's writing.

Further reading

Boyers, Robert, *Atrocity and Amnesia: The Political Novel since 1945* (Oxford: Oxford University Press, 1987).

Orr, John, *Tragic Realism and Modern Society: The Passionate Political in the Modern Novel* (Basingstoke: Macmillan, 1989).

Postcolonial literature

The dismantling of European empires in the 20th century, and particularly after the Second World War, created the conditions for an extraordinary explosion of literary creativity by writers from formerly colonised territories. Nations that were emerging out of their colonial past were intent on establishing their own national and cultural identities. One of the main ways in which they did this was through literature, the majority of which was written in English, the language of one of the main imperial powers, but also the international language of culture, commerce and business in the late 20th century. The labelling of this kind of writing under the single heading of postcolonial literature is arguably less than satisfactory, failing to take account of the very different experiences of colonialism out of which this body of writing emerged. For the purposes of academic study, postcolonial literature is generally taken to include writings by the formerly colonised from the Indian subcontinent, Africa and the Caribbean, but also from British Dominions like Canada, Australia and New Zealand. The literatures of all the above nations share common ground in that all have set out to challenge the dominance of Western cultural authority, which had been imposed upon them as part of the process of colonisation. Often those challenges have involved either rejection or subversive appropriation of the literary values, judgements, forms and language of the coloniser. In a contemporary period in which traditional literary conventions have been held up to scrutiny from a range of perspectives, postcolonial writers have instigated some of the most radical reworkings of those conventions.

The emergent national literatures of postcolonial nations have developed in different ways and at different rates of progress, but have tended to grow out of a dawning realisation by writers that the forms and language of the coloniser were inappropriate to the articulation of their own social and cultural experience. In order to address that experience, Caribbean writers, for example, inspired by the nationalist movements of the 1930s, began to draw on indigenous speech patterns and rhythms, and on imagery and metaphor that related to their own surroundings. Post-Second World War migration, especially to Britain, ensured that their writing strategies attracted wider attention and increased cultural authority, as literary validation was still achievable only through negotiation with Western values and standards of judgement when postcolonial writing was in its early stages.

Similar lines of development were apparent in other once colonised territories; the Nigerian novelist Chinua Achebe has spoken of the process of uncovering the history, culture and traditions of his ancestors, and of doing so through terms of reference that privilege indigenous experience, but which are mediated through the language of the coloniser. His novel *Things Fall Apart* (1958), widely regarded as the first major postcolonial novel, did just that. In the first half of the novel Achebe delineates the daily life, rituals and values of tribal society in vivid detail, using a proverbial, anecdotal style that evokes the original oral culture of his people, but within the traditional Western novel form. So successful is Achebe in recreating a sense of past tribal culture and society that the arrival of the coloniser in the second half of the novel comes as a defamiliarising shock, even to the Western reader.

One of the other key concerns of early postcolonial writers, in the period in which newly independent states and nations were coming into being, was with the ways in which freedom and independence were being used: how postcolonial societies were building an affirmative and assertive new identity that celebrated their own histories and traditions, and how they were reconciling this with their future role in a global context. The conclusions these writers reached were often pessimistic; the work of V. S. Naipaul, for example, is characterised by scepticism about the capability of postcolonial societies to benefit socially, culturally and economically in the new world order. His novel *A House for Mr Biswas* (1961) expressed this sceptical outlook symbolically in the quest of his main protagonist for economic survival and social status, which could be taken as analogous to the struggle for identity and stability that many newly independent states were undergoing at the time.

The subversive strategies of postcolonial writers, through which the perspective of the colonised takes precedence over the cultural values and authority of the coloniser, are often deployed as a challenge to the kind of thinking that Edward Said has shown underpins Western assumptions about the inherent superiority of European civilisation and values. Said saw such assumptions as part of the process whereby imperial powers maintained their control over the people and nations they colonised, and claimed that literature was one of the most potent means by which this control was culturally reinforced. The construction in Western writing of the colonised 'other', depicted in denigrating terms, was a strategy of such long standing that it became naturalised in a great deal of the writing that had traditionally been held to make up the canon of English literature.

The massive increase of postcolonial literature since around 1960, and the assimilation of much of that literature into the academic syllabus, has been one of the main contributory factors to the democratisation of English literature, or 'Literatures in English', as the subject is often now termed. Students are as likely to encounter the work of Nigerian writers like Achebe or the dramatist and poet Wole Soyinka, Indian-born novelists such as Salman Rushdie and Anita Desai, or Caribbean writers including Derek Walcott and V. S. Naipaul, as they are to come across the work of British and Irish writers who have traditionally been regarded as the main focus of the study of English literature. Postcolonial criticism has risen to a central position amongst the various forms of literary critical enquiry, due to the pioneering work of thinkers such as Said and Homi K. Bhabha, whose analyses of literary and cultural representations of national identity draw on psychoanalytical and poststructuralist theoretical approaches, and Gayatri Spivak, whose postcolonial perspectives are informed by Marxist and feminist ideas. The intellectual authority of postcolonial criticism has made a significant contribution to enhancing the status of the new literatures in English that have emerged in the postwar period.

See also *Contexts*: British Empire, decline and loss, Migrant experience and multiculturalism, Religion; *Texts*: Black British literature, Empire, end of, History, Magic realism, Political commitment.

Further reading

Ashcroft, Bill, Gareth Griffiths and Helen Tiffin, *The Empire Writes Back: Theory and Practice in Post-colonial Literatures* (London: Routledge, 1989).

Bhabha, Homi K. (ed.), *Nation and Narration* (London: Routledge, 1990).

Boehmer, Elleke, *Colonial and Postcolonial Literature: Migrant Metaphors* (Oxford: Oxford University Press, 1995).

King, Bruce (ed.), *New National and Post-colonial Literatures* (Oxford: Clarendon Press, 1996).

Postmodern literature

The pervasive influence of postmodern theory on cultural and critical practices has had a significant effect on ways in which the world is perceived, and has, unsurprisingly, extended its influence to techniques and thematic concerns reflected in literature of the contemporary period. Postmodernist scepticism about the capacity of major theoretical approaches – the 'grand narratives' of history and other intellectual disciplines – to describe and explain the social world and humankind's place within it, has inevitably had an influence on the writing strategies of contemporary poets, novelists and playwrights. The resurgence of interest in modernist literary techniques in the 1960s led many writers into further experimentation with narrative, poetic and dramatic forms that reflected postmodernist uncertainties about the stability of language and the survival of Enlightenment beliefs in reason, rationality and social, cultural and intellectual progress.

The first indications of what became recognisably postmodern concerns and techniques in contemporary writing were prefigured in experiments with narrative form and structure, by a number of novelists in the 1960s. Doris Lessing, in *The Golden Notebook* (1962), and John Fowles, in *The French Lieutenant's Woman* (1969), were among the first writers in Britain to adopt approaches in their novels that deliberately drew attention to the fictional status of the text, in Fowles's case openly discussing the techniques that were being used to relate the narrative. The self-reflexive and self-conscious narrative strategies pursued by these and other novelists with similar aims such as B. S. Johnson, whose work fell into critical neglect until a revival of interest in the early 21st century, were influenced to some extent by the *nouveau roman* movement that had come to the fore in the work of French writer Alain Robbe-Grillet in the previous decade. The *nouveau roman*'s rejection of the usual dominant characteristics of novelistic discourse – plot, setting and character – in favour of seemingly random perceptions was revised and reworked in many of the practices of postmodernist theory and postmodernist literature later in the century. Such techniques seemed eminently suited to textual reflection of the increasing fragmentation and discontinuity of modern life. Before that time, however, the economic downturn of the 1970s brought a period of retrenchment as publishers, operating with higher costs and fewer resources, became more circumspect about taking chances on writing that, in its experimental tendencies, was unlikely to be commercially viable. It was not until the 1980s, by which time postmodernist thought was culturally and intellectually established, that novelists turned with renewed experimental vigour to narrative procedures that self-consciously advertised their status as new kinds of literary conventions. Increasingly, too, at this time, writers began to interrogate the viability of narratives of all kinds, and especially of historical narrative, in much the same ways that postmodernist theories debated the same concerns. More distanced from the events of the Second World War, writers like Martin Amis, Ian McEwan and Graham Swift subjected historical perspectives on the past in general, and the war in particular, to sceptical scrutiny. Other writers experimented with subversions of temporal dimensions and chronological disjunctions. Peter Ackroyd's *Hawksmoor* (1985), for example, interweaves narratives that occupy the same London locations but shift back and forth between the present day and the 18th century. Among its other characteristics, *Hawksmoor* offers a pastiche of the detective novel genre, demonstrating another characteristic of much postmodern writing: the bringing together of high and popular cultural motifs in order to question traditional cultural categories.

There were identifiably postmodernist impulses at work also in some of the alternative directions followed by poets who rejected the more conventional approaches of the Movement poets, and those British and Irish poets who dominated the poetic mainstream in the later decades of the 20th century. Poets, including Douglas Oliver, Denise Riley, Andrew Crozier and the highly influential J. H. Prynne, stayed closer to the revived modes and procedures of modernism, the 'open field' strategies of Charles Olson, and, later, the practices and poetic concerns of the American Language poets. As with postmodernist fiction, the work of these poets was characterised by self-reflexivity and intertextual strategies. The deliberate abstraction of these poets' work, using patterns and juxtapositions of words and images, did not claim to offer a singleness of meaning that could be arrived at through traditional interpretative approaches. The emphasis was on drawing attention to the process of perception, rather than the object of that perception, as poetic convention dictated. The primary focus of such poems was on language itself, and how language, with its inherent instabilities, functioned as a means of recording perception.

British drama was less closely implicated with postmodernist thought and strategies, with only Tom Stoppard, among leading playwrights, engaging to a significant extent with key ideas about the unreliability of conventional intellectual and narrative approaches to making sense of the past and the present. His play *Arcadia* (1993), like much of Ackroyd's fiction, experiments with fractured temporal structures to cast doubt on the validity of historical narrative. The play takes place in one room, but shifts between the early 19th century and the present day as characters in the present try, and fail, to piece together the events of the past. In plays such as this, and in a considerable amount of fiction and poetry of the contemporary period, the fragmentary, self-conscious techniques and idioms are revealed as resistant to conventional modes of analysis:

those interpretative practices that depend on the kinds of large-scale theories and 'grand narratives' discredited in postmodernist thinking. In this respect these texts reflect, but do not attempt to interpret or explain, contemporary society at the end of a century in which established values and attitudes have shaken longstanding beliefs in the inevitability of human progress.

See also *Contexts*: Popular culture, War; *Texts*: Avant-garde poetry, Concrete poetry, Genre fiction, Holocaust literature, Language poetry, Modernism, legacy of, Realism; *Criticism*: Postmodernist theory.

Further reading

Gregson, Ian, *Contemporary Poetry and Postmodernism: Dialogue and Estrangement* (Basingstoke: Macmillan, 1996).

Holmes, Frederick M., *The Historical Imagination: Postmodernism and the Treatment of the Past in Contemporary British Fiction* (Victoria, BC: University of Victoria, 1997).

McHale, Brian, *Postmodernist Fiction* (London: Methuen, 1987).

Realism

For much of the contemporary period the concept of literary realism, that had been the dominant mode in fictional writing from the early 19th century until the around the time of the First World War, has been challenged by more experimental developments in narrative techniques. Realism, a style of fiction writing that aimed at conveying the impression of everyday life at a given time, through detailed description of settings, situations and characterisation, lent itself particularly to writing that aimed to reflect social, political and cultural attitudes, often by tracing the moral development of an individual character. This kind of narrative structure and trajectory was first challenged in the early 20th century by modernist writers like Virginia Woolf and James Joyce, who rejected many established literary conventions. Later in the 20th century, as traditional ways of reading and interpreting texts gave way to greater scepticism about the reliability of language and the stability of meaning, the strategies of realist writing were subjected to renewed scrutiny. Roland Barthes, for example, revealed the extent to which literary realism consisted of a set of conventions by which the illusion of reality was created. Realist conventions had been in place for so long as to have become naturalised, but were no more able, according to Barthes, to depict or even reflect 'real life' than other forms of literary discourse. As the limitations of literary realism became apparent, writers sought to find other modes of representation, through which their fictional worlds could be constructed.

In the early years of the post-Second World War era, literary realism enjoyed a resurgence in British fiction, in the work of a number of the newly emerging novelists of the 1950s, especially those whose main concern was with depicting contemporary Britain, often from a working-class or provincial perspective. These writers, who included Alan Sillitoe, John Braine and David Storey, tended more towards realist techniques than the experimentation and innovation that had characterised modernist writing of the interwar years. In the 1960s, however, a more culturally expansive and expressive spirit emerged, and writers moved on to wider thematic concerns. Literature in this period was largely characterised by its willingness to explore issues such as gender identity, self-expression, sex and sexuality, political ideologies and alternative social, cultural and moral values. The traditional techniques of realism seemed to many writers to be inadequate for meeting the new challenges facing the literature of the period, and this coincided with a revival of interest in modernist techniques. Doris Lessing and John Fowles were among the more innovative novelists of the 1960s, and continued to be influential in the following decade. Novels like Lessing's *The Golden Notebook* (1962) and *Briefing for a Descent into Hell* (1971), and Fowles's *The French Lieutenant's Woman* (1969) and *The Magus* (1966, revised 1977) were among the first to deploy the self-reflexive techniques and deliberately self-conscious engagements with intertextuality that became dominant features of British fiction by the end of the 20th century, as demonstrated in novels as different, for example, as Julian Barnes' *Flaubert's Parrot* (1985), A. S. Byatt's *Possession* (1990) and Lawrence Norfolk's *The Pope's Rhinoceros* (1996).

The magic realist techniques of South American writers such as Gabriel Garcia Marquez became another major source of influence on the narrative strategies of a number of British novelists. Angela Carter's work, from *The Magic Toyshop* of 1967 to her final novel, *Wise Children* (1991), exhibits perhaps the most sophisticated engagement with magic realism in British fiction. For women writers like Carter, and Fay Weldon in novels such as *The Lives and Loves of a She-Devil* (1983), the fantastic elements central to magic realism provided a means by which fictional worlds could be created that subverted or transcended patriarchal values.

For a brief period in the 1970s, more straitened economic circumstances affected British publishing, to the extent that more conventional modes of literary discourse offered greater likelihood of commercial success, bringing signs of a revival of literary realism. However, although the increased role played by market forces in the book trade has ensured a significant and majority place for realist modes in popular and genre fiction, realism was by no means the only, or even necessarily the most influential mode of narrative discourse in contemporary British literary fiction at the turn of the 21st century.

See also *Contexts*: Class structure; *Texts*: 'Angry young men', Class, Genre fiction, 'Kitchen-sink' drama, Magic realism, Modernism, legacy of, Political commitment, Postmodern literature.

Further reading

Gasiorek, Andrzej, *Postwar British Fiction: Realism and After* (London: Edward Arnold, 1995)
Sauerberg, Lars Ole, *Fact into Fiction: Documentary Realism in the Contemporary Novel* (London: Macmillan, 1991).

Regional identity

The democratisation of contemporary literature, resulting from an increased emphasis on once marginal perspectives of ethnicity and gender, and a rise in influence of Scottish, Welsh and Irish writing, is further demonstrated by the emergence of regional identity as a literary theme. This first became apparent in the 1950s with the sudden proliferation of what were sometimes called 'provincial novels', usually exploring aspects of working-class life in the changing social climate of the Welfare State era. Many of the writers of these novels were part of a new demographic that had taken advantage of the widening of educational opportunity. As a consequence, they found themselves distanced from the values and attitudes of the class into which they were born, and frustrated that social, political and economic power remained in the same hands as before the war, in spite of the egalitarian impulses informing the postwar national mood. However, the assertion of regional identity in contemporary British writing did not become strongly established until the 1970s, when, alongside developments in Scottish, Irish and Welsh writing, and amid the emergence of influential black British writers, various poets, novelists and dramatists who closely identified with their regional origins began to assert their presence and attract critical attention.

One of the earliest key texts in the period that explored issues of regional identity was Basil Bunting's long poem *Briggflatts* (1966), which prominently featured the Northumbrian landscape and alluded in its linguistic strategies to the characteristics of dialect speech, a practice that was to assume increasing significance in subsequent decades. The poetry of Tony Harrison from the late 1970s onwards, increasingly exploited the possibilities and potentialities of the dialect voice. In

Harrison's case, dialect was used in a conflicting relationship with Standard English and conventional poetic forms and metres, as in his widely anthologised poem 'Them & [uz]' (1978). The poem records an incident from the poet's schooldays, when Harrison was berated by his teacher for reading poetry aloud in his working-class Yorkshire accent. The teacher interrupts the young Harrison's reading of Keats's 'Ode to a Nightingale' by dismissing the boy as a 'barbarian', and claiming poetry as the preserve of those who speak in Received Pronunciation. The adult poet's response – 'So right, yer buggers, then! We'll occupy / your lousy leasehold Poetry' – is typical of the kind of combative dialectic in Harrison's work where poetic tradition is forced to accommodate voices and perspectives it had historically ignored or marginalised. Along with Seamus Heaney from Ireland and Douglas Dunn from Scotland, Harrison was regarded by Andrew Motion and Blake Morrison, editors of *The Penguin Book of Contemporary British Poetry* (1982), as heralding a shift of direction and a new spirit in poetry.

The impact of regional identity as a key theme in postwar literature was particularly noticeable for the ways in which it democratised poetic language. In the later 20th century, the wide linguistic range that readers of contemporary poetry encounter in the work of poets as diverse as Simon Armitage, Ian McMillan, Tom Paulin, Linton Kwesi Johnson, Liz Lochhead and W. N. Herbert, among others, no longer seems remarkable. In other genres, too, regional voices and locations have become increasingly prevalent. Since the emergence of the provincial novel in the 1950s, fiction has engaged with a significantly more diverse breadth of class experience and geographical location, though these tendencies are markedly more prevalent in Scottish and Irish writing, especially in the work of writers such as James Kelman and Roddy Doyle, who have presented very different but equally vivid representations of working-class life in Glasgow and Dublin respectively. In British drama, plays exploring provincial life have proliferated since the emergence of 'kitchen sink' drama in the 1950s. John Arden and Arnold Wesker were influential figures who built on John Osborne's radical transformation of the thematic and dramatic concerns of the British stage, and have been followed in subsequent decades by playwrights such as Trevor Griffiths in the 1970s, Jim Cartwright in the 1980s and the Scottish dramatist David Greig in the 1990s and beyond. The traditional exclusion or marginalisation of working-class voices and regional settings and concerns from literary consideration has given way to a plurality of perspectives that more accurately reflects the diversity of contemporary experience in Britain.

See also   *Contexts*: Class structure; *Texts*: Anglo-Welsh literature, Class, Englishness, Irish literature, Nature, Scottish literature.

Further reading

Crawford, Robert, *Identifying Poets: Self and Territory in 20th-Century Poetry* (Edinburgh: Edinburgh University Press, 1993).
Ludwig, Hans-Werner, and Lothar Fietz (eds), *Poetry in the British Isles: Non-Metropolitan Perspectives* (Cardiff: University of Wales Press, 1995).

Scottish literature

In common with other national and regional literatures within the United Kingdom, much Scottish writing of the period has been characterised by a preoccupation with national identity, defined in relation to the culture and literary tradition of England. This relationship, as constructed in the Scottish literary imagination, is analogous to that between coloniser and colonised explored in postcolonial literatures since the decline of British and European imperial power. The rise of English as an academic subject in the 20th century had the effect of either assimilating or marginalising the work of writers from Scotland, Ireland, Wales and the regions of England, leading to a narrowness of interpretation as to what constituted literariness. For much of the 20th century, English cultural domination had brought critical dismissal or marginalisation for Scottish and other literatures that sought to address the specific concerns of national identity. However, with the growing significance of once marginal perspectives in the postcolonial, post-modern period, British national literatures grew in confidence and began to assert and explore their own social, cultural and political concerns. Thematic and formal developments in the work of Scottish poet Douglas Dunn are emblematic of the changing status of Scottish literature. Dunn's early work clearly revealed the influences of Philip Larkin, in many ways the most English of postwar poets; Dunn's *Terry Street* (1969) charted his experiences as a Scottish exile in a northern English city, Hull, which often featured in Larkin's poetry. Increasingly, however, Dunn turned his attention to Scottish history and identity, in collections such as *St Kilda's Parliament* (1981), and explored the experiences of the socially and culturally excluded, often, as in 'The Come-On' (1979), relating that exclusion to issues of language and dialect. In that poem, Dunn, in a similar, but more subtle way than Tony Harrison, pledges to infiltrate the world of high culture and learning, while retaining a sense of national identity:

> Our honesty is cunning.
> We will beat them with decorum, with manners,
> As sly as language is.

One of the most significant ways in which Scottish literature has sought to establish a voice of its own is through the use of linguistic registers that seek to reflect Scottish dialect and speech rhythms. The debate about the validity of Scots as a literary medium, and the political implications of its use, has been current since the early decades of the 20th century. The spectrum of opinion on this issue ranged from Hugh MacDiarmid's advocacy of an uncompromising adherence to Scots dialect, to the more pluralistic approach of Edwin Morgan, for example, whose poetry incorporates the use of Scots dialect within a wider and more diverse linguistic range. Tom Leonard is another contemporary poet whose central concerns lie with analysing the relationship between language and political and cultural authority; his work rejects traditional forms and metres, and replaces Standard English registers and conventional notions of poetic language with transcriptions of Glaswegian dialect. His poems also display a sophisticated grasp of sociolinguistic ideas and a shrewd awareness of the political implications of speaking with the 'wrong' accent. Younger poets like Robert Crawford and W. N. Herbert have drawn on similar ideas and engaged in linguistic experimentation in a similar vein to Leonard, while also conveying national identity through a strong sense of place that is reflected also in the work of Scots women poets such as Kathleen Jamie and Liz Lochhead.

Wider critical and commercial acclaim has been directed at Scottish fiction of the period that has given similar prominence to Scots dialect. The novels and short stories of James Kelman, written entirely in a vernacular style, address urban working-class experience in the era of Thatcherism and post-Thatcher conservatism, examining the social and political consequences of policies imposed from Whitehall on the Scottish people. Irvine Welsh's *Trainspotting* (1993) is arguably one of the most significant novels in British as well as Scottish literature in the postwar period, exploring late 20th-century hard drugs culture in Edinburgh, and taking in issues of national identity. Welsh's novel, later turned into a highly successful feature film, attracted controversy for its explicit language and for the uncompromising attitudes expressed by the Edinburgh drug addicts at the heart of the novel. Their rejection of established authority and moral values eloquently reflect the disaffection of Scottish youth in the 1980s, that was echoed in decaying inner cities throughout Britain. Novelists such as Kelman and Welsh represent a strong impulse in contemporary Scottish writing, towards radical linguistic and narrative experimentation allied to a willingness to depict the social reality of demoralised industrial communities in a postindustrial era. Other writers of earlier generations continue to exercise a significant impact on the Scottish literary imagination, however. Muriel Spark, less exclusively concerned with issues of national identity and specifically Scottish locations, has continued to combine narrative innovation with acute social observation as exemplified in her 1961 novel *The Prime of Miss Jean Brodie* which depicted a very different Edinburgh from that in Welsh's fiction. Scottish devolution, achieved with the formation of the Scottish parliament in 1999, has done much to increase Scotland's sense of national self-confidence. Subsequent generations of Scottish writers may find in Spark's wider thematic range and outwardness more productive directions for future development, while not losing the acerbic assertiveness of Scottish identity and cultural authority of more overtly nationalistic writers of the period. It is clear, however, that Scottish writing at the turn of the 21st century had established a level of critical and cultural validity that canonical exclusion had denied it for much of the preceding century.

See also *Texts*: Anglo-Welsh literature, Class, Englishness, Irish literature, Regional identity.

Further reading

Crawford, Robert, *Devolving English Literature* (Edinburgh: Edinburgh University Press, 2000).

March, Christie Leigh, *Rewriting Scotland: Welsh, McLean, Warner, Banks, Galloway and Kennedy* (Manchester: Manchester University Press, 2002).

Neubauer, Jürgen, *Literature as Intervention: Struggles over Cultural Identity in Contemporary Scottish Fiction* (Marburg: Tectum, 1999).

Theatre of Cruelty

The French playwright and director Antonin Artaud coined the term 'Theatre of Cruelty' in his study of dramatic theory *The Theatre and its Double* (1938), a critique of traditional theatrical techniques that privileged text over action. Artaud did not intend a narrow definition of 'cruelty' as referring solely to acts of violence or sadism, though his own plays often depicted such scenes. The inherent cruelty of nature and the workings of the subconscious, rather than specific social and political circumstances, were, for Artaud, the main determinants of the human condition. To realise this in a theatrical context, he advocated the use of primitive ritual, powerful symbolic images and non-verbal communication, using the full physicality of the body in order to connect with primeval natural forces and the dream-like world of the unconscious.

Artaud's was one of a number of alternative philosophies of theatrical production that was current around the time of the Second World War, but like Brecht's epic theatre and the absurdist school of Ionesco and Beckett, it began to permeate British drama only in the late 1950s, coinciding with the first translation into English of *The Theatre and its Double* in 1958, and the growing public realisation of the magnitude of the Holocaust and other examples of genocide arising out of the Second World War. The director Peter Brook shared Artaud's disdain for conventional theatrical practices, adopting many of the Theatre of Cruelty's characteristic strategies in his critically acclaimed productions of the 1960s and beyond. Brook's production of Peter Weiss's *Marat/Sade* (1964) closely adhered to Artaudian principles, shocking audiences and critics with its intense physicality and ritualised violence, and exerting a lasting influence over British alternative and fringe dramatists. Brook also expounded his elaborations and variations on Artaud in his book *The Empty Space* (1968), a text that inspired future generations of dramatists. Brook's plays, including his landmark production of *A Midsummer Night's Dream* for the Royal Shakespeare Company in 1970, gave primary emphasis to the physical expressiveness of the body, heralding a shift in the balance between textual and visual language in theatrical staging. Over the same period, the abolition of the Lord Chamberlain's powers of censorship created a more favourable climate for the assimilation of the Theatre of Cruelty's key ideas and techniques into British drama in general, with striking and immediate effect. Collaborative stage shows such as the infamous nude musical *Hair* (1968), and *Oh! Calcutta!* (1970), a revue-style production staged by Kenneth Tynan, with contributions from many of the leading dramatists of the time, celebrated the body and explored various aspects of non-verbal theatrical communication.

During the 1960s and 1970s, many writers and directors, frustrated by the limitations of naturalistic drama, drew on elements of Artaud's Theatre of Cruelty, combined with Brechtian alienation techniques and absurdist strategies. The combined influence of Artaud and Brecht may seem somewhat unlikely, given the apparent conflict of interests between the latter's uncompromising insistence on drama as an ideological vehicle for political instruction, and the Theatre of Cruelty's emphasis on physicality as a means of exploring the workings of the unconscious. However, leading figures in British drama such as Brook were influenced in equal measure by Artaud and Brecht, seeing Brecht's techniques for 'distancing' the audience as compatible with the violent shock tactics of the Theatre of Cruelty. Although the significance of all three theatrical philosophies may have declined since the 1970s, it is possible to see the influence of Artaud on the work of the playwrights who came to prominence in the 1990s. Sarah Kane's *Blasted* (1995) provides arguably the most compelling evidence for this claim, with its graphic scenes of extreme physical and sexual violence, which provoked levels of shock unprecedented in the period since the relaxation of theatre censorship.

See also *Contexts*: War; *Texts*: Alternative theatre, Epic theatre.

Further reading

Artaud, Antonin, *The Theatre and its Double*, trans. Victor Corti (London: Calder, 1993).
Bermel, Albert, *Artaud's Theatre of Cruelty* (London: Methuen, 2001).
Brook, Peter, *The Empty Space* (London: MacGibbon & Kee, 1968).

Underground poetry

The 1960s has been cited as the period of most fundamental challenge to conventional social and cultural values in the years since the end of the Second World War. The emergence of counter-cultural attitudes had an impact on most areas of British life in this period, and even poetry, the most exclusive form of literary discourse, was affected by the influence of oppositional ideas. As with many cultural trends of the post-Second World War period, the initial impetus for the radical developments in British poetry came from the United States. In an era which championed self-expression, sexual liberation and unconventional life-styles, the vivid confessionalism and emotional expansiveness of American 'Beat' poets such as Allen Ginsberg caught the mood of a generation in Britain, who were also drawn to the ideas and philosophy of the hippy movement that originated in San Francisco in the mid-1960s.

The term 'underground', later used to describe the poetry movement closely associated with the counter-culture, was first coined to describe the wave of alternative magazines and newspapers that sprang up in the United States, Britain and elsewhere. These publications were emblematic of the counter-cultural ethos, advocating greater openness in personal relationships, more relaxed moral attitudes, the use of perception-altering drugs and challenges to social and cultural taboos. The same ideas and themes were explored in the poetry that developed out of the various counter-cultural movements of the mid-1960s, along with a heavily politicised sense of opposition to the norms of conventional society, and a passionate concern with contemporary world events, such as the Vietnam war, the threat of nuclear annihilation, apartheid in South Africa and various other issues around which political protest centred in the 1960s. Poetry, brought into the public arena by an increased emphasis on performance, and a perceived affinity with the increasing sophistication of rock music at the time, seemed to offer an effective platform for the articulation of these ideas. The period's emphasis on heightened states of consciousness and liberated self-expression had definite echoes of Blakean romanticism, and poetry's characteristic manipulation of imagery and metaphor offered distinct possibilities for the articulation of counter-cultural visionary utopianism. Other aspects of traditional poetic discourse, rigorous formal structures and metres, for example, were rejected in favour of incantatory free verse structures that lent themselves more easily to the immediacy and spontaneity associated with Underground poetry.

In 1965, the First International Poetry Incarnation, held at the Albert Hall, brought together most of the main practitioners of the Underground poetry movement, including Adrian Mitchell, whose poem 'To Whom it May Concern (Tell Me Lies about Vietnam)' (1968), in its vivid, disturbing imagery and fierce polemical anger, represents many of the typical characteristics of Underground poetry. The Albert Hall event confirmed the centrality of public performance to the strategies and concerns underlying this kind of poetry, and made a significant contribution to the increased emphasis on performance that has continued to characterise a great deal of poetry in the contemporary period. Many of the poets featured at the Albert Hall, and later in Michael Horovitz's anthology *Children of Albion* (1969), did not exert a lasting influence on poetry of the future, however. Others, including Lee Harwood, Tom Raworth and Roy Fisher, continued to work prolifically, becoming leading figures in the contemporary poetic avant-garde of the late 20th century.

See also   *Contexts*: Counter-culture, Political protest, Youth culture; *Texts*: Avant-garde poetry, Concrete poetry, Language poetry, Modernism, legacy of, Performance poetry, Political commitment.

Further reading

Nelson, Elizabeth, *The British Counter-Culture, 1966–73: A Study of the Underground Press* (Basingstoke: Macmillan, 1989).
Rexroth, Kenneth, *Alternative Society: Essays from the Other World* (New York: Herder and Herder, 1970).

Urban experience

Representations of the city have been a recurrent literary theme for much of the contemporary period, taking on particular significance from the early 1980s, as a means of illustrating the extent of social decay and division that affected many urban areas in that period. The disintegration of many industrialised inner-city areas, under the pressures of manufacturing decline and rising unemployment, provided striking visual evidence of the increasing gap between rich and poor, reinforced by the increasing corporate homogeneity of city centres, many possessing the same chain stores, fast-food outlets and coffee bars, creating a mood of soulless impersonality.

Contemporary writers have increasingly drawn on the depressed cityscapes of urban Britain as settings for their explorations and reflections of modern life: the novels and other writings of Martin Amis, Peter Ackroyd and Iain Sinclair are largely set in London, while James Kelman's fiction is as synonymous with Glasgow as that of his fellow Scot Irvine Welsh with Edinburgh and Roddy Doyle's with his native Dublin.

The heterogeneity of lived experience in urban Britain has expanded over the post-Second World War period; the greater emphasis on working-class life in the literature of the 1950s led to a shift of focus to industrial provincial settings. Nottingham provided the location for Alan Sillitoe's early novels, while fictional or unnamed industrial locations in Yorkshire provided the backdrop for David Storey's work. Female perspectives on urban experience have been provided by women writers throughout the period, from Australian-born Christina Stead, whose *Cotter's England* (1966) focused on the experiences of a working-class family on Tyneside, to Pat Barker, who set her 1998 novel *Another World* in the same region, and used a northern industrial background for her earlier novel, *Blow Your House Down* (1984), a story of a city, and particularly its women, terrorised by a serial killer.

The rise of immigration, as well as bringing greater cultural diversity into the inner cities, also led to an increase in racial tension. The positive and negative effects of immigration on British cities and their inhabitants have been anatomised by black British writers since the mid-1950s. The focus on difficulties of assimilation suffered by early immigrants was the focus of writers like Sam Selvon and George Lamming, for example. These difficulties have assumed different forms over the post-Second World War period, as the immigrant population has grown and become increasingly diverse. Novels like Hanif Kureishi's *The Buddha of Suburbia* (1990) and *The Black Album* (1995), and Meera Syal's *Life Isn't All Ha Ha Hee Hee* (1999), illustrate the pressures of urban living as they impact on minority communities.

The shift towards an emphasis on the contemporary urban world has been particularly noticeable in the poetry of the period, reflecting the declining appeal of the pastoral, a longstanding staple of British, and particularly English poetic discourse. The symbolic potency of pastoral, as depicting an idealised vision that in the earlier 20th century was linked in complex ways with conceptions of Englishness, diminished as postwar social change threatened established notions of national identity. Where Philip Larkin bemoaned the encroachment of urban conurbations on a rural England that he invested with almost magical properties, many of his contemporaries were exploring the imaginative possibilities of the city as a poetic construct, even before urban disintegration in the 1980s gave it a specifically political dimension. One of the most ambitious and innovative poetic treatments of urban experience of the postwar period was Roy Fisher's book-length poem *City* (1961). Drawing on modernist influences, Fisher presents a fragmented portrait of his home town, Birmingham, using a range of forms, styles and linguistic registers that mirror the diversity of city life. The re-emergence of modernist principles and strategies in British literature generally around this time may well provide another reason for the increase in literary attention on urban experience, given that modernist texts characteristically focused on city settings. The typical modernist concern with the alienated human condition was, for writers like T. S. Eliot and Virginia Woolf, encapsulated in the impersonality and anonymity of city life.

In the 1980s, social disintegration and decay in Britain's inner cities became a key theme for many writers, and again was examined with particular incisiveness by poets of the period. Ken Smith's critically acclaimed long poem *Fox Running* (1980) in some respects set the template for the decade, anticipating many of the concerns of late 1980s poetry. From the mid-1980s, when he published his uncompromising state-of-the-nation poem *Ukelele Music* (1985), to later collections such as *Stet* (1986) and *Evagatory* (1992), Peter Reading's work has exhibited a preoccupation with the despair, brutality and squalor of inner-city deprivation. Reading's bleak cityscapes are incongruously depicted within obscure but meticulously constructed traditional verse forms and articulated through a wide range of linguistic registers, from obscenity-laden urban demotic to convoluted, complex locutions that draw attention to their own procedures. In common with many other contemporary writers, Reading has helped to instigate a shift in British poetry from a predominant concern with rural and pastoral settings towards more experimental and innovative treatments of urban landscapes, through which the variousness of human experience in contemporary Britain can be more productively explored.

See also *Contexts*: Class structure; *Texts*: Black British literature, Class, Englishness, London, literary representations of, Modernism, legacy of.

Further reading

Barry, Peter, *Contemporary British Poetry and the City* (Manchester: Manchester University Press, 2000).

Women's writing

Women writers have historically found themselves cast in the role of 'outsiders', in relation to a canonical literary tradition formulated and perpetuated by the male-dominated professions of academia, criticism and publishing. As that tradition came under pressure from a range of hitherto marginalised perspectives, including that of gender, with increasing intensity from the end of the 1960s, the representation of female experience in poetry, fiction and drama by women assumed greater significance. This was due to a considerable extent to the rapid rise of feminism as an ideological and cultural phenomenon in the 1960s, and its impact on women's writing, which led to the emergence of numerous women's presses in the 1970s. In Britain, the most influential and successful of these was Virago, which not only sought to give greater opportunities to contemporary women writers of the present, but also made a huge contribution to the rediscovery and reappraisal of those from the past whose work had disappeared from critical view.

Writing by women in the post-Second World War era was often characterized by a greater willingness to embrace experimentation and innovation. The rejection of literary realism, and the revival and development of modernist techniques in the 1960s, held a particular appeal for women writers concerned with exploring female experience in a patriarchal society and demonstrating the constraints of conventional gender roles. Key texts such as Doris Lessing's *The Golden Notebook* (1962) anticipated themes such as gender identity and female sexuality, which shaped feminist consciousness later in the decade, and were central to women's writing throughout the remainder of the century. Changing attitudes to the depiction of intimate sexual detail, partly as a consequence of the outcome of the 'Lady Chatterley' trial, gave writers greater freedom to address sex and sexuality, and women writers in particular exploited this freedom. Nell Dunn's unsparing depiction of teenage motherhood in *Poor Cow* (1967), and Maureen Duffy's exploration of gay experience in London in *The Microcosm* (1966), were among the novels that set the tone for more explicit treatments of sex by women writers in subsequent decades. Feminist fiction of the 1970s and

1980s was more radical in terms of form as well as content, drawing on postmodern and magic realist narrative strategies in the writing of Fay Weldon and Angela Carter, among others. After this time, as feminist ideas and attitudes became more established, and some progress in correcting gender iniquities began to be achieved, women's fiction extended its imaginative and thematic range, often continuing to engage with gender issues, but less exclusively.

A similar pattern of development can be discerned in other literary genres. For women poets, canonical marginalization had been particularly acute: the difficulty of representing female-centred subject-matter, through poetic forms and symbolic language that were the preserves of male poets, proved insurmountable for all but a few female poets. As feminism extended its cultural influence in the later 20th century, many women poets made this obstacle a central theme in their work. Sylvia Plath, for example, illustrated the tension between the impulse to conform to the female stereotype associated with motherhood, domesticity and submissiveness, and her desire for fulfilment through artistic creativity. The gender-based dichotomy between public and private speech is arguably the most significant factor in the historical marginalization of women writers: in most societies the public world and the language through which its concerns are addressed have largely been male domains. Feminism's success in challenging this idea has been reflected in the renewed confidence with which women poets have asserted the validity of female experience as a theme for literary exploration. This has been clearly illustrated in the proliferation of anthologies of contemporary women's poetry in the period. Much of this poetry has sought to challenge rather than to replicate traditional forms and language. Some of the anthologies of the late 1970s and early 1980s expressed an explicitly feminist agenda: Lilian Mohin's *One Foot on the Mountain: An Anthology of British Feminist Poetry, 1969–1979* (1979) stated its purpose unambiguously, and advocated the rejection of monolithic poetic forms in favour of using innovative new techniques and devices, creating an alternative canon rather than forcing entry into the established one. From this uncompromising and radical starting-point women's poetry of the period has moved to a more sophisticated engagement with tradition and convention: like many postcolonial writers of the period, women poets have been particularly adept at manipulating traditional forms for their own purposes, placing female experience at the heart of their work. Carol Ann Duffy and Elizabeth Bartlett, for example, use male-dominated forms such as the dramatic monologue, undermining masculine pomposity and pretensions with subversive humour. The celebration of 'otherness' that underwrites much contemporary women's poetry also informs the work of Grace Nichols, who as a black woman poet recognizes the historical experience of marginalization on two counts. Nichols's response is to refuse the stereotype of oppressed womanhood, focusing instead on the affirmative aspects of black female experience; her 'Fat Black Woman' poems enact a critique of racial and sexual attitudes in relation to perceptions of idealised femininity. In 'The Fat Black Woman Goes Shopping' (1984), the protagonist's fruitless shopping expedition for 'accommodating clothes' to cope with the London winter, during which she is subjected to the 'slimming glances' of 'de pretty face salesgals', provides an opportunity for Nichols to subvert conventional racial and gender perceptions. The Fat Black Woman 'curses in Swahili / Yoruba / and nation language', demonstrating a linguistic and verbal dexterity that undermines the mute complicity of the white sales assistants, and the poem's final note of wry, incisive humour demonstrates the facility that poets like Nichols, Duffy and Bartlett possess for mocking social and cultural authority:

> The fat black woman could only conclude
> that when it come to fashion
> the choice is lean
>   Nothing much beyond size 14.

British drama had been as male-centred in its thematic concerns throughout the 20th century as fiction and poetry, and opportunities for women dramatists were rare even in the early years of the post-Second World War period. Only Shelagh Delaney, and to a lesser extent Ann Jellicoe, had any significant critical and commercial success in the 1950s, while Joan Littlewood's Theatre Workshop in the 1960s was unique in having a woman in a position of major influence. Again, the emergence of feminism and the growth of the women's movement had a significant effect in facilitating the greater involvement of women in British drama in the late 20th century. The formation of women's theatre groups had a major impact on the alternative theatre circuit: leading female playwrights like Pam Gems and Caryl Churchill were first given the chance to present and develop their work with the Women's Theatre Group and Monstrous Regiment respectively. Churchill went on to become a particularly influential figure in the theatrical mainstream in the 1980s, with plays such as *Top Girls* (1982), an examination of gender roles under Thatcherism that also incorporated an exploration of female experience from a wider historical perspective. Churchill's work is marked by radical experimentation, especially in relation to non-linear narrative progression and temporal juxtapositions: *Top Girls* opens with a scene that brings together characters from history, myth and art in a recognisably contemporary setting, who, through an innovative use of overlapping dialogue relate their different experiences of patriarchal oppression and their responses to it. Other female playwrights have also focused on the potentialities of a communal female ethos: Nell Dunn made this theme the central concern of her play *Steaming* (1979), depicting the sense of solidarity built up among a group of women who meet regularly at a Turkish baths. Other dramatists, like Sarah Daniels, marginalised or excluded male characters from central roles in their plays as a deliberate tactic to reverse the historical effacement of female experience from British theatre in the earlier 20th century.

The second half of the twentieth century saw radical changes in the role and status of women in British society. Improvements in their legal rights and standing, the greater representation of women in what were historically male-dominated professions and a weakening of the influence exerted by traditional patriarchal values on social, cultural and sexual attitudes have all been significant consequences of the campaigning work of women's movements in British and elsewhere. As a result, the continuing relevance of the original aims of 1960s feminism and the extent to which they can be said to have been fulfilled are issues that are open to debate. It is, however, clear that literature by women since that time has provided an effective platform for the clarification and exploration of those aims, not only at the level of subject-matter, but also through formal innovation and experimentation that has challenged the conventions of the male-dominated literary tradition. The increasing recognition and acceptance of women writers, allied to the growth of feminist scholarship and feminist literary theory, have ensured a greater centrality for notions of female experience and gender identity. As a consequence, women writers have become less likely to define themselves solely by their gender and have expanded the range of their thematic concerns, though these are still often refracted through a feminist perspective to a lesser or greater degree.

See also   *Contexts*: Feminism and the role of women, Sex and sexuality; *Texts*: Alternative theatre, Gay and lesbian writing, History, Magic realism, Modernism, legacy of, Political commitment, Realism; *Criticism*: Feminist criticism, Gender criticism, Psychoanalytic criticism.

Further reading

Anderson, Linda R. (ed.), *Plotting Change: Contemporary Women's Fiction* (London: Edward Arnold, 1990).

Cousin, Geraldine, *Women in Dramatic Place and Time: Contemporary Female Characters on Stage* (London: Routledge, 1996).

Duncker, Patricia, *Sisters and Strangers: An Introduction to Contemporary Feminist Fiction* (Oxford: Basil Blackwell, 1991).

Mark, Alison and Deryn Rees-Jones, *Contemporary Women's Poetry: Reading/Writing/Practice* (Basingstoke: Palgrave Macmillan, 2000).

3 Criticism: Approaches, Theory, Practice

Introduction

Literary criticism has changed fundamentally since the Second World War, in ways that reflect challenges to the canonical literary tradition from once marginalised constituencies and the questioning of social and cultural orthodoxies that characterised the period. At the mid-point of the 20th century, the most influential British literary critic was F. R. Leavis. In critical studies such as *The Great Tradition* (1948), Leavis presented the case for literature as an antidote to a contemporary society characterised by the rise of mass culture. The role of the critic, for Leavis, was to analyse how literary texts represented human experience and the moral imperatives that he considered were in retreat in modern culture and society. The close reading that this kind of criticism necessitated drew heavily on practical criticism, the analytical approach developed by I. A. Richards in the 1920s, which focused on the text to the exclusion of literary, cultural and historical context, or biographical detail about the author. The emphasis on the text-in-itself was also a key element of New Criticism, the dominant analytical approach in America during the same period. Unlike Leavis, critics such as John Crowe Ransom, Cleanth Brooks and Allen Tate were more concerned with the aesthetic than the moral dimensions of the text. They concentrated on the structural relationships and formal elements that gave a specific text its literariness. Both Leavisite criticism and New Criticism shared a belief that textual meaning could be determined through rigorous analysis of form and language, along with a general consensus about what literariness was, and in which texts it could be found. These kinds of assumptions were questioned over subsequent decades as attitudes towards the function of criticism changed and literary theory came to assume a more central role in critical practice.

New approaches to literary analysis and interpretation began to emerge in the 1960s, a period in which attitudes to the arts and culture, both 'high' and 'popular', were dramatically transformed. Many of the major developments in literary theory at this time originated in France, and gradually extended their influence to the English-speaking academic world. In particular, the rise of structuralism and poststructuralism brought to the fore the work of French intellectuals, including Jacques Derrida, Roland Barthes and Michel Foucault; Jacques Lacan's crucial developments of psychoanalytic theory were taken up and revised by Luce Irigaray, Julia Kristeva and Hélène Cixous, while Louis Althusser and Pierre Macherey made vital contributions to advances in Marxist literary criticism and theory.

However, for all the undoubted significance of French intellectual thought in this period, the growth of contemporary literary theory cannot be fully understood without reference to ideas that were first articulated earlier in the 20th century. The pioneering lectures of Ferdinand de Saussure, published posthumously as *Course in General Linguistics* (1913), and the linguistic approach to literary analysis pioneered by the Russian Formalist movement at around the same time, were little known in the West until the 1960s, but were to have a lasting impact in providing the theoretical basis for both structuralism and post-structuralism, two of the most influential theoretical movements of the late 20th century. Saussure defined language as a sign system, each sign consisting of two elements, signifier and signified. The former represents the physical form of the sign, for example a printed word, sound or image, and the latter the mental concept of the thing evoked by the signifier. Saussure claimed that the connection between signifier and signified was inherently arbitrary and only a matter of convention within a specific language. This can be demonstrated by the fact that different languages have different words (signifiers) for the same object (signified). Thus, for example, the English word 'dog' and the French word *chien* denote the same animal. This key principle of Saussurean linguistics, posited in similar terms in Russian Formalism, had wide-ranging implications for literary theory and criticism, bringing into question the possibility of ascribing fixed and definite meanings to language in general, and by extension to any literary text.

The work of Russian Formalists such as Viktor Shlovsky and Roman Jakobson applied linguistic principles to the task of defining literariness, coining the term *ostranenie* – 'making strange' – to illustrate how literary language, unlike language in its everyday communicative use, defamiliarised conventional perceptions and definitions. Russian Formalists brought a rigorously scientific approach to the study of literature that required emphasis on close reading, similar to that of Leavis and the New Critics later in the century, but the Formalists' concern was more with the way language and formal devices worked than with what a literary text might have to say about human experience, moral or aesthetic values, or so-called universal 'truths'. This shift of emphasis was highly influential in the growth of structuralist and poststructuralist theory in the late 20th century.

Structuralism posed a fundamental challenge to the humanist and moral-aesthetic preoccupations of Leavis and the New Critics, questioning the validity of attributing unitary meaning to any act of textual interpretation. But, by the end of the 1960s, structuralism itself was being overtaken by more innovative applications of Saussurean theory, leading to even more radical critiques of traditional critical practices. Roland Barthes, in questioning the usual preoccupation with the role of the author in textual criticism, became one of the major figures in poststructuralism. In his essay 'The Death of the Author' (1968), Barthes claimed that the authorial presence limits the possibilities available for textual interpretation and fails to take account of the extent to which all literary texts are in a permanent state of negotiation and interaction with each other, an idea summed up in the term 'intertextuality', which came into critical usage around this time. For Barthes, it is only in the act of reading that the multiplicity of meanings and interpretations that result from the inherent intertextuality of the text can be revealed, and then only provisionally.

Barthes's idea of the fragmentary and transient nature of meaning is taken further in another of the more controversial strands of poststructuralist theory: the practice of 'deconstruction' associated with Jacques Derrida, a form of close reading that focuses on the instability of the text. Saussure's key proposition, of the arbitrariness of the sign, informs Derrida's insistence that all language is predicated on differentiation: that the signifier achieves its identity not in being the essence of the thing it signifies, but in its difference from other signifiers. Deconstruction seeks to exploit this difference by analysing textual language for its range of possible or potential meanings, many of which are incompatible and reveal contradictions that destabilise the text. The aim of deconstruction is not to try to draw together these multiple meanings, but to use them to reveal the impossibility of any fixed textual interpretation.

Other prominent theoretical approaches since the late 20th century have echoed the idea of textual instability, but have attached more importance to the relationship between language and the social world it inhabits. The social dimension of literary language is perhaps most fully explored in the dialogic theories of Mikhail Bakhtin, which grew in significance towards the end of the 20th century. Bakhtin's key works were produced in the Soviet Union between the First and Second World Wars, but achieved wider recognition in the West only when his work began to be widely distributed in translation in the 1980s. Bakhtin proposes a distinction between literary texts that are predominantly monologic, that is, controlled by a single authoritative voice, and those that are fundamentally dialogic, in which multiple voices or discourses interact or engage in conflict with each other. Bakhtin saw the novel as the genre which most embodied dialogism, though he also claimed that no literary text could be purely monologic: in the act of narration other voices or perspectives will inevitably break through. The existence of multiple voices within the text, and their effect on the disruption of textual meaning, mirror poststructuralist concerns with the instability of interpretation. However, Bakhtin also insists that all language is comprised of 'utterances' that interact with and respond to each other, generating a diversity of meanings that have a concrete existence in the social world, an idea that poststructuralist thought is less willing to accommodate.

Theoretical approaches such as Marxism, feminism and postcolonialism, that have also been prominent during the contemporary period, depend crucially on placing literature within a political, historical and social context. The first of these, Marxist theory, was central to the development of a particular strain of British social literary criticism that was associated with the political and cultural values of the 'New Left' in the 1950s, though its roots could be found in the literary criticism of George Orwell. Orwell's political identity as a democratic socialist permeated his entire literary output, including a substantial body of critical writing, though he rejected Marxism, or indeed any other form of theorising about literature. Orwell died in 1950, but his influence can be seen in the work of leading 'New Left' critics such as Raymond Williams, whose insistence on the central relationship between literature and society was increasingly mediated through a Marxist perspective. The Marxist influence on British social literary criticism was also evident in the more explicitly theoretical approach of Arnold Kettle, and survives in the early work of Terry Eagleton in the 1970s and 1980s.

Marxist literary theory has developed in various directions, from the crude social realist position of analysing textual content for what it revealed about class relationships, to a more sophisticated demonstration of the complex connections between text and ideology that involves some degree of negotiation with poststructuralist ideas. The relationship between literature and ideology that lies at the heart of Marxist criticism can be either conscious or unconscious, and in ways similar to the deconstructionist practices of Derrida, Marxist textual analysis can reveal unintentional and contradictory impulses within the text. For theorists such as Louis Althusser, literature, intentionally or not, represented and perpetuated the ideological values of the society it depicted. For others, like Pierre Macherey, significant absences from the text – the gaps and silences that betray a text's unconscious ideological slant – can be at least as instructive as the text's conscious reflection of ideology.

Modern feminism could be said to have its roots in seminal works such as Simone de Beauvoir's *The Second Sex* (1949), but it was not until the late 1960s and early 1970s that feminist literary criticism began to assume a coherent theoretical perspective. Kate Millett's *Sexual Politics* (1970) was particularly significant in this respect, examining literary representations of female experience in the work of canonical male writers. Millet's work helped to lay the foundations for later feminist critics, who shifted their focus to the status and nature of canonicity, and drew attention to texts by women which had fallen into critical neglect. The questioning of canonical assumptions, the rediscovery and reassessment of historically marginalised women writers of the past, and an increasing emphasis on contemporary women's writing and its representation of female experience, are some of the main achievements of the feminist literary critical movement.

The process of constructing a theoretical framework within which literature from traditionally marginalised perspectives could be productively evaluated, was also undertaken in the rapidly expanding field of postcolonial studies. Critics such as Edward Said have shown how colonialism was ideologically driven to depict and perceive the colonised world in terms of 'otherness' that reinforced stereotypes of cultural inferiority. As an increasing number of writers from formerly colonised countries sought to address their historical experience of subordination, postcolonial criticism developed a methodology through which their work could be analysed and validated.

In some respects, it is misleading to discuss individual theoretical or critical movements in isolation, given that there is a considerable degree of interaction between them, as demonstrated, for example, in the close relationship between some aspects of feminist thought and Jacques Lacan's psychoanalytic theories. Lacan, in turn, had synthesised Freudian psychology and Saussurean linguistics to illustrate his belief that the unconscious was structured like a language. Lacan's explorations of the process of the creation of self-identity, the acquisition of language, and the workings of the unconscious mind, came to have significant implications and consequences for literary theory. According to Lacan, the child recognises its status as an independent self only when it enters what he termed the 'mirror' stage. This realisation brings with it a desire to possess that which it now recognises as separate from itself (particularly the mother), coupled with a wish to compete for the object of desire. In turn, the process of projecting beyond the self involves the child in a construction of its own self consequent on the perception of itself by others. Crucially, this construction was seen by Lacan as disguising an absence or lack of being: the human subject is forever desiring that which it lacks or is not.

The 'mirror' stage also brings about perceptions of gender differences, which, for the male child, involves recognition of the father's status as a powerful rival for the mother's attentions. This point in the child's development coincides, too, with the entry into language, which Lacan terms the 'symbolic order', because of the figurative nature of all language: like Saussure, Lacan makes the distinction between language and the things it signifies. Lacan's further claim, that boys, having submitted to 'the law of the father' in renouncing claims to the mother, find entry into the symbolic order easier and more natural than girls. This equation of maleness with dominance of the symbolic order was taken up and challenged by feminist theorists and critics, who have further explored the relationship between language and gender.

The emphasis on language and the text-in-itself that characterised post-Second World War criticism and theory, from New Criticism through structuralism to poststructuralism, was tempered somewhat by other developments, beginning in the 1980s with the advent of New Historicism, which revived the practice of placing texts in their historical context. The New Historicist conception of history, however, differed considerably from that used in traditional historical scholarship, focusing more centrally on the history of political and class structures and the conflicts within them. New Historicism shared with Marxist literary criticism a belief that literary texts are inherently political, reflecting the power relations, social attitudes and economic factors of the period in which they were written. New Historicism first made its impact in the areas of Renaissance and Romantic literature, though its emphasis on contextualisation offered a more general corrective to the text-based approaches that had dominated the period.

Connections can also be drawn between Marxist literary theory and the cultural materialist school of critical thought that emerged at around the same time as New Historicism. Cultural materialism had its roots in Marxist theory; the term was coined by Raymond Williams to demonstrate how the forms which culture and cultural production took were dictated to a considerable extent by economic, social and political forces. Where New Historicism tended to show that literature represented and dramatised the impact of class and power structures on social relationships, consciously or otherwise, reinforcing the dominant ideology, cultural materialism focused more on the subversive potentialities of literature, both at the time of production and in later periods, as it revealed social inequalities in the spheres of, for example, race, class and gender.

This brief survey of developments in literary criticism and theory since the Second World War demonstrates how ways of reading and interpreting texts have multiplied over the period, just as the expanding range of styles and forms of literary expression, and the widening of definitions of the literary have expanded the canon. The post-Second World War period has often been described as the age of postmodernism. This problematic term is also used to describe literature characterised by experimentation in form and language, breaks with literary conventions and traditions, and a thematic emphasis on the futility and alienation of modern existence, in which literature itself is no longer seen as able to transcend the failings of contemporary civilisation or to offer redemption or restoration. It is no surprise, then, that the interpretative approaches which dominated literary criticism at the start of the period have been superseded by a postmodern melange of reading practices, many of which question the validity of textual meaning and the extent to which interpretation is possible at all.

Further reading

Barry, Peter, *Beginning Theory: An Introduction to Literary and Cultural Theory* (Manchester: Manchester University Press, 1995).

Eagleton, Terry, *Literary Theory: An Introduction* (Oxford: Basil Blackwell, 1983).

Murfin, Ross and Supriya M. Ray, *The Bedford Glossary of Critical and Literary Terms* (Boston and New York: Bedford Books, 1997).

Peck, John and Martin Coyle, *Literary Terms and Criticism*, 3rd edn (Basingstoke: Palgrave Macmillan, 2002).

Rice, Philip and Patricia Waugh (eds), *Modern Literary Theory: A Reader*, 2nd edn (London: Routledge, 1992).

Wolfreys, Julian, Ruth Robbins and Kenneth Womack, *Key Concepts in Literary Theory* (Edinburgh: Edinburgh University Press, 2002).

Cultural materialism

The idea that the literariness of texts resides in their capacity to offer universal truths, transcending the historical concerns and conditions in which they were written, and in which they are encountered by subsequent generations of readers, has been challenged from a variety of perspectives. One such corrective is offered by cultural materialism, a concept first defined by the Marxist critic Raymond Williams. Cultural materialism has in common with New Historicism an insistence on studying literary texts in relation to their historical, social and cultural contexts, rejecting the words-on-the-page approach of earlier critics, including F. R. Leavis and I. A. Richards in Britain, and the American New Critics. Leading cultural materialists such as Catherine Belsey, Jonathan Dollimore and Alan Sinfield maintain that critical engagement with literature of a particular period can be fully achieved only through textual analysis alongside examination of the historical circumstances and conditions under which texts were written, disseminated and read. Such readings can uncover the potentially subversive elements of literary texts: what they say about the dominant ideas of the period in which they were written, and what ideological perspectives, intentional or unintentional, they reveal. Cultural materialist approaches often focus on what a text has to say about specific determinants of social identity such as race, class and gender.

Cultural materialist literary theory has focused mostly on literature of earlier periods, but its emergence is directly related to some of the main cultural and political developments of the contemporary era, being born out of frustration with the limitations of the post-Second World War consensus that gave rise to the Welfare State. That consensus posited the belief that 'high' culture, including literature, should be available to all. In the late 20th century, the very concept of 'high' culture came under scrutiny, first with the emergence of the counter-culture in the 1960s, and later with the rising influence of previously marginal literary constituencies. In contemporary writing from Scotland, Ireland and Wales, as well as that of women writers of various geographical origins, black British writers of either gender, and class-conscious 'regional' authors, can be found considerable evidence of the subversive potential that cultural materialists see as crucial to the function of literature in all ages.

One such text is Tony Harrison's long poem v. (1985). The poem was partly inspired by Harrison's discovery, on a visit to the cemetery in which his parents were buried, that their graves had been sprayed with obscene graffiti. Harrison invents an imaginary skinhead figure, with whom his narrator engages in a forceful dialectic, itself peppered with the kind of language sprayed on the tombstones. The poem plays off themes of class conflict and social division, articulated through the use of obscene language and working-class dialect speech, against the connotations of Harrison's chosen form, a conventional cross-rhyming iambic pentameter stanza form that deliberately echoes Thomas Gray's famous and deeply canonical 'Elegy Written in a Country Churchyard' (1751). From a cultural materialist perspective, Harrison's poem needs to be read with recognition of both contemporary and historical issues relating to the political, social and cultural marginalisation of the working class. The poem is partly a state-of-the-nation polemic – it was written at the time of the miners' strike of 1984–5, and contains passing references to the conflict – and partly as a wider exploration of how literature, and particularly poetry, has tended to exclude certain areas of social experience. Harrison's borrowing from Gray's poem is particularly instructive in this respect, given that the 'Elegy' also addressed issues of marginalisation and exclusion in a different period, though with less polemical intent than Harrison brings to his late 20th-century reworking of the earlier poem.

Cultural materialists and new historicists differ in the extent to which they claim that textual subversiveness has a destabilising effect on cultural and other forms of authority, including the literary canon. New historicists tend to focus on the extent to which potential subversion is controlled by, among other factors, the process of canonisation, as demonstrated in the contemporary period by the shift of once marginal literary voices and perspectives to a more central position at the heart of academic study and intellectual debate. Cultural materialism, in its determination to challenge established categories of literature and the validity of the concept of canonicity, views such shifts in definitions of the literary in a more optimistic light, acknowledging the readiness of new writings of various kinds to appropriate literary forms and language for the purpose of exploring themes, and social and cultural perspectives, that were not conventionally regarded as appropriate subject-matter for literature. The close conjunction between text and context that characterises cultural materialism also has implications for other contemporary theoretical approaches, such as Marxism, feminism and postcolonialism, all of which adduce a similarly close relationship between literature and the historical moment of its production and reception. On the other hand, the rise of postmodern theory, with its mistrust of historical and other forms of 'grand narrative', has posed a considerable challenge to cultural materialist methodology, casting doubt on the influence on literary texts of extrinsic forces and circumstances.

See also Contexts: Class structure; Literature: Class, History; Criticism: Marxist criticism, New Historicism.

Further reading

Brannigan, John, New Historicism and Cultural Materialism (Basingstoke: Palgrave Macmillan, 1998).
Ryan, Kiernan (ed.), New Historicism and Cultural Materialism: A Reader (London: Arnold, 1996).
Williams, Raymond, The Long Revolution (Harmondsworth: Penguin, 1961).

Deconstruction

The critical concept of deconstruction constitutes one of the most radical and influential strands of poststructuralist theory. The term 'deconstruction' was first used in this sense by Jacques Derrida, the French linguistic philosopher who became its leading advocate and exponent, to describe a process through which texts are analysed for the range of inherently contradictory meanings they contain. The existence of multiple textual readings undermines the traditional view that literary works contain a fixed and unified core of meaning that can be deduced by rigorous explication of their linguistic and formal structures. As such, deconstruction is less a method of interpretation than a way of reading that anticipates and reveals the unreliable nature of language, the existence of textual uncertainty and undecideability, and the impossibility of ascribing final and unambiguous meaning.

For Derrida, the whole of Western cultural production, including literature, has historically been predicated on the existence of binary oppositions – connected but mutually exclusive pairs of concepts, objects or ideas, in which one always takes precedence over the other. Derrida sought to question the validity of such hierarchies, and focused particularly on the binary opposition between speech and writing, which, in privileging the former, dictated what he saw as the essentially logocentric tradition of Western thought. For Derrida, logocentrism reflected a belief that the spoken word inherently possesses a greater claim to truth than the written word, because the physical presence of speaker and auditor is inherently superior to its binary opposite, absence, which is the condition implicit in the written word. Derrida based his challenge to Western logocentrism on a radical reworking of Ferdinand de Saussure's linguistic theories of the early 20th century. Saussure sought to demonstrate the shifting and unstable relationship between words and the things they describe. Derrida, developing this idea, claimed that the arbitrariness of the connection between the word, or in Saussure's term the 'signifier', and what it represents, the 'signified', undermined the claim that speech, and therefore presence, should take precedence over writing, or absence. The relationship between signifier and signified is no closer in speech than it is in writing: the thing described is no more actually present to the spoken than the written word. The word represents a 'deferred presence', in Derrida's phrase; he coined the punning term *différance* to describe this concept, deriving from the French verb *différer*, which contains both the meaning 'to differ' and 'to defer'. In this coinage Derrida encapsulated Saussure's idea that the meaning of signifiers resides in their difference from other signifiers, rather than any inherent attributes they may possess, as well as illustrating the logocentrism of Saussure's own privileging of speech over writing.

The implications of Derrida's approach are made manifest in his own critical practices, in which he sought to demonstrate that the principle of *différance* negated any possibility of textual interpretation that could produce a single fixed meaning. Deconstruction consists of close textual analysis intended to bring to light the inherent contradictions in the text, arising from the multiplicity and continual slippage of possible meanings that prove ultimately irreconcilable. In this way, the artificiality of the concept of binary oppositions is revealed, and the text is shown to contain within its own structures elements that destabilise its purported wholeness and unity; faced with an almost limitless range of potential interpretations, the reader is forced to recognise the impossibility of deciding among them. Deconstruction also rejects the claims of formalism and New Criticism, that textual meaning can be derived out of analysis of the relationship between a text's formal and linguistic constituent parts, and in particular its deployment of figurative language, including metaphor and imagery. Such an approach depends on an evaluation of the significance of different aspects of the text; deconstruction brings into question the validity of this kind of practice. Different readings of the same text may focus on different aspects of its form, language, structure and narrative techniques, all of which will produce contradictory readings.

Deconstruction, then, aims to challenge Western notions of logocentrism, and the supposed structural and thematic logic that this conveys upon literary texts. Attention is focused on textual language, as with formalist, structuralist and New Critical approaches, but with the intention of uncovering inconsistencies, contradictions and instabilities underpinning the text's attempt to construct meaning. Texts are shown to exist in a complex and problematic relationship with textuality in a wider sense: with language as a whole, and with the world beyond the text, which is expressed and understood through language that is inherently unstable.

The implications of deconstruction for literary criticism have been fundamental and far-reaching, causing a reassessment of traditional notions of the function of literary study as an interpretative process that leads towards the identification of fixed textual meaning. Critics of deconstruction have seen the strategies of Derrida, J. Hillis Miller, Paul de Man and others, as tending to distance literature from its social, historical and political contexts; textual analysis is reduced, according to these critics, to mere academic 'playfulness', or at worst a reduction to hopeless nihilism, as a consequence of a belief that textual meaning is indeterminable. Deconstructionists might argue in response that what their methods prove is a multiplicity of possible interpretations, rather than an absence of meaning. Furthermore, they claim that the emphasis on the text and textual language in deconstruction does not preclude engagement with literature's relationship to wider contextual issues: indeed, deconstruction's definition of 'text' embraces all aspects of human discourse and communication, not merely the literary. It is also clear that deconstruction has exerted an influence on other critical and theoretical approaches, that are more overtly political or ideological in orientation. Postcolonial approaches to literary analysis, for example, draw heavily on the binary oppositions between West and East, coloniser and colonised, and Occident and Orient, while similar dichotomies in terms of gender and sexual identity have closely informed feminist and gay and lesbian criticism. The implications of deconstruction can be difficult to grasp in the abstract, and the term has become to some extent synonymous with the process of textual analysis in general. This reductive definition undermines the significance of deconstruction's contribution to critical thinking and especially its idea of textual instability. That instability is given almost tangible form in the work of poems such as Paul Muldoon's 'Immram' (1980) and 'The More a Man Has the More a Man Wants' (1983). Muldoon's narrators metamorphose across time and place; the narratives of both poems are pervaded with deliberate inconsistencies, contradictions and false trails that pose fundamental questions about the reliability of language itself. Similar techniques are apparent in the dream-like sequences that make up the central narrative of Kazuo Ishiguro's novel *The Unconsoled* (1995). The experiences of Ishiguro's central protagonist, a famous pianist called Ryder, who is on tour in Eastern Europe, defy conventional notions of narrative logic and structure, in a novel that explores the untrustworthiness of memory and of the workings of the conscious and unconscious mind.

See also *Criticism*: Dialogic theory, Feminist criticism, Gender criticism, New Criticism, Postcolonial criticism, Postmodernist theory, Post-structuralism, Structuralism.

Further reading

Bloom, Harold, Paul de Man, Jacques Derrida, Geoffrey Hartman and J. Hillis Miller, *Deconstruction and Criticism* (London: Routledge & Kegan Paul, 1979).

Culler, Jonathan, *On Deconstruction: Theory and Criticism after Structuralism* (London: Routledge & Kegan Paul, 1983).

Derrida, Jacques, *Writing and Difference*, trans. Alan Bass (London: Routledge, 2001).

Norris, Christopher, *Deconstruction: Theory and Practice* (London: Methuen, 1982).

Wolfreys, Julian, *Deconstruction: Derrida* (Basingstoke: Macmillan, 1998).

Dialogic theory

The concept of dialogism, as it relates to literary criticism and theory, draws heavily on the ideas of the Soviet critic Mikhail Bakhtin, whose major works spanned a period from the late 1920s to the 1960s, but were little known in the Western world until the first translations appeared in the 1980s. The key element of Bakhtinian literary theory is the contention, first posited in *Problems of Dostoevsky's Art* (1929), that all literary texts can be characterised as either predominantly monologic or dialogic. A monologic text is dominated by a single authoritative voice or discourse; other voices that the text may give rein to are subordinated to the control of a narrative presence that reflects the authorial perspective, which in turn, according to Bakhtin, usually reinforced the prevailing cultural and social values of the period in which the text was written. The dialogic text, on the other hand, allows numerous, often conflicting and contradictory, voices and discourses to emerge and interact, beyond authorial control. In this way, the text gives scope for the expression of a range of social, cultural and political attitudes and values. For Bakhtin, the subversive potential of literature derives out of its deployment of multiple voices and perspectives. He developed this idea further in *Rabelais and his World* (1940), introducing the concept of the carnivalesque, which took its name from the festivals, held in many societies, in which the usual hierarchical order is temporarily overturned, permitting the lower orders a brief period of sanctioned transgressive behaviour. Bakhtin detected an analogous process in literature, which through its dialogic properties challenged and attempted to subvert dominant ideas, often through the interpolation of elements of low or popular culture, representations of the grotesque or the use of mocking humour.

Bakhtin saw language as an essentially social construct, depending on its status as a medium of communication. Each individual speech act, or 'utterance', is in continuing interaction with other utterances past and present; language is shaped and develops as a result of its use in social communication. Different social groups understand the same utterances differently; at any particular moment in history there will be a specific set of social, cultural and material conditions that govern the meaning of an utterance at that time, so meaning and interpretation are in a constant state of flux. Bakhtin coined the term 'heteroglossia' to describe this permanently shifting sense of language and meaning, that accounts for the existence of the conflicting multiplicity of voices that Bakhtin sees as characterising the literary text, the language of which is subject to the same social pressures and influences as all other linguistic communication.

In Bakhtin's view, no literary work could be totally monologic, in spite of authorial intention to the contrary: the creation of a plausible fictional world, populated by a diversity of characters, for example, inevitably allowed into the text a plurality or polyphony of voices and competing discourses. The consequence of textual polyphony was disruption of the authoritative narrative perspective, the dominant status of which could no longer be taken for granted. All literary texts were, for Bakhtin, dialogic to some degree, but it was the novel that he regarded as the most dialogic of literary forms. Bakhtin's essay 'Discourse in the Novel', written in the late 1930s, developed his dialogic theory, privileging discourse, which consists of the various strategies used to convey narrative, over plot, that is to say, the events that occur in the course of the narrative. The novel lends itself more readily than poetry, for example, to the presentation of multiple perspectives, which pose a challenge to the dominant values and ideas of the time in which the text was written. Those ideas, for Bakhtin, are mediated, consciously or otherwise, through authorial discourse. Meaning and interpretation, therefore, as in later poststructuralist critical approaches, become more problematic, shifting and indeterminate.

Bakhtinian theory has gained rapidly in currency and influence since the 1980s. There are interesting parallels to be drawn with the deconstructionist theories of Jacques Derrida, given Bakhtin's equally emphatic insistence on demonstrating contradictions inherent within a given text. Similarly, Bakhtin's identification of the carnivalesque as a defining characteristic of novelistic discourse provides a vehicle for Marxist and cultural materialist critics to engage with literature's subversive possibilities and its relation to the social world in which it is written and received. Furthermore, Bakhtin's recognition of the existence of the interplay between high, or 'official', culture and low, or popular, cultural forms within the novel, has clear implications for those aspects of postmodern criticism that focus on the dissolution of boundaries between cultural categories previously regarded as monolithic and impermeable. Although Bakhtin's most significant work was written between the late 1920s and the 1940s, and the emphasis in his critical work was on medieval, Renaissance and 19th-century literature, his theoretical approach anticipates many of the concerns of poststructuralism, and lends itself effectively to the analysis of much contemporary literature, which is often characterised by a self-consciousness awareness of its narrative strategies, and deploys shifting multiple perspectives and experiments in narrative structure, as for example, in novels such as Julian Barnes's *Flaubert's Parrot* (1984) and Martin Amis's *London Fields* (1989). In spite of Bakhtin's view of poetry as essentially monologic, his critical perspectives have been drawn upon to considerable effect by critics striving to explore the formal and linguistic developments in contemporary poetry. In a period in which literary categories and literary language have become markedly more democratic, Bakhtinian theory has exerted considerable influence on literary criticism.

See also *Criticism*: Deconstruction, Narratology, Postmodernist theory, Poststructuralism, Structuralism.

Further reading

Bakhtin, Mikhail, *The Dialogic Imagination: Four Essays*, ed. Michael Holquist, trans. Caryl Emerson and Michael Holquist (Austin: University of Texas Press, 1981).
Holquist, Michael, *Dialogism: Bakhtin and his World* (London: Routledge, 1991).
Morris, Pam (ed.), *The Bakhtin Reader: Selected Writings of Bakhtin, Medvedev and Voloshinov* (London: Edward Arnold, 1994).
Pearce, Lynne, *Reading Dialogics* (London: Edward Arnold, 1994).

Feminist criticism

The revival of interest in feminist thought, that precipitated the emergence of the women's movement at the end of the 1960s, gave rise to one of the most significant and influential developments in literary criticism in the late 20th century: the formulation of a critical approach to textual analysis that drew attention to the gendered nature of writing, reading and interpretation. Feminist criticism itself has undergone a number of fundamental changes of direction and emphasis since its inception. Its critical practices have become more sophisticated over time, taking greater account of differences in female experience in different societies and cultural environments at different historical moments.

In the 1970s and early 1980s the main developments in feminist criticism were centred on France and North America, and reflected contrasting preoccupations. One of the main influences on French feminism at this time was Simone de Beauvoir's pioneering study, *The Second Sex* (1949), which examined the idea of gender identity as a social construct. De Beauvoir highlighted the ways in which female experience had been marginalised in male-dominated societies throughout history. French feminist critics used de Beauvoir's ideas as informing principles for their particular concern with the ways in which language reflected and reinforced patriarchal values and assumptions. The psychoanalytic theories of Jacques Lacan were equally important in this respect. The Lacanian idea that children's acquisition of language – their entry into the linguistic order – occurred as they began to recognise their separateness from the mother, was of major significance to French feminist theorists who challenged and refined Lacan's views. They emphasised the extent to which language was structured along the lines of the binary opposition between masculine and feminine, with the masculine identified as the dominant side of the pairing. Thus, from the feminist perspective, language was regarded as inherently phallocentric – a male-oriented discourse – in that masculine experience was automatically privileged above the feminine. Women had either to adapt to masculine modes of expression and imagination or retreat into silence. As a consequence, the expression of female experience through language is subject to limitations and constraints.

In analysing women's experience and their ways of presenting it through language, and particularly through writing, French feminist critics claimed that just as women experience life differently from men, so they write in a different way, or must learn to do so in order to escape the narrowness of patriarchal language structures. This led female French critics and theorists, not all of them comfortable with the label 'feminist', to posit the existence of a style of women's writing that they termed *écriture féminine*. According to Julia Kristeva, female language derives from a stage in human development before the child becomes aware of her distinct identity, rather than from the point at which Lacan defined entry into the symbolic order. Language at this stage, for Kristeva and others, is more rhythmic and fluid, and lacks the capacity for categorisation and evaluation that characterises male language, thus posing a potential threat to the patriarchal order. Sylvia Plath's poem 'Daddy' (1962) could be read as an example of *écriture féminine*. The poem's repetitive use of internal and end-rhymes based around long vowel sounds, set up by the opening line – 'You do not do, you do not do' – and the childlike diction of lines like 'Barely daring to breathe or Achoo' at the end of the first stanza, give an almost jaunty, nursery-rhyme-like quality to a poem that is intensely dark in its subject-matter: the oppression of women by the structures of patriarchy, symbolised by the narrator's dead father. The father is variously described as a fascist, and a Nazi, while the speaker pictures herself in

> An engine, an engine
> Chuffing me off like a Jew.
> A Jew to Dachau, Auschwitz, Belsen.

The incongruous combination of form, language and theme, further reinforced by the use of logical inconsistencies, as in the lines:

Daddy, I have had to kill you.
You died before I had time –

encapsulates the subversive potential of *écriture feminine* for undermining the linear structures of patriarchal thought.

Other French feminist critics developed Kristeva's ideas in still more radical directions, proposing closer associations between women's writing and the body. For Hélène Cixous, that connection was naturally rather than socially constructed, and related also to women's sexual potential, which she saw as repressed by their gender identity and the dictates of patriarchal society. Luce Irigaray employed a similar focus on women's sexual experience, demonstrating that female sexual pleasure, or *jouissance,* could not be articulated through masculine language. Again, a fundamental relationship was posited between the body and writing: the potential multiplicity of female sexual pleasure, compared to that of men, was mirrored by the greater potential fluidity and diffusiveness of women's language.

North American feminist critics did not totally ignore or reject the preoccupations of their French counterparts, but the prevailing emphasis in their work in the 1970s was more closely related to textual analysis through a gendered perspective. This originally took the form of rereadings and revisions of canonical texts by male writers, to reveal the inherent patriarchal attitudes and prejudices embedded in those texts. Kate Millet's *Sexual Politics* (1970) was arguably the first major contribution to this debate, showing how the depictions of women in the work of writers such as D. H. Lawrence were compromised by male-centred perspectives that resulted in distorted representations of female experience. Criticism of this kind stopped short, however, of challenging the patriarchal nature of the process of canon formation, and the next major development in North American feminist scholarship, labelled 'gynocriticism', sought rather to bring about the conditions for the creation of an alternative, female canon. The work of feminist critics such as Sandra Gilbert, Susan Gubar and Elaine Showalter aimed to rediscover a lost tradition of women's writing by subjecting canonical women writers to reassessment, and reviving interest in women writers whose work had been long neglected. In the 1980s, as feminist criticism broadened its range and became more sophisticated in its analytical practices, the limitations of working within a male-centred critical tradition became apparent, although feminist theory benefited from drawing on other critical models such as psychoanalytic and Marxist theory. As a consequence, many feminist critics advocated the development of a more radical separation from other theoretical approaches. At the same time, there was growing dissatisfaction with the emphasis in feminist criticism on the universality of female experience and identity, which many argued reflected only issues and concerns affecting white, middle-class women in Western societies, who had made up the majority of activists in the women's movement. This led to a greater representation of different kinds of female experience in feminist theory and criticism, based on racial identity or sexual orientation, reflected in the rise of feminist postcolonial and third world studies, and gay and lesbian criticism.

Feminist theory and criticism has helped to bring about massive changes in textual analysis and interpretation, questioning the male-dominated process of canon formation, bringing to light lost or effaced traditions in women's writing, rediscovering women authors who had not received their critical due and widening opportunities for contemporary female novelists, poets and dramatists. Major works of feminist scholarship, including Elaine Showalter's *A Literature of their Own* (1977) and Sandra M. Gilbert and Susan Gubar's *The Madwoman in the Attic* (1979), as well as anthologies such as Germaine Greer's collection of 17th-century women's poetry, *Kissing the Rod* (1988), are among the key texts that have enabled the validation of female experience as a literary theme and asserted the significance of women's writing past and present.

See also *Contexts*: Feminism and the role of women, Sex and sexuality; *Texts*: Women's writing; *Criticism*: Deconstruction, Gender criticism, Marxist criticism, Postcolonial criticism, Psychoanalytic criticism.

Further reading

Belsey, Catherine and Jane Moore (eds), *The Feminist Reader: Essays in Gender and the Politics of Literary Criticism* (Basingstoke: Macmillan, 1993; first pub. 1989).

Eagleton, Mary (ed.), *Feminist Literary Criticism* (Harlow: Longman, 1991).

Greene, Gayle and Coppelia Kahn (eds), *Changing Subjects: The Making of Feminist Literary Criticism* (London: Routledge, 1993).

Humm, Maggie, *A Reader's Guide to Contemporary Feminist Literary Criticism* (Hemel Hempstead: Harvester Wheatsheaf, 1994).

Moi, Toril, *Sexual/Textual Politics: Feminist Literary Theory* (London: Methuen, 1985).

Showalter, Elaine (ed.), *The New Feminist Criticism: Essays on Women, Literature and Theory* (London: Virago, 1985).

Gender criticism

By the mid-1980s, feminism had become firmly established as one of the most influential theoretical approaches to cultural criticism and literary analysis, and the increasing sophistication of the movement's practices was fostering an intense and rigorous debate about its methodologies and terms of reference. The emergence of gender criticism, which opened out new directions for literary and cultural studies in relation to issues such as sexual identity and sexual orientation, was one consequence of this debate.

Gender critics such as Eve Kosofsky Sedgwick, whose study *Between Men: English Literature and Male Homosocial Desire* (1985) could be described as the first major work in gender criticism, questioned the status of the basic gender categories of masculine and feminine. The mainstream of feminist thought had devoted little attention to this question, accepting traditional conceptions of masculinity and femininity as natural, or 'essential' characteristics of human identity. Sedgwick proposed the view that gender was in fact a social and cultural construct; that categories of male and female, beyond biological and anatomical differences, were created by the way society and culture regarded masculine and feminine behaviour and attributes. This position, held by the majority of gender critics, has been termed constructionist, to differentiate it from the essentialist view, that women and men are naturally different. It would, however, be somewhat simplistic to divide gender and feminist critics strictly along constructionist and essentialist lines. Many feminist critics adhere to the constructionist view; similarly, many gay and lesbian critics, who comprise a prominent element within gender criticism, tend towards a more essentialist view.

The formulation of a specifically gay and lesbian critical movement constitutes one of the most radical developments within gender criticism. Homosexuality and heterosexuality have conventionally been regarded as binary opposites, but gay and lesbian critics have drawn attention to the diversity of sexual identities between these two poles, and the multiplicity of sexual practices and types of sexual behaviour beyond reproductive sex, which has tended to be taken as the social and cultural norm. Practitioners of gay and lesbian criticism, or 'queer theory', as it is sometimes called, foreground homosexual difference and have constructed ways of reading that focus on homosexual identity and issues. The representation of such issues in contemporary literature is often depicted in ways that undermine literary, social and cultural convention, as, for example, in the novels of Jeanette Winterson. Gender criticism might focus on the subversion of traditional narratives of religious conversion in Winterson's first novel, *Oranges Are Not the Only Fruit* (1985), which uses the titles of books of the Old Testament as chapter headings, and details the struggle of her protagonist, raised, like Winterson, in a fundamentalist Christian environment, to assert her lesbian identity in the face of ferocious, and often psychologically violent, attempts by her elders to suppress her true sexuality. Later novels, including Sexing the Cherry (1989) and Written on the Body (1992), manipulate conventions of narrative time and gender identity in ways that evoke parallels with earlier subversive texts like Virginia Woolf's Orlando (1928).

In addition to the emphasis on texts that explicitly address homosexual experience, gay and lesbian criticism is concerned with re-evaluating those in which engagement with such experience has been subliminated or repressed. Gay and lesbian critics have explored in this way canonical texts by writers such as Henry James and Emily Dickinson, as well as contemporary authors like the African American novelist Toni Morrison.

One of the most contentious issues that gender criticism has addressed is the notion of écriture féminine, promoted by French feminist critics including Hélène Cixous and Luce Irigaray, which cites the inherently patriarchal nature of language as a justification for women to find new styles of writing, expressive of female sexuality and the body. Gender critics do not deny that there are differences in the way women and men write, or that women's literary expression has been constrained by patriarchy, but they see such differences and difficulties as resulting from social and cultural conditioning, rather than inherent biological differences. In their critical practices they speak of feminine or masculine ways of writing and reading texts, but deny that feminine or masculine writing and reading strategies are necessarily the exclusive province of female or male writers. It should be noted that in this respect they are not dissimilar to some of the advocates of écriture féminine, who do not necessarily believe that male writers are unable to replicate such styles, citing, among others, Andre Gide and James Joyce. In practice, there are considerable areas of similarity in the basic assumptions and critical methods of feminist and gender critics. The key contribution of gender critics to the debate about the complex relationship between gender, language and literature has been to hold up to scrutiny some of the central notions of the nature of sexual identity and sexual orientation. In doing so, they have formulated more sophisticated approaches to the analysis of literary texts for what they say, or perhaps significantly do not say, about gender and sexuality.

See also   *Contexts*: Feminism and the role of women, Sex and sexuality; *Texts*: Gay and lesbian writing, Women's writing; *Criticism*: Deconstruction, Feminist criticism.

Further reading

Hall, Donald E., *Queer Theories* (Basingstoke: Palgrave Macmillan, 2003).
Sedgwick, Eve Kosofsky, *Between Men: English Literature and Male Homosexuality* (New York: Columbia University Press, 1985).
Sinfield, Alan, *Cultural Politics – Queer Reading* (London: Routledge, 1994).
Winders, James A., *Gender, Theory and the Canon* (Madison, WI: University of Wisconsin Press, 1991).

Leavisite criticism

F. R. Leavis, who taught at Cambridge University from before the Second World War to the early 1960s, and edited the influential literary journal *Scrutiny* between 1932 and 1953, was arguably the first British literary critic to introduce a more rigorously analytical approach to the study of English literature, contributing greatly to the enhanced academic status of the subject. In the earlier 20th century, literary study had largely confined itself to generalised comments about the aesthetic properties of literature, combined with an awareness of literary history and biographical details about the author of a given text. Leavis, following the example of I. A. Richards's classes in practical criticism at Cambridge, placed close textual reading at the core of his critical approach, focusing attention not just on what the text said, but also on how its content was expressed in terms of language and formal techniques. For Leavis, the central theme of literature, the key that defined a text as literary and worthy of study, was the extent to which it could, in highly complex ways, reflect, comment on and offer guidance about lived experience. The purpose of Leavisite literary criticism was to demonstrate how texts achieved these aims.

In effect, Leavis saw literature as having a moral and social function, though morality in his terms was less to do with a set of ethical guidelines by which life should be lived, and more to do with the totality of human experience, the role and responsibilities of the individual in society and universal values. From a Leavisite perspective, literature presented a potential corrective to the deleterious effects of modern mass culture, modern technology and the growth of consumerism and commercialism. Literature could present an alternative vision of what society could be and how human experience could be exploited to its full potential. Texts that Leavis regarded as constituting the best in literary expression did not present their preoccupation with moral seriousness in an overt or programmatic way; it was the task of the educated critic to tease out textual meaning, through detailed attention to the text and the effects of its formal and literary devices. Leavis regarded the novel as the most appropriate and effective form for serious exploration of the potentialities of lived experience, and though he also wrote extensively on poetry, he is best known for his critical study *The Great Tradition* (1948), in which he cited novelists such as Jane Austen, Joseph Conrad and D. H. Lawrence as cornerstones of a canonical tradition.

The Leavisite approach was the dominant model of literary criticism in Britain up until the 1970s, offering a seemingly objective and ideology-free justification for the inclusion of certain texts within the literary canon and the exclusion of others. It was only with the advent of new critical approaches such as structuralism, poststructuralism and Marxism in the 1970s that the subjectivity and lack of theoretical rigour that underpinned Leavisite criticism became more apparent. The beliefs that fixed textual meaning could be extracted by close reading, and that literary texts could be said to reflect and make statements about lived experience, were held up to question by the emphasis in structuralist and poststructuralist theories on the instability of language and the undecidability of textual interpretation. Similarly, the focus on the text itself, to the exclusion of extrinsic considerations, was challenged from Marxist and other perspectives that insisted on the need to contextualise literary production. Nevertheless, Leavisite insistence on the importance of close reading has survived and holds a central place in most critical and theoretical approaches since the 1970s, even if few of these devote the sort of attention to moral imperatives that preoccupied Leavis and his followers earlier in the 20th century.

See also   *Criticism*: Cultural materialism, Marxist criticism, New Criticism, New Historicism.

Further reading

Day, Gary, *Re-reading Leavis: Culture and Literary Criticism* (Basingstoke: Macmillan, 1996).
Leavis, F. R., *The Great Tradition* (London: Chatto & Windus, 1948).
Mulhern, Francis, *The Moment of 'Scrutiny'* (London: New Left Books, 1979).
Samson, Anne, *F. R. Leavis* (London: Harvester Wheatsheaf, 1992).

Marxist criticism

The need to place literary texts within a social and historical context is common to many contemporary critical approaches, but is arguably more central to the various forms of Marxist criticism than to any other. The complex relationship between literature and the social world in which it is produced, disseminated and received has maintained its primary importance in Marxist criticism and theory, which has developed from a relatively crude mechanism for analysing the political content of literary texts and their representations of class struggle, to more sophisticated engagements with poststructuralism and other theoretical movements, and an emphasis on the ways in which texts create and reflect, not always intentionally, ideological perspectives.

Marxist criticism aims to explain and interpret literary texts with reference to their content, their formal and stylistic characteristics and the meanings they convey, all of which are acknowledged as products of a particular historical moment and social, political, cultural and economic climate. Specific kinds of literature have been particularly amenable to Marxist analysis: narrative realism, for example, in aiming at a mimetic representation of the social world and its material conditions was, for leading Marxist critics such as Georg Lukàcs, the literary form which seemed to demonstrate most effectively the relationship between literature, reality and ideology. The subjectivity, fragmented narrative structures and isolated or alienated characters represented in modernist writing, on the other hand, were for Lukàcs antithetical to an understanding of the underlying political and social forces that realist literature could depict. Modernist literature, according to Lukàcs, presented characters lost in an apolitical, asocial, ahistorical landscape bereft of social interaction. Other critics, like Theodor Adorno, disagreed, recognising the capacity in literary innovation and experimentation for creating a necessary sense of distance, enabling Marxist critics to discern the workings of ideology that permeated a given text.

Ideology is a key term in Marxist criticism, one that has been open to different emphases of interpretation. The ways in which contemporary critics understand ideology owes much to the work of Louis Althusser, who viewed it as a set of beliefs that are socially constructed and unconsciously absorbed by individuals in order to make sense of, and accept, their position in society. In capitalist societies, according to Althusser, these beliefs are inculcated through institutional structures which he termed 'ideological state apparatuses', and which present as natural the values and attitudes necessary for the propagation of the capitalist system. Religion, law, media and the arts, including literature, are all examples of ideological state apparatuses. In Althusser's analysis, literary texts reflect the prevailing ideology of the period and society in which they were written; like ideology itself, they present an imaginary or fictionalised version of social relations, but the mediation of ideology in literature is a complex process. One of the key tasks of Marxist criticism, from Althusser's point of view, is to highlight the role of ideology in literary texts, which is often a presence of which an author may not be aware, and to demonstrate how the transformative

effect of literature on ideology points up fractures in the ideology represented in the text.

Althusser's influential analysis of the nature of ideology and its literary manifestations were developed further by Pierre Macherey, who
focused attention on what he termed textual 'gaps and silences'. For
Macherey, what was often most informative was not what the text said
but what it did not say: the significant absences that an author,
consciously or unconsciously, leaves out of the version of social reality
depicted in the text. These absences are crucial because their inclusion
would point up inconsistencies and contradictions in the ideology of the
text. The narrow social milieu of the upper middle classes depicted in
Anthony Powell's vast novel sequence *A Dance to the Music of Time*
(1951–75) may, according to Macherey's theory of textual gaps, suggest
a subliminal ideological aversion to the impact of the wider social
democratisation of the period in which they were written.

The developments in Marxist criticism inspired by Althusser and
Macherey are typical of the trend towards more complex textual engagements, taking account of formal and stylistic considerations as well as
theme and content that can be seen in the greater emphasis on narrative strategies in the work of later Marxist critics such as Fredric
Jameson and Terry Eagleton. Jameson's *The Political Unconscious* (1981),
for example, constructs a politicised narrative theory that he uses to
explore texts by Balzac, Gissing and Conrad, while Eagleton's *Myths of
Power* (1975, revised 1988) contextualises close readings of the novels of
the Brontës within an account of the historical and material conditions
in which they were produced.

Marxism's emphasis on social relations and the power of ideology to
perpetuate hierarchical structures, thus defending the interests of the
status quo, has also rendered its preoccupations and methodology of
interest to feminist and postcolonial critics, who acknowledge the significant role played by historical, social, cultural and economic context in
informing the study of literature. On the other hand, postmodernist
scepticism about 'grand narratives', and the extent to which historical
analysis, or indeed any form of discourse, can be relied upon, has posed
a particularly rigorous challenge to the materialist procedures of Marxist
criticism, which has undergone something of a decline of authority since
its period of greatest influence in the 1970s and 1980s.

See also   *Contexts*: Class structure; *Texts*: Class, History; *Criticism*: Cultural materialism,
Feminist criticism, Marxist criticism, New Historicism, Postcolonial criticism,
Poststructuralism.

Further reading

Eagleton, Terry, *Marxism and Literary Criticism* (London: Methuen, 1976).
Elliott, Gregory (ed.), *Althusser: A Critical Reader* (Oxford: Blackwell, 1994).
Jameson, Fredric, *The Political Unconscious: Narrative as a Socially Symbolic Act* (London: Routledge: 1989; first pub. 1981).
Macherey, Pierre, *A Theory of Literary Production* (London: Routledge & Kegan Paul, 1978).
Mulhearn, Francis (ed.), *Contemporary Marxist Literary Criticism* (London: Longman, 1992).

Narratology

The basic methodologies and practices of structuralist poetics have given rise to a range of related critical approaches, many of which have helped to shift critical attention onto the underlying structures of textual narrative. Narratology is the term used to describe one of the more significant strands of narrative analysis, strongly influenced by the work of the Russian Formalists in the 1920s. Like the Russian Formalists, narratologists' main concern is with textual structure, with identifying and defining the significant elements that are common to all narratives, and describing the ways in which those elements interact to create a sense of narrative cohesion. Narratologists are less concerned with the process of textual interpretation than with establishing and explaining the general rules that characterise narrative structure; technical analysis rather than critical exploration is the key aspect of their work.

The construction of a methodology for describing general principles of narrative structure has necessitated the creation of various categories of narrative components, such as those proposed by Gérard Genette, whose *Narrative Discourse* (1972) has become recognised as one of the seminal explanations of narratology. Genette, following the model of Russian Formalism, formulated a distinction between what he called *récit*, the sequence of narrative events as related in a given text, and *histoire*, the chronological sequence that those events would have followed if they had really happened. Such a distinction is helpful in demonstrating the effects created by a text's handling of time, such as the creation of suspense, the deferral of explication, the varying amounts of textual space taken to address specific periods of time, and the consequences of departure from temporal linearity. In conjunction with other categories relating to narrative perspectives, actions, settings and language, narratologists such as Genette were able to construct a detailed framework that could be adapted to various kinds of narrative, not only fictional and printed, but performative, verbal and filmic. Other narratologists have pioneered additional developments in the exploration of narrative structure. Roland Barthes and Seymour Chatman have both posited the existence of hierarchical categories of narrative events, for example, that privilege those that are integral to narrative cohesion – 'kernels', in Chatman's phrase – over 'satellites', that is to say, those textual components that could be removed without affecting the reader's sense of narrative progression. The absence of these elements in the narrative would, however, deprive the text of many of the qualities that compel the reader to read on, such as character development, psychological consistency, motivation or sense of place. The notion of narrative as a hierarchical structure makes clear the distinction between the succession of events and actions that make up the 'story', and the 'discourse', that is to say the formal techniques that are used to tell that story.

Fictional writing since the emergence of modernism in the early 20th century has often focused as much, if not more, on the processes by which narrative is produced: discourse frequently dominates over story, in effect, and many crucial developments in literary theory have taken account of such shifts of emphasis. Narratology is not concerned with exploring and evaluating the possibilities of authorial intention, or the disjunction that often occurs between that intention and the text itself. In this respect it shares common ground with many structuralist and poststructuralist approaches, reflecting the drift in late 20th-century criticism and theory away from a concern with the author and the significance of contextual background. Narratology, by demonstrating the rules and principles that govern all types of narrative construction, offers a means of making sense of the increasing complexity of contemporary narrative strategies, especially those that self-consciously draw attention to their own construction of discourse. John Fowles's *The French Lieutenant's Woman* (1969) was one of the most influential novels of the period in this respect. A narratological reading of Fowles's novel could profitably scrutinise the deliberately self-conscious manipulation of literary conventions that provide Fowles with his narrative framework. His narrator repeatedly draws attention to the artificiality of those conventions, particularly the realist techniques that recall much fiction of the period in which the novel is set – the mid-19th century. Fowles also uses the well-established perspective of the omniscient narrator, but that narrator's temporal distance from the events described gradually becomes apparent, as he repeatedly points out contrasts between Victorian attitudes towards sex and sexual relationships, and those of the 1960s. The novel's self-referentiality becomes increasingly apparent when the narrator breaks off from his task to admit, 'This story I am telling is all imagination. These characters I create never existed outside my own mind', and, in a digression on the art of narrative creation, invokes the names of contemporary writers and critics like Robbe-Grillet and Barthes. The kind of authorial self-consciousness that permeated *The French Lieutenant's Woman*, culminating in the use of alternative endings, that again draws attention to, and undermines, narrative convention, prefigures in many ways the postmodernist techniques that later novelists such as Julian Barnes, Martin Amis and Peter Ackroyd, among others, were to develop.

See also *Criticism*: Poststructuralism, Structuralism.

Further reading

Bal, Mieke, *Narratology: Introduction to the Theory of Narrative* (Toronto: University of Toronto Press, 1985).

Chatman, Seymour, *Story and Discourse: Narrative Structure in Fiction and Film* (Ithaca and London: Cornell University Press, 1993; first pub. 1978).

Genette, Gérard, *Fiction and Diction*, trans. by Catherine Porter (Ithaca and London: Cornell University Press, 1993).

Genette, Gérard, *Narrative Discourse*, trans. Jane E. Lewin (Ithaca, NY: Cornell University Press, 1988).

Rimmon-Kenan, Shlomith, *Narrative Fiction: Contemporary Poetics* (London: Routledge, 1983).

New Criticism

For a period of around 30 years, from the 1940s to the 1970s, the dominance of New Criticism's textual practices in the American academy was unchallenged. Some of its main influences and antecedents were British, such as the practical criticism techniques of I. A. Richards, and William Empson's theory of the functions of ambiguity in literature. Both critics were discussed in John Crowe Ransom's *The New Criticism* (1941), which gave the movement its name, although the differences between the critical practices of its leading exponents, such as Ransom, Cleanth Brooks, Robert Penn Warren and Allen Tate were as numerous as the similarities. What these critics shared, however, was a commitment to close reading and detailed textual analysis that focused only on the language of the text, and not on issues such as authorial intention, biography and literary historical context. Many New Critics held views close to those of F. R. Leavis and his followers, regarding literature as an aesthetic corrective to the decline of contemporary culture.

The New Critics tended to focus mainly on poetry, treating the individual poem in isolation, as a self-contained object that generated meaning through the confluence of its use of language and its formal poetic techniques. In some respects, New Criticism echoed the procedures of the Russian Formalists, though without the scientific methodological emphases of that movement: New Critics sought to interpret the structures and meanings of individual texts, rather than establish general principles which could be applied to all kinds of textual analysis, or indeed to any act of linguistic communication. New Critics invested particular significance in poetic techniques such as imagery, symbolism, rhythm and repetitions of sound; the ways in which these devices cohered were as crucial to the decoding of the text as its thematic content and subject-matter. New Criticism proved more assertive than many later critical movements in its claims to objectivity, which were predicated on the premise that textual meaning would yield itself up to rigorous close analysis. That is not to say that New Critical techniques guaranteed that texts would be shown to have straightforward meanings; it was more likely that close critical reading would highlight ambiguity than transparency, given the complex relationships between literary form and language, but there was an overriding assumption that interpretation, however provisional, was achievable, a belief that would later be challenged by structuralist, poststructuralist and postmodernist theories.

The rise of structuralism on the one hand, and the range of theoretical and critical approaches that stressed the value of placing literature in a wider social, cultural and historical context – feminist, Marxist and postcolonial, for example – on the other, gradually undermined the authority of New Criticism. Nevertheless, many of those same approaches continue to adhere closely to an emphasis on analytical practices of close reading, albeit with a greater emphasis on literature's indivisibility from the social world.

See also *Criticism*: Leavisite criticism, Structuralism.

Further reading

Jancovich, Mark, *The Cultural Politics of New Criticism* (Cambridge: Cambridge University Press, 1993).
Spurlin, William J. and Michael Fisher, *The New Criticism and Contemporary Literary Theory: Connections and Continuities* (New York and London: Garland, 1995).
Wimsatt, W. K., *The Verbal Icon: Studies in the Meaning of Poetry* (London: Methuen, 1970; first pub. 1954).

New Historicism

The emergence of New Historicism, in the mid-1980s, owed something to the methodologies of socially and politically oriented theoretical approaches such as Marxism, feminism and postcolonialism, as well as to formalist emphases on the value of close reading. The interests of New Historicists also harked back to the emphasis on the relationship between literature and history that had dominated literary study between the First and Second World Wars. The conception of history that informed New Historicism was, however, very different, reflecting shifts in thinking about the validity of absolute and objective historical knowledge, which had been accepted as natural half a century earlier.

The key informing principle of New Historicism, so named by Stephen Greenblatt in 1988, is that literature is inevitably and inescapably bound up with political and historical considerations: the kinds of writing made possible at any given time both reflected and were a consequence of prevailing conditions at the time in which they were produced. The difficulty that New Historicism acknowledged was the fragmentary and partial nature of historical evidence of the conditions in which texts were written, disseminated and read. Deconstructive theory had by this time posited the unreliability of language, thought and perception, with implications for disciplines such as history, especially in relation to its claims to absolute authority. New Historicists rejected traditional perceptions of history that emphasised chronological linearity and periodisation, being suspicious of definitions of specific historical periods according to fixed sets of characteristics or prevalent values and attitudes. Where literary historical scholarship of the 1930s and 1940s adhered to a narrow sense of historical context in which the characteristic values and attitudes of a period could be extrapolated from the available evidence, New Historicists drew on a wider and more fluid range of historical sources and discourses, taking in economics, social history, social science, anthropology and the recovered histories of the marginalised and excluded. The work of the French historian and philosopher Michel Foucault was a key influence on New Historicism in this respect: Foucault went beyond obvious areas of historical enquiry, in favour of bringing together disparate sources, through the analysis of which a necessarily provisional historical sense of a given period and its social world could be produced. New Historicists, following Foucault, placed less importance on major historical events and more on exploring how life was lived and on the influence of social, economic, political and cultural forces in a particular time.

The basic assumption of New Historicism is that the relationship between literary texts and the diverse range of historical contexts in which they were produced is reciprocal: texts are informed by and inform their historical contexts. Furthermore, texts are open to a multiplicity of historical contextual influences, making for a more symbiotic

relationship between history and literature than earlier literary histori-
ans allowed. History is not merely a backdrop to the study of the text,
but permeates and informs textual practice. New Historicists recognised
that the historical evidence available to them was inevitably incomplete.
Furthermore, that evidence was susceptible to the subjective interpretation of the historian or the literary critic, and was mediated through the
values, attitudes, and prejudices of the present. Their conclusions were,
therefore, open to continual reinterpretation; for this reason New
Historicism tends to focus on the potentially subversive nature of literary production, rather than on actual examples. Textual analysis may
reveal values and intentions that run counter to the prevailing ideology
of the time in which the text was written.

Unlike cultural materialists, however, New Historicists tend towards
scepticism about this kind of evidence: their historicised perspective
takes into account the capacity of a dominant ideology to assimilate and
incorporate oppositional views and contain the danger of subversion.
Tony Harrison, for example, whose poem *v.* (1985) is discussed in this
chapter under 'Cultural materialism', is now a central figure in the canon
of contemporary British poetry, for all the oppositional tendencies in his
work. His poem *v.*, which attracted considerable controversy and noto-
riety when it was broadcast on television in 1987, because of its use of
obscene language, is now regularly featured on university curricula and
reading lists. New Historicists could also point to the fate of the precur-
sor poem to *v.*, Gray's 'Elegy', neutralised by its canonical acceptance
and familiarity over time, to the extent that any element of critique of the
social order at the time it was written has all but evaporated.

Another text that, like Harrison's poem, provoked controversy, especially after its transformation into film, was Anthony Burgess's *A
Clockwork Orange* (1962). A full engagement with that text from a New
Historicist perspective would focus on what it revealed, intentionally or
otherwise, about a range of political, social and cultural attitudes of the
period, and what the reception of the filmed version, around a decade
later, might have to say about how those attitudes might have changed.
One of the functions the text performs is to satirise the emergence of a
distinct youth culture in the period, by setting the novel in a near future
featuring gangs of young males, notable for their outlandish fashions,
drug consumption and a language of their own, 'Nadsat', for which
Burgess drew on Russian vocabulary. These gangs terrorise society with
sadistic acts of physical and sexual violence, and society's response is
draconian, as extreme psychologically as the behaviour of the youths is
physically. The underlying theme of the novel – the existence of evil and
the debate about how it can be confronted – is one that would clearly

have resonated with a contemporary readership, given recent historical events. Other concerns are also present in the text. The Cold War, for example, is an underlying theme. The gangs' fashions, slang and cultural habits allude to the Americanisation of British culture that was a particular issue in the period, while the Russian origins of their dialect reinforce the Cold War connection, and offer an implicit critique of Britain's role in the new world order, suggesting that the dystopian vision the novel presents may be an inevitable consequence of the way society in general was developing in the postwar period. The validity and effectiveness of that critique, was, New Historicists might argue, undermined by other aspects of the narrative, such as its representations of violence, which were all the more emphatic in Stanley Kubrick's 1971 film. The film aroused such controversy that it was withdrawn by Kubrick himself for over a quarter of a century. The book's reception was invariably affected by this, compromising its effectiveness as a vehicle of social commentary.

New Historicist practices have permeated many different critical movements and perspectives since the 1980s, and their diffusiveness renders them particularly resistant to simple definition. The eclectic range of influences to which New Historicists are receptive, due to their willingness to draw on a broad spectrum of historical sources, adds to the difficulty of accurately summarising exactly what New Historicism is, as does the refusal of its practitioners to accommodate traditional notions of the nature of historical enquiry, leaving their practices continually subject to revision and redefinition in the light of changes in historical circumstances and contemporary theorising about the past. By its very nature, New Historicism focuses largely on the literature of the past; its strategies are less easily applicable to contemporary writings, but the basic methodology of reading the text with an awareness of external factors and influences is one that can be usefully adapted to the literature of any period, including the present.

See also   *Contexts*: Class structure; *Texts*: Class, History; *Criticism*: Cultural materialism, Marxist criticism.

Further reading

Colebrook, Claire, *New Literary Histories: New Historicism and Criticism* (Manchester: Manchester University Press, 1997).

Gallagher, Catherine and Stephen Greenblatt, *Practising New Historicism* (Chicago: University of Chicago Press, 2000).

McGann, Jerome, *The Beauty of Inflections: Literary Investigations in Historical Method and Theory* (Oxford: Clarendon Press, 1985).

Postcolonial criticism

Materialist criticism has maintained a significant presence since the 1970s, in response to the text-based practices of structuralism and post-structuralism, and the questioning of historical authority that characterises postmodern theory. Marxist and feminist criticism, for example, have retained their prominent status in literary study in the late 20th century, but have in some respects been overtaken by postcolonial criticism as arguably the most influential interpretative practice of the contemporary period.

One of the main tasks facing postcolonial theory and criticism has been to take account of the diversity of the experiences of nations and peoples that have escaped the constraints of colonial rule. Postcolonial criticism has attempted to recognise that the perceptions and responses of colonised peoples in India or Africa, where European settlers have brought and imposed their own social, cultural and political values on indigenous populations, may be very different from the experience of Caribbean peoples who have suffered exile and diaspora, losing contact with the lands of their origins. Similarly, women in many colonised societies may have perceived their situation very differently from men, especially in those cultures in which the external pressures of colonialism combined with indigenous patriarchal attitudes to place them under a double burden of oppression. Third world feminist critics, such as Gayatri Spivak, pioneer of subaltern studies, have drawn productively on postcolonial theories to explore just these issues. Conversely, many postcolonial theorists, critics and activists have appropriated Marxist thinking, in support of their response to colonial subjection and the reassertion of national, social and cultural identity in the postcolonial era. Many of the 20th-century nationalist movements that helped to bring about independence for colonised states were influenced and inspired by Marxism, as were later critics from Franz Fanon, who advocated the creation of national literatures as a crucial means of forging postcolonial identity, to Homi K. Bhabha, who has explored the relationship between nationhood and cultural production from a wide range of perspectives.

Postcolonial criticism covers a wide range of cultural and critical practices, reflecting the diversity of colonial experience. The fundamental literary critical focus of postcolonial studies is twofold: the study of texts written by authors who originate from imperialist nations, about aspects of the colonised culture, and the study of texts written by inhabitants of those cultures, usually concerned with the experience of colonisation and its aftermath. One of the key factors about texts by writers from colonialist backgrounds that postcolonial criticism aims to reveal, is how those texts, consciously or otherwise, depict the colonised culture and its inhabitants as inferior to their Western and European counterparts. The leading postcolonialist critic Edward Said, in theoretical and critical studies such as *Orientalism* (1978) and *Culture and Imperialism* (1993), has demonstrated how colonialist writing confirms, consolidates and perpetuates the political, social and cultural dominance of the coloniser, by describing the colonised in terms that evoke a sense of 'otherness'. As Said and other critics have shown, many texts, particularly novels, that are at the heart of the canonical tradition of English literature represent the colonised in this way, either explicitly or implicitly: Joseph Conrad's *Heart of Darkness* (1902), with its racial stereotyping of African natives, is one such case. The decline of European imperial power in the second half of the 20th century inspired inhabitants of formerly colonised territories to reconnect with their own histories and traditions, which had been effaced or marginalised by the imposition of the cultural values of the coloniser. In literature, this was manifested in the emergence of a vast corpus of postcolonial writing. Many postcolonial writers, like the Nigerian novelist Chinua Achebe, were also acutely aware of the wider theoretical issues informing their work, and were conscious of the implications of their use of particular narrative strategies. Achebe's novel *Things Fall Apart* (1958) has claims to be the first major work of postcolonial fiction; his use of recognisably Western literary forms, and his decision to write in English, generated intense discussion across the spectrum of postcolonial thought, with some critics questioning Achebe's choices, advocating instead the use of tribal or native languages and forms more closely reflecting the original oral traditions of many colonised societies. Achebe's defence was to point to the wider audience he could reach by writing in English, and the potency of using the language and cultural traditions of the coloniser to articulate critiques of imperialist attitudes and values.

One of the most striking consequences of both the volume of postcolonial literature, and the intense critical attention it has received, has been a fundamental change in the kinds of texts that are now subjected to academic scrutiny. There is now a greater tendency to use the descriptive term 'literatures in English', rather than 'English literature', to reflect this, which is indicative of the extent to which postcolonial writing and criticism has posed a fundamental challenge to traditional conceptions of canonicity. The growing sophistication of postcolonial criticism has seen its practices and strategies develop from textual readings of texts such as Conrad's *Heart of Darkness* that aim to reveal its underlying imperialist perspective, embedded in the novel's title and its representations of Africa as a place of primitive barbarity, to a fuller engagement with the work of writers like Achebe and his contemporaries, as well as the theoretical debates that inform and underpin such writing.

See also *Contexts*: British Empire, decline and loss, Migrant experience and multiculturalism; *Texts*: Black British literature, Empire, end of, Postcolonial literature; *Criticism*: Feminist criticism, Marxist criticism, Postmodern theory.

Further reading

Ashcroft, Bill, Gareth Griffiths and Helen Tiffin, *Key Concepts in Post-colonial Studies* (London: Routledge, 1998).

Boehmer, Elleke, *Colonial and Postcolonial Literature: Migrant Metaphors* (Oxford: Oxford University Press, 1995).

Chrisman, Laura and Benita Parry (eds), *Postcolonial Theory and Criticism* (Woodbridge: D. S. Brewer, 2000).

Harrison, Nicholas, *Postcolonial Criticism: History, Theory and the Work of Fiction* (Cambridge: Polity Press, 2003).

Moore-Gilbert, B. J., Gareth Stanton and Willy Maley (eds), *Postcolonial Criticism* (London: Longman, 1997).

Said, Edward, *Orientalism* (Harmondsworth: Penguin, 1995; first pub. 1978).

Walder, Dennis, *Post-colonial Literatures in English: History, Language, Theory* (Oxford: Blackwell, 1998).

Postmodernist theory

Literary critical debate, from the 1980s to the turn of the 21st century, has been dominated by postmodernist theoretical approaches that have interrogated traditional modes of cultural enquiry. Notions of objectivity, and of the validity of overarching theories that claimed to offer interpretations of the social world, and the role within it of cultural production, including literature, have been held up to scrutiny by postmodernist critics and theorists.

The term 'postmodernism' was first used as early as 1947, by Arnold Toynbee, who used it to describe a contemporary Western world in crisis, whose inhabitants struggled to make sense of a century characterised by conflict and mass genocide, leading to the questioning of traditional moral values and beliefs. By the early 1970s, the term 'postmodernism' had come to refer to the extension and development of cultural modernism, the artistic and literary style that had enjoyed a period of massive influence between the wars, and experienced a revival of interest in the 1960s. Later still, postmodernism took on the wider definition with which it is now more usually associated: a critical apparatus through which contemporary society and culture could be examined, though not interpreted, or explained, along conventional theoretical, historical or philosophical lines.

Central to postmodernist thinking was a radical challenge to intellectual attitudes that dated back to the 18th-century Enlightenment, such as the belief that reason and rationalism held the key to progress in all spheres of human endeavour, including science, philosophy, politics and culture. Throughout the 20th century, the evidence of two world wars, and recurrent acts of genocide and inhumanity, had cast doubt on the basic assumptions and premises of Enlightenment thinking, though its values had largely survived. The belief in reason as the key to knowledge and progress had survived many developments in criticism and theory. Cultural products, including literature, were still generally held to offer ways of reflecting and understanding the world and the place of humankind within it, in spite of the rise of structuralist and poststructuralist theories. Postmodernism, however, in developing some key poststructuralist ideas, was more effective in holding Enlightenment rationality to account. Jean-François Lyotard, in his influential study *The Postmodern Condition* (1979), traced the erosion of confidence in Enlightenment ideals back to the revelation of the mass extermination of 6 million Jews in the Holocaust. The pessimism and scepticism this engendered was evident everywhere in human society and culture in the postwar period, and preoccupied movements and modes of thought that looked for alternative ways of explaining the world. The various counter-cultural movements of the 1960s, culminating in the near-revolutionary events in Paris in 1968, were crucial examples of the quest for new values and beliefs to replace those that had survived since the Enlightenment, but the ultimate failure of these movements led to a dwindling of idealism and optimism in the closing decades of the 20th century. Moral progress, a given of Enlightenment beliefs, seemed not just to be in doubt, but almost impossible to envisage. Western capitalism and its attendant features, the rise of mass culture and mass communications, the growth of advertising and the consumer society were all seen as complicit with the creation of an increasingly fragmented society in which traditional moral, social and political values and beliefs had been eroded.

For postmodernists, the failure of Enlightenment rationality showed that theories and intellectual thought-systems that claimed to be able to offer an objective vantage point from which to observe and interpret human behaviour were illusory. These 'grand narratives', as they were termed, included academic disciplines such as philosophy and history, and cultural products such as literature. In undermining the validity of these disciplines and their attendant belief systems, postmodernism drew on poststructuralist scepticism about the reliability of linguistic meaning, but extrapolated these ideas further into a comprehensive analysis of the nature of the contemporary social world. If language itself lacked stable referentiality, as structuralists and poststructuralists claimed, and was fundamentally arbitrary in its relationship to the objects and concepts it described, then all kinds of intellectual theories and processes of cultural enquiry, consisting of nothing more than discourse, could have no claim to reflect reality or posit objective truths. The consequence of these claims was a crisis of representation in the modern world, that critics like Fredric Jameson saw as heightened by the power of the mass media, with its capacity to create versions of reality that acquired authoritative status. Jean Baudrillard explored the role of the media still further, showing how its use of images presented through television, print and advertising resulted in a plethora of alternative realities that were complicit with rapidly changing tastes, styles and fashions. As a consequence, the contemporary world came to be seen as ephemeral, lacking in depth, and without solid moral, social and cultural foundations. The effect of this on the consciousness of the individual was another factor that postmodernism sought to explore, again with pessimistic conclusions, as human identity found itself marooned without stable referents of reality against which to define itself.

Critics of postmodernist thought, like the Marxist theorist Terry Eagleton, claimed that its reduction of all intellectual and cultural enquiry to the status of discourse removed it from engagement with the social world. For other critics there was also the disquieting consequence that postmodernist scepticism might bring the entire concept of moral judgement into question. Postmodernist theorists such as Lyotard, however, continued to hold up the example of the Holocaust, and its psychological and emotional legacy, as proof that some vestige of moral relativism still survived, even after the end of 'grand narratives' and the disintegration of Enlightenment optimism.

Postmodernism's rejection of 'grand narratives' and the implicitly elitist values that informed Enlightenment thinking about culture had some positive implications, contributing to the creation of a more liberal and open cultural climate, allowing greater freedom to constituencies historically marginalised on grounds of ethnicity and gender, for instance. Those constituencies have been able to fashion their own narratives in the contemporary period, recovering a sense of identity and tradition that had been obscured by imperialist and patriarchal imperatives. Postmodernism has in this respect contributed to the lessening of canonical authority, and the greater democratisation of literature, in the contemporary period. The concomitant rise of feminist and postcolonial theories has been another consequence of the emergence of these alternative narratives.

As postmodernism has become an established critical discourse, the problem of defining its key concepts and vocabulary has become increasingly acute, given that those concepts and terms are themselves predicated on the undecidability and instability of language and discourse. Nevertheless, postmodernist criticism has proved a particularly useful methodology for the study of contemporary literature, much of which shares its concerns with intertextuality, self-referentiality, narrative fragmentation and ironic and sometimes playful manipulations of language.

See also *Texts*: Genre fiction, Postmodern literature; *Criticism*: Deconstruction, Feminist criticism, Postcolonial criticism, Poststructuralism.

Further reading

Docherty, Thomas (ed.), *Postmodernism: A Reader* (London: Harvester Wheatsheaf, 1993).

Frow, John, *Time and Commodity Culture: Essays in Cultural Theory and Postmodernity* (Oxford: Clarendon Press, 1997).

Jameson, Fredric, *Postmodernism; or, The Cultural Logic of Late Capitalism* (London: Verso, 1991).

Lyotard, Jean-François, *The Postmodern Condition: A Report on Knowledge*, trans. Geoff Bennington and Brian Massumi (Manchester: Manchester University Press, 1984; first pub. 1979).

Woods, Tim, *Beginning Postmodernism* (Manchester: Manchester University Press, 1999).

Poststructuralism

There is no single theoretical approach that can be defined as post-structuralist. The term covers a range of critical practices, all of which respond to, and in some way extend, the basic methodology of structuralism. The relationship between the two critical models is problematised by the emergence of poststructuralism in France, in the late 1960s, as an almost immediate response to structuralism. Leading poststructuralists, like Jacques Derrida and Roland Barthes, had also been at the forefront of the development of structuralist theory. In Britain and America, the situation is even more complex, as translations of the key structuralist and poststructuralist texts entered the academy at roughly the same time in the mid-1970s.

Jacques Derrida's deconstructionist practices are often regarded as synonymous with poststructuralism. The fundamental concept at the heart of Derrida's theory, that determinate textual interpretation is an impossibility, given the belief that the relationship between language and the things it represents is arbitrary and subject to constant slippage of meaning, is a central tenet of poststructuralist thought in its various manifestations. Deconstruction can be seen as poststructuralism at its most radical, given its total denial of the possibility of a final, determined meaning; but poststructuralism informs a diversity of other critical perspectives and methodologies, which are also 'anti-foundationalist' in their orientation: that is, they reject the basic assumption of conventional analytical procedures that a text can be said to have a single fixed meaning. Psychoanalytical theory or certain types of reader-response theory, for example, draw heavily on poststructuralist strategies, but although they acknowledge the multiplicity of possible meanings, and their provisional status in a given text, they also maintain that under those plural meanings lies an actual meaning that can be uncovered by the interpretative process.

The key difference between structuralism and poststructuralism is located in the latter's more radical extension of Saussurean linguistic theory. Structuralism recognised language as a system predicated on differentiation: signifiers locate their identity in their difference from other signifiers, rather than from inherent qualities that relate them to their signifieds, making their relationship with their signifiers arbitrary. However, once this relationship had been fixed in language, signifier and signified become defined and stable. Poststructuralism denies that stability of this kind is possible: rather, it posits that any attempt to define a particular word sets off a chain of signifiers, all of which differ slightly, but crucially, in their relationship to the original word and the thing, or concept, it signifies. Furthermore, each of these signifiers can be open to a further multiplicity of meanings, creating an even greater degree of uncertainty between signifier and signified. Where structuralism proposed a system of language that offers a key to all acts of textual communication, predicated on the relationship between signifier and signified, poststructuralism extends the notion of undecidability to all language use. The consequence of this is that all aspects of literary critical discourse, including its component concepts and vocabulary, are susceptible to slippage and indeterminacy, existing in the same arbitrary relationships as all other kinds of signifiers and signifieds. As a result, by challenging the stability of those concepts and categories that provide the foundation for traditional literary critical enquiry, poststructuralism rejects the notion that textual interpretation can produce determinate meaning.

Many of the key terms of literary critical debate have been radically revised by poststructuralist theorists. Roland Barthes, in his seminal essay 'The Death of the Author' (1968), rejected analytical approaches that placed the author at the heart of the critical enterprise. If all language is subject to indeterminacy, the status of the author as creator and controller of textual meaning is denied, and authorial intention is shown to have no more validity than any other interpretative perspective. For Barthes, texts are more productively categorised as either 'readerly' (*lisible*) or 'writerly' (*scriptible*). The 'readerly' text demonstrates a close dependence on commonly used forms and narrative structures, and is more readily comprehensible along conventional analytical lines. Novels that stay close to the traditions of literary realism, giving emphasis to the development of plot and character, fall into this category. The 'writerly' text is more innovative and experimental, and more resistant to traditional methods of critical analysis. It may also draw on mainstream literary conventions, as in John Fowles' *The French Lieutenant's Woman* (1969), discussed earlier (see 'Narratology'). However, texts like Fowles's draw attention to the artificial and somewhat arbitrary nature of those conventions, through the use of other, more radical and deliberately self-conscious techniques. A more comprehensively 'writerly' text from roughly the same period is B. S. Johnson's *Albert Angelo* (1964), a novel that rejected, rather than manipulated established forms and strategies such as realist description, linear narrative progression, psychologically consistent characterisation and plot development. The structure of *Albert Angelo* is deliberately fragmented, with short, disconnected passages of narrative presented seemingly at random for the most part. Towards the end of the novel, the narrative voice dispenses with all pretence of authorial objectivity, in a section entitled 'Disintegration', which begins with a barely coherent, unpunctuated tirade against the act of narration itself: 'Im trying to say something not tell a story telling stories is telling lies.'

For Barthes, both 'readerly' and 'writerly' texts illustrate the extent to which literature is a cultural and artistic construct. Texts do not reflect or mimic reality, but are the product of formal and linguistic conventions that become established by the text's relationships with other texts, and with the larger text, as poststructuralists perceive it, of language itself. The definition of text itself is brought into question by poststructuralism, and is used to refer not just to an individual work of creative writing, a literary artefact produced by a specific authorial consciousness, but rather to a collection of arbitrary signifiers whose potential meaning is subject to continual revision and reassessment. The role of the reader, too, is radically altered in poststructuralist theory. The reader, in more culturally located forms of criticism, has an identity as a specific subject, whose interpretative strategies are governed by his or her perception and experience of the world the subject inhabits; in poststructuralism, on the other hand, the subject's personal experience has no influence on textual interpretation. The reader is perceived as the point at which the multiplicity of contending, often contradictory and provisional meanings offered by the text congregate.

Poststructuralist theory has had a profound and pervasive influence on literary criticism since the 1970s. The competing claims of the coalition of anti-foundationalist approaches that make up poststructuralism, from deconstruction to postmodernism on the one hand and those of the various forms of cultural criticism – Marxism, feminism, postcolonialism and cultural materialism – on the other, have set up a continuing dialogue about the validity of literary interpretation. That debate is further problematised by the poststructuralist belief that all language is subject to negotiation and slippage, so even the terms of the debate become indeterminate and open to constant questioning. Critics of poststructuralism claim that the classification of all critical and theoretical concepts as discourse removes the practice of literary criticism from the social world in which texts are produced and received, but it should also be noted that key elements of poststructuralist methodology have permeated the structures of cultural criticism to some degree. At the very least, poststructuralism has forced critical enquiry to question the status of its key terms of reference in ways that reflect a general scepticism about language, meaning and interpretation.

See also *Criticism*: Deconstruction, Dialogic theory, Postmodernist theory, Psychoanalytic criticism, Reader-response criticism, Structuralism.

Further reading

Barthes, Roland, *Image-Music-Text* (London: Fontana, 1977).
Barthes, Roland, *S/Z* (London: Jonathan Cape, 1976).
Belsey, Catherine, *Critical Practice* (London: Methuen, 1980).
Lavers, Annette, *Roland Barthes: Structuralism and After* (London: Methuen, 1982).

Psychoanalytic criticism

The beginnings of psychoanalytic literary criticism can be traced back to Sigmund Freud, who in addition to founding the practice of psychoanalysis, at times used literary analysis to demonstrate his theories of human psychology. Freud is widely credited with expanding knowledge of the unconscious workings of the human mind, especially in his contention that the human psyche consisted of three interrelated aspects. The id, representing the unconscious, Freud described as the location of instinctive, physical impulses and desires. The superego, by contrast, is the aspect of the conscious mind that represents the conscience and operates in response to learned social behaviour. The third part of the mind, the ego, operates as mediator between the id and superego, between the conscious and unconscious mind, interpreting reality and constructing a sense of self. Part of this process involves repressing the socially unacceptable wishes and desires of the id to the unconscious mind, from where they periodically surface, disguised in, for example, dreams, linguistic slips, neurotic behaviour, and artistic and creative activity. For Freud, one of the most important unconscious desires in human psychology was that which occurred in childhood development: the wish to supplant the parent of the child's own sex in the affections of the other parent. Freud termed this impulse the 'Oedipus complex', after the figure in Greek myth and tragedy who unknowingly murdered his father and married his mother. The gender implications of Freud's theory, as it was taken up by later generations of psychoanalysts and psychoanalytic critics, were influential and far-reaching.

One of Freud's main psychoanalytical tools was dream analysis, which he deployed in order to reveal the repressed feelings, wishes and fantasies of his patients. Freud contended that such repressed desires appeared in dreams in symbolic forms, the true meaning of which could be arrived at by a process of interpretation, just as the meaning of the literary text was traditionally believed to be attainable through analysis of form and language. In the early 20th century a number of literary critics drew on Freud's psychoanalytic theories to explain literary texts, either through analysis of the author's psychological motivation or that of the text's characters, who were often read as projections of the authorial presence. For psychoanalytic literary critics in the first half of the 20th century, literary devices such as metaphor, metonymy and various other kinds of figurative language functioned in similar ways to the symbolic nature of dreams, and were interpreted along similar lines. Freud's theories of the unconscious mind were largely accepted without question by these critics; it was not until after the Second World War that critics began to challenge fundamental Freudian ideas, with radical consequences for psychoanalytical and other forms of literary criticism.

The first indication of a shift in the focus of psychoanalytic literary criticism in the second half of the century came with a move away from emphasis on the influence of the unconscious on authorial intention, in favour of greater exploration of the psychological response of the reader to the literary text. More attention was paid to the text's engagement with the unconscious wishes and desires of the reader, an approach that laid the foundations for the various reader-response theories that emerged in the 1970s. The main development in psychoanalytic theory after the Second World War, however, was inspired by the pioneering work of Jacques Lacan, who extended and modified Freudian thinking on the unconscious mind to examine the relationship between language and social identity.

Lacan's theory held that the process by which a child comes to realise its separate identity, and becomes aware of its relationship with others and its position in the wider social world, occurred at around the same time as its acquisition of language. Lacan described the latter process as the child's entry into the 'symbolic order'; language for Lacan was symbolic because it 'stands in' for, or symbolises, the things and concepts it describes. Lacan was influenced in this respect more by Saussurean linguistics and structuralist models of language systems than by Freud. According to Lacan, at the pre-oedipal stage of child development, when the child is still unaware of its existence as an entity distinct from the mother, it can also be said to be in a pre-verbal state. The child has no access to symbolic language: the sounds it uses in communication have no direct reference to the things that exist in the world around it. As the child begins to enter what Lacan termed the 'mirror stage', the phase of development in which it begins to distinguish itself from the mother, and later from others, it learns both empathy with and fear of those others and begins to desire what is beyond itself. The first object of desire is usually the mother, from whom it has recently come to realise its separateness. At this point, the child has begun to learn to project beyond itself, as part of the process by which the self is created, a self which Lacan sees as a construct dependent on the perception of others. For Lacan there is no self beyond this constructed identity, which in fact disguises an absence or lack of being.

The mirror stage is followed by the oedipal stage, the point at which the child becomes aware of its own gender and the concept of gender difference. Lacan followed Freud in seeing this as a more problematic stage of development for the boy child, whose recognition of the phallus as the difference between father and mother also brings recognition of the father's status as rival for the mother's affection. The boy child subsequently learns that social convention demands that the object of desire cannot be achieved except indirectly, and that the father occupies a superior hierarchical position to the child. Lacan claimed that the oedipal stage coincided with the child's entry into language, in which words are substitutes for the things they stand for, rather than the things themselves. Thus the process of acquiring language is similar to the male child's experience of having to submit to what Lacan called 'the law of the Father', in which acceptance of the loss of the mother stands in for the socially unacceptable desire for the forbidden object. Consequently, Lacan argued, the entry into the symbolic order was inextricably linked to the child's recognition of gender difference. This led him to the contentious conclusion that entry into language is more difficult for female than male children, because recognition of their own gender identity has not forced them to concede that which they initially saw as indistinguishable from themselves (the mother) to a more powerful rival, and are not required to use language as a way of subliminating their desire for the unattainable object.

Psychoanalytic literary criticism takes many forms, most of which draw to some extent on Lacanian theory. Often these kinds of critical approaches focus either on aspects of the text that receive unusual or intense emphasis, or on that which is absent, that is, unconsciously excluded, or on that which is treated ambiguously. Themes related to absences of various kinds – unfulfilled or frustrated desire, loss, denial or prohibition – can often be productively explored through psychoanalytic critical practices. Such themes are prevalent in the fiction of Ian McEwan. His first novel, *The Cement Garden* (1978), describes the experiences of four children, aged between 5 and 16, suddenly orphaned by the deaths of both parents in quick succession. The death of the father, through a heart attack, has Oedipal overtones, in that it is most closely connected with, and mediated through the perspective of his eldest, 14-year-old son. When the mother dies soon after, the children bury her body in cement, and secrete it in the basement of their house. Their refusal to articulate their loss to the outside world, and especially the burying of the mother, could be said to symbolically mirror the repressive functions of the superego, from a psychoanalytic viewpoint. The children respond in various ways to the deaths of their parents; fantasy, dreams and role-play, all psychologically revealing activities, shape their social and sexual development over the course of the novel, which culminates in the eldest girl and boy, Julie and Jack, assuming the parental role, which they reinforce through an incestuous sexual relationship, the discovery of which leads Julie's boyfriend, the only non-family member to play a prominent role in the novel, to inform the authorities of the body buried in the basement.

The connections Lacan drew between language and gender were highly significant in relation to the development of psychoanalytic and other forms of literary criticism; Lacan's ideas carried substantial implications for poststructuralist theories, especially deconstruction, in positing the ego as a socially determined construct that disguised an actual lack of selfhood. This absence is analogous to the absence of fixed and unitary meaning in any linguistic sign. In addition, Lacan's belief that male and female children have different experiences of acquiring language has fundamental implications for the ways men and women's writing might be perceived, and suggests that language use may be dictated by gender as well as social considerations. In this respect, Lacanian theory had a profound impact on feminist thought and criticism, especially among French theorists such as Hélène Cixous, Julia Kristeva and Luce Irigaray, who adopted and adapted Lacan's ideas to explore issues of language and gender. Their developments of Lacanian theory led these critics to identify or advocate different kinds of writing and reading practices, free of socially constructed patriarchal assumptions, that could more fully reflect female experience.

See also   *Contexts*: Feminism and the role of women; *Literature*: Women's writing; *Criticism*: Deconstruction, Feminist criticism, Poststructuralism, Reader-response criticism, Structuralism.

Further reading

Felman, Shoshana, *Jacques Lacan and the Adventure of Insight: Psychoanalysis and Contemporary Culture* (Cambridge, MA: Harvard University Press, 1987).
Lacan, Jacques, *Ecrits: A Selection* (London: Routledge, 2001; first pub. 1977).
Vice, Sue (ed.), *Psychoanalytic Criticism: A Reader* (Cambridge: Polity Press, 1996).
Wright, Elizabeth, *Psychoanalytic Criticism: A Reappraisal* (Cambridge: Polity Press, 1998).

Reader-response criticism

In the 1970s, the emphasis in some of the newer forms of literary criticism shifted towards more rigorous attention to the role of the reader, and the interpretative processes that derive from the act of reading. A number of distinct theories emerged that are generally encapsulated in the terms 'reader-response criticism' or reception theory, but the attachment of greater significance to the reader's contribution to textual meaning has also permeated across the spectrum of critical enquiry, from cultural critical movements such as feminism, to psychoanalytic theory and various aspects of poststructuralism.

The German critic Hans Robert Jauss has been cited as the main influence on the emergence of reader-response criticism. For Jauss, the interpretative process was one that clearly emerged only through a historical perspective: the reader and the text are always located in history, and the act of reading in any historical period is informed by the conventions and expectations of that period, as well as social and cultural influences surrounding the reader and helping him or her to make sense of the wider world. The process by which the reader acquires lived experience and perceptions of the world is crucial to the development of the reader's interpretative skills and the ability to produce textual meaning from the act of reading. Jauss used the term 'horizon of expectations' to account for the particular historical conditions that inform the act of reading; awareness of those expectations enables the critic to understand how and in what ways a text was received, and what it was taken to mean at a specific point in the past. This approach implies that textual meaning is something that changes constantly and is open to revision and reassessment – a process that is also affected by the attitudes and values of the present time, which the critic brings to bear on the text, and on the past in which the text was written. The past, as New Historicists also claim, can be known only imperfectly and is refracted through the perspective of the present. For Jauss, therefore, historical textual reception, the ways in which readers read and understand a text, are interpreted through the lens of the present in order to arrive at the creation of textual meaning.

Another influential German critic of the period, Wolfgang Iser, adopted a similar, if less historically located, theory to that offered by Jauss. In Iser's version of reader-response theory, the text is only a site of potential meaning in itself; it requires the contribution of the reader to render it concrete. The reader, as in Jauss's theory, brings to the text perceptions and perspectives based on his or her own experience, values, attitudes and understanding of the world. Iser also allowed that the text guides the reader towards a particular interpretation to some degree; the extent to which this will be the case depends on the individual text and on the reader's level of competency. However, even where a text provides considerable direction there will be 'gaps', as Iser termed them, which the reader's interpretative strategies 'fill in', according to his or her world-view. Iser extended his theoretical position still further: the reader's experience will be changed throughout the process of reading, leading to a continuing process of re-evaluation and modification, according to how the reader's textual expectations are met. In Iser's view, the human compulsion to make sense of the world by establishing coherence on events and experience is one that also translates to the act of reading, which becomes a process of continuing interpretation and reinterpretation, to arrive at possible and provisional meanings that most closely reflect the individual reader's perceptions and experience, rather than a single universal and determinate meaning.

Iser's caveats about the text's capacity to limit the reader's potential responses, thus preventing the emergence of radical misreadings, were viewed with suspicion by some reader-response theorists. The American critic Stanley Fish, for example, was more ready to accept the notion of subjectivity entering into the interpretative process, to the extent that wilful misreadings could take place and should be taken into consideration. Fish's concept of 'affective stylistics' focused on the ways in which texts work psychologically on readers, and posited a more radical role for the reader than Iser. No text, according to Fish, can ever be self-contained; its language exists in negotiation with all acts of linguistic communication, or 'utterances', which impact on the consciousness of the reader and contribute to the reader's interpretation of the text: the meanings of the words in the text do not depend solely on their relationships with each other and their textual context, but on what they mean in a wider sense to the individual reader. The natural extension of Fish's theory would be that all readings, even those arrived at in error, would be valid. His later work, especially his formulation of the concept of interpretative communities, offered a way of delimiting possibilities of meaning. Among all the readers of a text, there will be groups who share common expectations and levels of competency, who will therefore reach the same or markedly similar conclusions about textual meaning, thus conveying greater validity on those readings and reducing the influence of overly subjective misinterpretations.

Reader-response criticism, while it did not offer as radical a rejection of traditional forms of critical enquiry as poststructuralists (for example, Barthes, who around the same time was proclaiming the 'death' of the author), nevertheless made a significant contribution to the shift away from concerns with the text as a self-contained unit, or with the author as having a privileged perspective on textual meaning. More significantly for contemporary literature, the emphasis on the implications for the interpretative act of the reader's extra-literary experience, and perceptions of the social world in which the text is produced and received, was of a part with the liberalising and democratising tendencies of the period. Interpretative communities of hitherto marginalised status, for example, had their experience validated by such approaches, and a more receptive climate was created for the acceptance of literatures and critical practices arising out of those communities.

See also   *Criticism*: Feminist criticism, New Historicism, Poststructuralism, Psychoanalytic criticism.

Further reading

Davis, Todd F. and Kenneth Womack, *Formalist Criticism and Reader-Response Theory* (Basingstoke: Palgrave Macmillan, 2002).

Fish, Stanley, *Is There a Text in This Class? The Authority of Interpretive Communities* (Cambridge, MA: Harvard University Press, 1980).

Iser, Wolfgang, *The Act of Reading: A Theory of Aesthetic Response* (London: Routledge & Kegan Paul, 1978).

Tompkins, Jane P. (ed.), *Reader-Response Criticism: From Formalism to Post-Structuralism* (Baltimore: Johns Hopkins University Press, 1980).

Structuralism

Structuralist theory, which first began to make an impact across a range of academic and intellectual disciplines in France in the late 1960s, is generally regarded as being the single most radical development in literary criticism in Britain and the United States from the mid-1970s onwards. Most if not all subsequent critical approaches have responded in some way to the central assumptions and methodology of structuralism, and structuralist analytical strategies have informed a wide range of other critical practices. By shifting the focus of attention to the way language functions, structuralism precipitated a thoroughgoing critique and re-evaluation of traditional modes of textual criticism.

The main theoretical influence behind structuralist criticism was the work of the Swiss linguist Ferdinand de Saussure in the early 20th century. Saussure's ideas were developed in a series of lectures which were published posthumously under the title *Course in General Linguistics* in 1913. For Saussure, the object of linguistic study was to uncover the systems of codes and conventions that governed all language use, and give meaning to language. Language, in Saussure's theory was made up of a system of signs which manifested themselves verbally or visually as words, but had no inherent or intrinsic relationship to the things or concepts for which they stood. Each individual sign constituted a basic unit of meaning and consisted of two elements: the signifier, that is, the word itself, and the signified, which can be described as the mental concept of the thing the word represents. Saussure argued that the sign itself was arbitrary, as was the relationship between signifier and signified: there was no necessary connection between the two; the meaning ascribed to a sign was simply a matter of convention within a particular language, as can be demonstrated by the fact that different languages have different signs for the same concept or object. Saussure also perceived arbitrariness at the level of the signifier, in that signifiers do not always have direct equivalents in different languages. The absence of any intrinsic connection between the sign and the mental concept it represents implies for Saussure that language is predicated on a system of differentiation: the meaning of a sign is defined by what it is not, that is to say the sign has meaning only by way of its differential place within the overall system of signs.

The application of structuralist methodology to literary study incorporated a radical shift from the traditional emphasis on the text's aesthetic and formal qualities, its literary merit and its meaning, to a focus on its underlying linguistic structure. Structuralism offered a more scientific approach to literary criticism, through which general principles and rules governing textual language could be adduced. According to structuralist thinking, any literary text, or indeed any kind of cultural product that depended on linguistic communication, was constructed according to a system of signs, and the relationship between the elements of that system was what dictated textual meaning. Structuralism rejected traditional literary critical methods that presupposed a relationship between the text and the external reality it was claimed to reflect. It also offered a rigorous critique of the idea that the authorial self and authorial intention are crucial keys to unlocking the meaning of the text. The idea of the text as a unique product of an author's creative imagination gave way to a recognition that the form, language and meaning of a text are governed by a set of rules that constitute the particular language system of a text. Texts are not reflections or representations of reality, a concept which is cast into doubt by the arbitrary nature of linguistic relationships between signs, and between signifiers and signifieds. According to structuralist modes of analysis, literary styles such as realism are only the product of a set of conventions that readers have unconsciously absorbed, just as the author produces the text having internalised the same set of conventions. Readers are able to make sense of a text, to arrive at its meaning, only through an understanding of the underlying linguistic structures that have shaped it. For many structuralist critics, the reader became a more significant focus of the process of critical analysis, though he or she is not accredited with the capacity for creative interpretation, any more than the author is allowed to have produced the text through his or her unique imagination. The role of the reader is much less active and participative than in the various reader-response theories that emerged in the 1970s; the reader is not regarded as a specific individual, mediating the text through his or her personal experience and world-view. Structuralism is an essentially text-oriented approach to literary criticism, though structural linguistic analysis replaced the aesthetic approaches of New Criticism and similar critical practices that preceded it.

By the late 1960s, structuralism in France was coming under increasing pressure from poststructuralist critiques, many of them formulated by critics and theorists who had been central figures in structuralism's emergence, such as Jacques Derrida and Roland Barthes. Poststructuralism widened the implications of Saussurean linguistic theory in ways that cast doubt on the possibility of constructing a scientific analysis of sign systems, arguing that the very instability of language that results from the arbitrary relationship between signifier and signified fundamentally compromises meaning on all levels, which is, in the terms of Jacques Derrida's theory of deconstruction, endlessly deferred, revealing contradictions, shifts and multiplicities of meaning. Poststructuralism's refutation of some of structuralism's basic premises does not entail complete rejection of the strategies of the latter movement, however, as refinements and modifications of structuralist methodology continued to occupy a prominent role in many poststructuralist approaches throughout the remainder of the 20th century.

See also *Criticism*: Deconstruction, Narratology, Poststructuralism.

Further reading

Culler, Jonathan, *Structuralist Poetics: Structuralism, Linguistics and the Study of Literature* (London: Routledge & Kegan Paul, 1975).
Hawkes, Terence, *Structuralism and Semiotics* (London: Methuen, 1977).
Saussure, Ferdinand de, *Course in General Linguistics*, trans. Roy Harris (London: Duckworth, 1983).
Sturrock, John, *Structuralism* (London: Fontana, 1993).

Notes

1 Contexts: History, Politics, Culture

1. Seamus Heaney, 'Englands of the Mind', in *Finder's Keepers* (London: Faber & Faber, 2002), pp. 77–95 (p. 95).
2. Mervyn Griffith-Jones, quoted in Arthur Marwick, *The Sixties: Cultural Revolution in Britain, France, Italy, and the United States, c.1958–1974* (Oxford: Oxford University Press, 1998), p. 146.
3. Margaret Thatcher, quoted in *Woman's Own*, 31 October 1987.
4. Harold Wilson, speech at Labour Party Conference, 1 October 1963.
5. A. Alvarez, *The New Poetry* (Harmondsworth: Penguin, revised edn, 1966), p. 26. First published 1962.

2 Texts: Themes, Issues, Concepts

1. Edward Kamau Brathwaite, *The History of the Voice: The Development of Nation Language in Anglophone Caribbean Poetry* (London: New Beacon, 1984), p. 10.
2. George Orwell, *The Lion and the Unicorn: Socialism and the English Genius* (Harmondsworth: Penguin, 1982; first pub. 1941), p. 54.
3. Robert Conquest, *New Lines: An Anthology* (London: Macmillan, 1956), p. xv.

Chronology

1945   VE day (Victory in Europe): end of war in Europe

Labour wins general election in landslide, defeating Winston Churchill's Conservatives; Clement Atlee becomes Prime Minister

United States drops atom bombs on Japanese cities (Hiroshima and Nagasaki)

VJ Day (Victory in Japan): end of Second World War

George Orwell, *Animal Farm*; Evelyn Waugh, *Brideshead Revisited*

1946   National Health Service Act and National Insurance Act passed, leading to creation of National Health Service and beginning of creation of Welfare State

Postwar division of Berlin and East and West Germany between Allies and USSR; start of Cold War

Dylan Thomas, *Deaths and Entrances*

1947   Indian Independence from British Empire, led by Mahatma Gandhi

Malcolm Lowry, *Under the Volcano*

1948   SS *Empire Windrush* arrives at Tilbury, bringing first postwar immigrants to Britain from the Caribbean

1949   Eire (southern Ireland) gains independence from British Empire

T. S. Eliot, *The Cocktail Party*; George Orwell, *Nineteen Eighty-Four*

1950   General Election: Labour returned with slashed majority of five seats

British troops sent to Korea in support of American military action

William Cooper, *Scenes from Provincial Life*

1951 Festival of Britain

Defection of spies Burgess and Maclean to USSR

Conservatives win General Election; Churchill returns as Prime Minister

Anthony Powell, *A Question of Upbringing*, first volume of *A Dance to the Music of Time* (1951–75)

1952 Death of George VI; Princess Elizabeth becomes Queen Elizabeth II

First British atom bomb tested

1953 Coronation of Queen Elizabeth II

Samuel Beckett, *Waiting for Godot*; John Wain, *Hurry On Down*

1954 End of food rationing (which had been brought in during Second World War)

Kingsley Amis, *Lucky Jim*; William Golding, *Lord of the Flies*; George Lamming, *The Emigrants*; Iris Murdoch, *Under the Net*

1955 Churchill resigns as Prime Minister; succeeded by Anthony Eden

Conservatives re-elected at General Election

First commercial television channel launched

Philip Larkin, *The Less Deceived*

1956 Suez crisis; Britain forced to cease military action against President Nasser of Egypt by American pressure and international condemnation

Rock and roll music makes impact in Britain

John Osborne, *Look Back in Anger*; Sam Selvon, *The Lonely Londoners*

1957 Harold Macmillan becomes Prime Minister after resignation of Eden

Independence from Britain for Ghana and Malaya

Samuel Beckett, *Endgame*; John Braine, *Room at the Top*; Ted Hughes, *The Hawk in the Rain*

1958 Founding of CND (Campaign for Nuclear Disarmament)

Race riots in Nottingham and Notting Hill, London

Chinua Achebe, *Things Fall Apart*; Shelagh Delaney, *A Taste of Honey*; Harold Pinter, *The Birthday Party*; Alan Sillitoe, *Saturday Night and Sunday Morning*; Arnold Wesker, *Chicken Soup with Barley*

1959 Conservatives re-elected at General Election

John Arden, *Sergeant Musgrave's Dance*; Geoffrey Hill, *For the Unfallen*; Colin Macinnes, *Absolute Beginners*

1960 Cyprus and Nigeria gain independence from Britain

'Lady Chatterley' trial; Penguin Books cleared of charge of obscenity for publishing paperback edition of D. H. Lawrence's *Lady Chatterley's Lover*

Stan Barstow, *A Kind of Loving*; Wilson Harris, *Palace of the Peacock*; Harold Pinter, *The Caretaker*; David Storey, *This Sporting Life*

1961 South Africa leaves British Commonwealth

Berlin Wall built to separate West Germany from communist East Germany

Contraceptive pill introduced into Britain; prescribed only for married women

Roy Fisher, *City*; V. S. Naipaul, *A House for Mr Biswas*; Muriel Spark, *The Prime of Miss Jean Brodie*; Raymond Williams, *Border Country*

1962 Commonwealth Immigration Act introduced; Commonwealth citizens no longer have right to free entry to Britain

Independence from Britain for Uganda, Jamaica, Trinidad and Tobago, and Tanganyika

Cuban missile crisis

Compulsory national military service abolished

Anthony Burgess, *A Clockwork Orange*; Doris Lessing, *The Golden Notebook*

1963 Conservative minister John Profumo forced to resign after sex scandal involving prostitutes

Harold Macmillan resigns on health grounds; Alec Douglas-Home becomes Prime Minister

American President John F. Kennedy assassinated in Dallas, Texas

Independence for Kenya

John le Carré, *The Spy Who Came in from the Cold*; Sylvia Plath, *The Bell Jar*

964 Labour wins General Election; Harold Wilson becomes Prime Minister

Race Relations Act passed

American involvement in Vietnam War

Second BBC television channel launched

B. S. Johnson, *Albert Angelo*; Philip Larkin, *The Whitsun Weddings*

1965 Death of Winston Churchill

Abolition of death penalty

Race Relations Act passed, leading to creation of Race Relations Board

Rhodesia (now Zimbabwe) declares itself independent from British Empire

Edward Bond, *Saved*; Joe Orton, *Loot*; Harold Pinter, *The Homecoming*

1966 Labour wins General Election with increased majority

England wins football World Cup

Basil Bunting, *Briggflatts*; Maureen Duffy, *The Microcosm*; Seamus Heaney, *Death of a Naturalist*; Jean Rhys, *Wide Sargasso Sea*; Tom Stoppard, *Rosencrantz and Guildenstern are Dead*

1967 Legalisation of abortion

Decriminalisation of homosexuality

'Summer of love': beginnings of hippy movement in San Francisco

Edward Kamau Brathwaite, *Rights of Passage*; Nell Dunn, *Poor Cow*; Roger McGough, Brian Patten and Adrian Henri, *The Mersey Sound*

1968 Mass demonstration in London and elsewhere against Vietnam War

American civil rights leader Martin Luther King assassinated

Student protests in Paris leading to mass demonstrations and strike action by workers and students

Enoch Powell makes inflammatory 'rivers of blood' speech against immigration

Colour TV introduced in Britain

Abolition of Lord Chamberlain's office; lifting of theatre censorship

Geoffrey Hill, *King Log*

1969 Outbreak of 'troubles' in Northern Ireland

London School of Economics closed for one month by student protests

Divorce Reform Act

US moon landing

Brigid Brophy, *In Transit*; Douglas Dunn, *Terry Street*; John Fowles, *The French Lieutenant's Woman*; Seamus Heaney, *Door into the Dark*

1970 Conservatives defeat Labour in General Election; Edward Heath becomes Prime Minister

British government introduces internment without trial in Northern Ireland

Voting age lowered to 18

The Beatles split up

Trevor Griffiths, *Occupations*; Tony Harrison, *The Loiners*; Ted Hughes, *Crow*; Muriel Spark, *The Driver's Seat*

1971 Introduction of decimal currency

Women's Liberation movement organise mass protest march in London

Expulsion of Asians from Uganda by President Idi Amin; many sought refuge in Britain

Edward Bond, *Lear*; Geoffrey Hill, *Mercian Hymns*; Doris Lessing, *Briefing for a Descent into Hell*; V. S. Naipaul, *In a Free State*

1972   National miners' strike for improved pay

'Bloody Sunday': 13 civilians shot by British troops in Londonderry, Northern Ireland; direct rule from Westminster imposed on Northern Ireland

Margaret Atwood, *Surfacing*; John Berger, *G.*; Seamus Heaney, *Wintering Out*; R. S. Thomas, *H'm*

1973   Britain joins European Economic Community

Miners announce ban on overtime in pay dispute, state of emergency declared by Edward Heath; three-day working week imposed to conserve energy supplies

IRA bombs English mainland

Ceasefire announced in Vietnam

Athol Fugard, John Kani and Winston Ntshona, *The Island*; Paul Muldoon, *New Weather*; Iris Murdoch, *The Black Prince*; Derek Walcott, *Another Life*

1974   General Election; Harold Wilson becomes Prime Minister of minority Labour government

Miners call off strike action; three-day weekends

Second General Election of year; Labour returned with larger majority

16 people killed in IRA bombing of Birmingham pub

Nadine Gordimer, *The Conservationist*; Philip Larkin, *High Windows*; Tom Stoppard, *Travesties*

1975   Sex Discrimination Act passed; establishment of Equal Opportunities Commission

Margaret Thatcher becomes leader of Conservative party

Inflation reaches record levels of 25 per cent

Malcolm Bradbury, *The History Man*; Seamus Heaney, *North*; Linton Kwesi Johnson, *Dread Beat and Blood*; Paul Scott, *The Raj Quartet*

1976   Harold Wilson resigns as Prime Minister; succeeded by James Callaghan

National Theatre founded

David Edgar, *Destiny*; Thom Gunn, *Jack Straw's Castle*; Wole Soyinka, *Death and the King's Horseman*

1977 Queen Elizabeth II's Silver Jubilee

Emergence of punk rock movement as national phenomenon causes controversy

Angela Carter, *The Passion of New Eve*; Ted Hughes, *Gaudete*; Paul Scott, *Staying On*

1978 Strike action closes *Times* newspaper

First 'test-tube' baby born

Soviet coup in Afghanistan

David Hare, *Plenty*; Tony Harrison, *The School of Eloquence*; Geoffrey Hill, *Tenebrae*; Iris Murdoch, *The Sea, The Sea*

1979 'Winter of discontent': widespread strike action brings many public services to standstill

Conservatives win General Election; Margaret Thatcher becomes Britain's first woman Prime Minister

Buchi Emecheta, *The Joys of Motherhood*; William Golding, *Darkness Visible*; Seamus Heaney, *Field Work*; Craig Raine, *A Martian Sends a Postcard Home*; Emma Tennant, *Wild Nights*

1980 Inner-city rioting in Bristol

Conservatives announce privatisation of major industries and utilities

Unemployment rises above 2 million

Howard Brenton, *The Romans in Britain*; Russell Hoban, *Riddley Walker*; Paul Muldoon, *Why Brownlee Left*; Ken Smith, *Fox Running*

1981 Formation of Social Democratic Party (SDP; now Liberal Democrats) after a number of MPs split from Labour Party

Nine IRA hunger-strikers die in Maze prison

Inner-city riots in London, Liverpool and Manchester

Wedding of Charles, Prince of Wales, to Lady Diana Spencer

Brian Friel, *Translations*; Salman Rushdie, *Midnight's Children*; D. M. Thomas, *The White Hotel*

1982 Falklands War; Argentina invades Falkland Isles; defeated by British forces

Channel 4 begins broadcasting

Caryl Churchill, *Top Girls*; Timothy Mo, *Sour Sweet*; J. H. Prynne, *Poems*

1983 Conservatives win General Election with increased majority

American Cruise missiles stored at Greenham Common air-base leads to formation of women's peace camp

J. M. Coetzee, *The Life and Times of Michael K*; Paul Muldoon, *Quoof*; Graham Swift, *Waterland*

1984 Miners' leader Arthur Scargill calls strike against proposed pit closures

IRA bomb in Brighton during Conservative Party Conference kills four

Ted Hughes becomes Poet Laureate

Martin Amis, *Money*; J. G. Ballard, *Empire of the Sun*; Angela Carter, *Nights at the Circus*; Seamus Heaney, *Station Island*; Grace Nichols, *The Fat Black Woman's Poems*

1985 Miners end strike and return to work

Live Aid concerts, in London and Philadelphia, organised by Bob Geldof raise £40 million for famine relief in Ethiopia

Greater London Council abolished by Conservative government

Inner-city rioting in Birmingham, Brixton and Tottenham

Unemployment rises to 3.5 million

Heysel stadium disaster: fighting between Liverpool and Juventus fans at European Cup Final results in 38 deaths

Peter Ackroyd, *Hawksmoor*; Anita Desai, *In Custody*; Tony Harrison, *v.*; Peter Reading, *Ukulele Music*; Jeanette Winterson, *Oranges Are Not the Only Fruit*

1986 US bombing of Libya, using British-based military aircraft

Growing AIDS crisis debated in Parliament

Margaret Atwood, *The Handmaid's Tale*; Kazuo Ishiguro, *An Artist of the Floating World*

1987 Conservatives win General Election

Stock market crash

Caryl Churchill, *Serious Money*; Ian McEwan, *The Child in Time*

V. S. Naipaul, *The Enigma of Arrival*; Tom Paulin, *Fivemiletown*

1988 Liberal and Social Democratic Parties join forces to form SDLP

Three IRA suspects shot in Gibraltar by British troops

National Schools Curriculum introduced

Alan Hollinghurst, *The Swimming Pool Library*; David Lodge, *Nice Work*; Salman Rushdie, *The Satanic Verses*

1989 Ayatollah Khomeini of Iran imposes a *fatwa* (death sentence) on novelist Salman Rushdie for perceived blasphemy in *The Satanic Verses*; Rushdie forced into hiding

Hillsborough stadium disaster: 94 Liverpool football supporters killed in crush at FA Cup match.

Conservatives introduce community charge (poll tax)

Fall of Berlin Wall

Tiananmen Square student demonstration in China crushed

Simon Armitage, *Zoom!*; Kazuo Ishiguro, *The Remains of the Day*; Derek Walcott, *Omeros*

1990 Reunification of East and West Germany

Mass demonstrations against poll tax

Margaret Thatcher resigns as Conservative leader after leadership challenge; John Major becomes Prime Minister

A. S. Byatt, *Possession*; Hanif Kureishi, *The Buddha of Suburbia*; Ian McEwan, *The Innocent*

1991 Gulf War: British and American forces take action against Saddam Hussein's Iraqi regime after invasion of Kuwait

End of Soviet Union

Apartheid ends in South Africa

Martin Amis, *Time's Arrow*; Pat Barker, *Regeneration*; Angela Carter, *Wise Children*; Caryl Phillips, *Cambridge*

1992 Conservatives win fourth consecutive General Election but with reduced majority

'Black Wednesday': economic crisis forces Britain out of Exchange Rate Mechanism

World Wide Web launched

Thom Gunn, *The Man with Night Sweats*; Ian McEwan, *Black Dogs*

1993 Downing Street Declaration: attempt to find solution to Northern Irish problem

Black teenager Stephen Lawrence murdered in racist attack in London

David Hare, *The Absence of War*; Vikram Seth, *A Suitable Boy*; Irvine Welsh, *Trainspotting*

1994 Negotiations between British and Irish governments leads to IRA ceasefire

Homosexual age of consent lowered to 18

Death of Labour Party leader John Smith; succeeded by Tony Blair

Opening of Channel Tunnel from Folkestone to Calais

First women priests ordained by Church of England

National Lottery founded

Romesh Gunesekera, *Reef*; James Kelman, *How Late It Was, How Late*

1995 Frederick West, in prison awaiting serial murder charges, found dead in cell; wife Rosemary found guilty of serial murder

Sarah Kane, *Blasted*; Patrick McCabe, *The Dead School*

1996 IRA ceasefire ends as peace talks founder

Dunblane massacre: gunman Thomas Hamilton breaks into Scottish primary school and kills 16 children and their teacher

IRA bombs Canary Wharf in London and Manchester city centre

Roddy Doyle, *The Woman who Walked into Doors*; Mark Ravenhill, *Shopping and Fucking*; Graham Swift, *Last Orders*

1997 Labour wins General Election with massive landslide; Tony Blair becomes Prime Minister

Hong Kong returned to Chinese sovereignty

Death of Princess Diana in car accident

Ian McEwan, *Enduring Love*; Arundhati Roy, *The God of Small Things*; Iain Sinclair, *Lights Out for the Territory*

1998 'Good Friday Agreement': renewal of peace process brings elections for Northern Ireland assembly

Julian Barnes, *England, England*; Ted Hughes, *Birthday Letters*; Paul Muldoon, *Hay*

1999 Devolution measures lead to creation of Scottish Parliament and Welsh Assembly

Conflict in former Yugoslavia leads to ethnic cleansing

Andrew Motion becomes Poet Laureate

J. M. Coetzee, *Disgrace*; Salman Rushdie, *The Ground beneath her Feet*

2000 Euro becomes legal tender in several European countries

Anti-capitalism demonstration in London ends in rioting

Fuel protests: hauliers and farmers take action against rises in fuel prices

Legal age for gay sex reduced to 16

Margaret Atwood, *The Blind Assassin*; Zadie Smith, *White Teeth*

2001 Foot-and-mouth epidemic has serious consequences for British farming

Inner-city race riots in Oldham, Leeds, Bradford and Burnley

Labour re-elected with second landslide majority

'9/11': series of terrorist attacks on 11 September; hijacked passenger planes crash into World Trade Center towers, and the Pentagon, killing almost 3,000 people; Taliban terrorist group led by Osama bin Laden held responsible; America declares 'war on terror' and attacks Afghanistan, believed to be home of Taliban

Pat Barker, *Border Crossing*; Ian McEwan, *Atonement*; Salman Rushdie, *Fury*

2002   Death of Queen Mother

Hundreds killed in terrorist bombing in Bali

Peace process runs into difficulties: Northern Irish government suspended after allegations of Republican espionage

American and British military put on standby for war against Iraq, where Saddam Hussein is believed to be stockpiling 'weapons of mass destruction'

Michael Frayn, *Spies*; Yann Martel, *Life of Pi*; Caryl Churchill, *A Number*

2003   Military invasion of Iraq by US and British forces after UN efforts to ensure Iraq has no weapons of mass destruction prove inconclusive

Dr David Kelly, government scientist, commits suicide after being revealed as implicated in allegation that government manipulated evidence to strengthen case for war

US troops capture former Iraqi leader Saddam Hussein

Monica Ali, *Brick Lane*; Graham Swift, *The Light of the Day*

2004   Hutton inquiry into death of David Kelly exonerates government

Iraq Survey Group rejects claim that Iraq possessed weapons of mass destruction; Prime Minister Tony Blair admits intelligence was flawed but stands by decision to go to war

Massive earthquake in Indian Ocean causes tsunami leading to death and destruction on massive scale in Indonesia, the Maldives, Sri Lanka and Somalia: 300,000 killed

Gurpreet Kaur Bhatti, *Behzti*; Alan Hollinghurst, *The Line of Beauty*

2005   Labour wins historic third consecutive term in General Election but majority significantly reduced

Bob Geldof organises Live Eight, a series of rock concerts and demonstrations in favour of reduction of third-world debt

'7/7': London suicide bomb attacks linked to al-Qaeda: 52 people killed in explosions on three underground tube trains and a London Transport bus; second attack two weeks later fails and perpetrators arrested

Massive hurricane floods American city of New Orleans

Geoffrey Hill, *Scenes from Comus*; Salman Rushdie, *Shalimar the Clown*; Zadie Smith, *On Beauty*

General Index

(References for specific topics are given in **bold type**)

abortion, legalisation of, 6, 24, 45–6
absurdist theatre, 49, 59, **62–4**, 96,
  100, 109, 134
Achebe, Chinua, 123, 124, 176, 177
Ackroyd, Peter, 90, 102, 103, 104, 126,
  137, 170
Adcock, Fleur, 47, 58
Adorno, Theodor, 92, 95, 119, 166
Agard, John, 57
AIDS (acquired immuno-deficiency
  syndrome), 46, 88
Ali, Monica, 56, 103
Al-Qaeda, 4–5
alternative theatre, 23, 27, 60, **64–6**,
  77, 88–9, 100, 121, 134
Althusser, Louis, 145, 147–8, 166–7
Alvarez, A., 48, 56, 112
Amis, Kingsley, 54, 56, 68–9, 74, 111,
  112
Amis, Martin, 29, 55, 78, 96, 102, 103,
  121, 126, 137, 157, 170
Anglo-Welsh literature, xi, 57, **66–7**,
  114, 129, 131, 151
'angry young men', 35, 37, 58, 60,
  68–9, 74, 81, 99
Arden, John, 10, 59, 60, 65, 81, 85–6,
  130
Armitage, Simon, 58, 117, 118–19, 130
Artaud, Antonin, 133–5
Ashbery, John, 58, 117
Auden, W.H., 37, 76, 119
Austen, Jane, 90, 165
avant-garde poetry, 58, **69–71**, 79,
  101–2, 110, 116–17, 118, 126, 136
Aw, Tash, 115

Bakhtin, Mikhail, 146–7, 156–8
Ballard, J.G., 44, 91, 93
Balzac, Honoré de, 167

Banks, Iain, 90
Banville, John, 98–9
Barker, Howard, 17, 37, 60, 65, 77
Barker, Pat, 49, 77, 78, 92, 137
Barnes, Julian, 90, 92, 128, 157, 170
Barnes, Peter, 60, 96
Barthes, Roland, 101, 127, 145, 146,
  168–9, 170, 180, 181–2, 189, 191
Bartlett, Elizabeth, 140–1
Baudrillard, Jean, 179
'beat' poetry, 22, 56, 71, 88, 118, 135
Beatles, the, 22, 38, 41, 51, 56, 117
Beauvoir, Simone de, 148, 158
Beckett, Samuel, 49, 59–60, 62–3, 109,
  134
Belsey, Catherine, 151
Berger, John, 23, 55
Bergvall, Caroline, 44, 70, 118
Berlin Wall, fall of, 20
Berliner Ensemble (theatre company),
  59, 85–6
Bernières, Louis de, 49
Bernstein, Charles, 70, 101
Berry, James, 32, 73
Berryman, John, 48, 56
Beveridge Report, 1, 14
Bhabha, Homi K., 124, 175
Bhatti, Gurpreet Kaur, 13
black British literature, xi, 31–2, 53, 57,
  71–4, 76, 84–5, 107, 118, 120, 129,
  137, 141, 151
Black Mountain poets, 58, 69, 101
Blair, Tony, 4, 16
Blake, William, 79
Boland, Eavan, 57
Bond, Edward, 12, 59, 60, 77, 87
Booker Prize, 98–9, 107
Borges, Jorge Luis, 104
Bradbury, Malcolm, 74–5

Index of Works Cited